CULTURE AS GIVEN, CULTURE AS CHOICE

Second Edition

DATE DUE

CULTURE AS GIVEN, CULTURE AS CHOICE

Second Edition

DIRK VAN DER ELST

WAVELAND
PRESS, INC.
Prospect Heights, Illinois

For information about this book, write or call:
Waveland Press, Inc.
P.O. Box 400
Prospect Heights, Illinois 60070
(847) 634-0081
www.waveland.com

To the students who asked questions.

What about the anthropologists? The scientists who study the cultures of humankind also have power and responsibility. They have the power to see beyond the immediate greed of quick profits or the sudden enthusiasm of shortsighted "answers" to complicated social problems. They have the responsibility to make their voices heard. If governments or private corporations refuse to listen to their advice, the anthropologists must take their case to the general public, and make their knowledge available to all.

—Ben Bova (1932–)

❧ Contents ❧

৯ Foreword ৯

Paul Bohannan

Two events in 1871 put cultural anthropology on the road it has followed since. American lawyer Lewis Henry Morgan, who grew up in upstate New York with a number of Iroquois friends, had discovered that some middle-western Native Americans, whose languages were totally different from Iroquoian, did nevertheless classify their kinfolk in exactly the same way as the Iroquois— which is very different from the way kinship is reckoned in English, Latin, or Greek. Morgan prepared a questionnaire and got the U.S. State Department to distribute it throughout the world to people who were in a position to ask about kinship terms in many languages. The result was a book titled *Systems of Consanguinity and Affinity in the Human Family,* the first "comparative study" that remains significant today. Morgan's idea of fieldwork was rudimentary, but the idea of going "out there" to gather the information had been introduced.

The second event in the same year was the publication of a book called *Primitive Culture* by England's Edward Burnett Tylor. His was the first systematic exploration of culture as the mechanism that differentiates one group of people from another. Because of it, those differences no longer can be blamed on race or climate or any other irrelevance. Tylor got the idea of culture from English poets like Matthew Arnold, who learned it from German poets. Tylor's definition of culture—"that complex whole which includes knowledge, belief, art, morals, law, custom and any other capabilities and habits acquired by man as a member of society"— is still current, although many restatements of it have been made.

Anthropological theory had been launched.

In the early days of fieldwork the unwitting assumption was that one's own way of doing things was "the" way to do them (later generations came to call that "ethnocentrism"). By 1900, anthropologists had become aware that they themselves had culture, that European nations differed culturally just as societies of "natives" did, and that one's own culture gets in the way of looking at other cultures.

It was a short but difficult step to the next point: the reason Others act as they do cannot be explained by recourse to Western values and habits of thought. Once anthropologists recognized that the people they called "natives" were rational and comprehensible as soon as you looked at the world the way they did, "native" ways of thinking about their own actions and institutions became a core part of every descriptive study of an alien people.

Out of this insight, anthropologists developed a principle called "cultural relativism," which holds that every culture explains itself, and that to interpret what its people do without understanding their reasoning can lead you to grievous error.

This idea is difficult only if you can't bring yourself to question your own assumptions, and only if you therefore cannot provide options for yourself by entertaining (I did not say blindly accepting) other ideas.

Fieldworkers also told themselves they should go to the field not to change the culture they studied, but to record it. Eventually this idea also became distorted: some said it meant that anthropologists should not "judge" any culture. But human beings are built to judge—they probably can't help making judgments. People survive by making choices based on judgments. In order to make better judgments, you have to enlarge what in today's world would be called "your database." But even with the smallest database, you *will* judge.

Teachers cannot expect students not to bring their moral concerns to class with them—even as they learn that those moral concerns are part of their culture and may limit their own potential. We also cannot expect them not to seek refuge in some doctrine (today it tends to be political conservatism; fifty years ago it was communism); there are prerequisites before they can realize that a successful life depends not on doctrine, but on critique and analysis of what is actually out there.

Among the many factors that determine the path a human life takes, two of the most important are your reaction to the events that go on around you and the education you allow yourself to receive.

So how did Dirk van der Elst get to be who he is? Born in 1933, he grew up during World War II in Nazi-occupied Holland—a good place and time to learn to distrust the use of coercion and power and, incidentally, to question the sanity of some human behavior. When he was 14 years old, his parents brought him and his younger sister and brother to Salt Lake City, Utah—a good place and time to experience changing your culture from the ground up and, incidentally, to question the sanity of your own choices. After high school he joined the U.S. Army just in time to participate in the last four months of the Korean War—there could have been no better place to discover the self-serving nonsense that sometimes accompanies authority.

These reactions to what went on around him, plus a graduate degree in psychology and a doctorate in anthropology, turned Dirk into a knowing participant-observer of the American experience. Teaching at a state university in central California, which draws its students from a hinterland populated by more than a hundred ethnic groups from all over the world, forced him to become aware of the contrast between the cultures that people absorb willy-nilly as children and the culture they purposefully choose (or more commonly, stumble into) as adults.

His point—and the point of this book—is that, though you may not be aware that you even have options about your culture, you will be a lot better off if you recognize that you *do* have them, and know what they are. This useful insight, presented here by a "new" but decidedly *American* American (who believes that anthropology is a tent under which every rational viewpoint can be assembled) is a guide in your conscious creation of a better culture for yourself.

❧ Why This Book ❧

The main point of higher education, I believe absolutely, is its liberating effect. I further believe that the introductory course in any field of study should showcase its intellectual contribution to that purpose.

An introductory course to cultural anthropology is the one place in a general education curriculum where you can gain objective insights into your own culture's manipulation of the choices you will have to face in life. If it is presented in that vein, an anthropological perspective can help you recognize and evaluate alternatives and achieve "adaptive fitness" in a shrinking but still polycultural world. Most traditional textbooks, however, are geared to another purpose: to acquaint you with the findings and explanations of the discipline. That's an excellent goal—but when the emancipation involved in "liberal" arts is put front and center, quite a different virtue of anthropology emerges.

When knowledge about other people is presented so that you learn things about yourself whenever you contrast your own experience with that of people who grew up with a different history and culture, it vastly broadens your areas of awareness—and therefore of choice. And isn't that the purpose of a liberal education?

The book you are holding is the distillation of a thousand Socratic skirmishes with my students in the well over 100 sections of Introduction to Cultural Anthropology I've taught over 25 years. The facts it deals with are familiar to most people in the discipline and found in standard textbooks for this course. But my way of presenting and interpreting them may raise a few eyebrows: I don't bother to hedge every declarative statement with modifiers, and I don't fear the occasional broad generalization. We have to cover a lot of ground fast, so I won't burden you with footnotes or citations either. My intent, after all, is not to write a legal brief or dissertation, but to present you with a coherent argument from an anthropological perspective, which, even where it does not convince you, will at least make you look at your personal interdependence with your culture in ways you hadn't considered before.

You live in a world in which individuals and agencies are endlessly trying to manipulate you, to steer and guide your behavior for purposes you may not be aware of. And I, of course, am one of those. I have had the time and the opportunity to learn and to think about culture, and to have developed a very definite point of view. Since subtlety is not my long suit, you will recognize my bias.

Note that I've been saying "*an* anthropological perspective," not *the* anthropological perspective. It may be acceptable to talk about "*the* physics of X" or "*the* chemistry of Y" because in those disciplines facts may be subject to dispute but never to interpretive viewpoint—in the physical sciences, personalization of facts is something righteously to be shunned. The speed of light or the atomic weight of lead remain constant no matter who measures them—if they aren't, you're "doing it wrong."

But human behavior has infinitely more degrees of freedom than the physical universe. It is therefore less predictable and less amenable to rigid measurement. Moreover, it can only be perceived and communicated through other human behavior; its description actually gains meaning and value when the attitudes of *both* the observer and the observed are stipulated. An account called *The Cultural Anthropology of Z* would have an arrogant title for the simple reason that another observer, or the same one on a different day, would have brought a somewhat different viewpoint to exactly the same data—and on paper it would look different even when it is not demonstrably contradictory.

As I hope to convince you, perspectives—viewpoints, ways of looking—can be judged only by their usefulness. Every discipline has a viewpoint. In anthropology at least, so does every writer, and an honest one makes it clear. You'll know mine.

Let's get back to your adaptive fitness—you will need it over the next few decades. Your future holds dangers never even imagined by your ancestors—not even your grandparents. Although it may hold opportunities to match, those may not always be distinguishable instantly from the threats.

If you are to live well with the results of the decisions that life will force you to make, you'll need to recognize your options. To do that optimally, you need to know what culture is, what *your* culture is, and how it operates on you and your world. And for *that*, you need to understand culture's biological roots.

You may wonder why I begin a book on culture with two chapters that look like psychobiology and postpone a definition of its subject matter until chapter 3. I could simply tell you that all culture is based on biological and genetic factors, but I'd rather convince you. So let me explain my reasoning.

You are flesh and blood; you were born and you will die like any animal. Yet there are things you do routinely that no other species can even imagine, things that your ancestors would have called miracles just a century ago, and things even you cannot explain.

You are a creature of habits. The beliefs and assumptions you live by and through are habits so primal and so practiced that you are probably not even aware that you have them.

You are the outcome of a tree of decisions, most of which you do not remember making. Nevertheless, those decisions have formed the person you've become. Your intellect, your morality, your habits of mind all bias your perceptions, color your thinking and predispose you to respond to problems in certain ways. You are therefore far more likely to lose your life—or love, or freedom—through some learned propensity than from ignorance or some willful mistake.

So how did something as complex as you come to be this way? How did you acquire those habits, and why? Well, sure, through your parents' genes and teachings, through your own adaptations to life as you found it. But your parents had parents too, and so on and so on until you're looking for original causes in some dim and unknowable past. How did things progress from them to you?

As long as there have been human beings, there have been attempts at answering questions like these. But until the advent of modern science, there really weren't any answers that could be backed up with hard evidence. Even then, it took a while before there evolved a field of study, anthropology, which was willing and able to tackle subjects of that sort. Its practitioners have now gone out for over a century to record and analyze everything that they could think of that was typically human, from our physiology to our cultures, and tried to fit the parts of the human puzzle together. In the process they amassed a libraryful of information and several disciplines' worth of insights. But there is a cornucopia of alternatives still to be considered in the anthropological record; there are implications still not fully realized.

One of those is that today it is *your* task, not just the anthropologists', to evaluate and judge—and even select!—the culture you live by. *Culture as Given, Culture as Choice* was written to make you aware of that.

Beginning with Sex

Why Males Exist and
How Women Are Unique

"Two of the worst things we commonly teach our children are that a knowledge of science is nice but not necessary, and that a knowledge of sex is necessary but not nice."

—Marilyn vos Savant (1948–)

"After all," as a pretty girl once said to me, "women are a sex by themselves, so to speak."

—H. C. Beeching (1859–1919)

*Sexual reproduction allows a species
to adapt more readily to changing
environmental situations. Human sexual
dimorphism is more cultural than biological
but remarkable either way—
and it is absolutely astonishing
that you are here at all.*

*U*sually the first thing you notice about another person is the stranger's sex. You have been doing so since you were very young, because the men around you treated you differently than the women did, and they still do.

Since those innocent days you have learned a great deal about things sex can mean and do and influence, but you should still have a few questions. Like why are you one sex instead of the other? What really causes all those differences between men and women? And if sex is to be tied up with love and loneliness, which can cause so much unhappiness, why are human beings saddled with it?

The answers are complicated; they begin in physiology.

Reproduction is the foundation on which the life process has to be built. If life cannot reproduce, it cannot adapt, and a species that cannot adapt cannot, in the long run, survive. One-celled animals reproduce when the cell splits into two identical cells. That system works, but it does not help in adaptation to changing environmental forces.

Everything changed when two cells found a way to merge and mix their DNA together *before* dividing. The two cells became dependent on one another. This process developed and ultimately evolved into sexual reproduction. Therefore, just as life is dependent on reproduction, sociality—the dependency of two or more creatures on one another for their survival—requires sex.

Note that sex is not the same thing as depending on each other for survival. Perhaps the *species'* survival may depend on sex, but not the individual's. For many organisms, the only time they act social at all (after their "childhood") is when they meet briefly for procreation before resuming their separate ways.

The fact that distinguishing men from women was among the first things people insisted you learn reflects the universal expectation (even among populations without this vocabulary) that men and women will react differently to you because of your and their sex, and that you will act differently to them because of both their sex and your own. People are taught as soon as possible how to behave toward each other—and these ways become ingrained and

3

habitual. They will forever affect the way you respond to the universe around you. Like all human beings you are a creature of habit and culture; think of culture (for now) as "everything people aren't born with" or as "habit writ large."

The biologic software program for your physical construction lies encoded in your genes, in those tightly spiraling strings of DNA that scientists call "the double helix." The same is true for every other creature composed of cells. But what you see in your mirror reflects a lot more than your genetic blueprint, for you, unlike any other life form, require the intercession of culture just to exist and survive.

SEX IN NATURE

The major biological importance of sexual reproduction is that it allows a reshuffling of genes in every generation. By randomly producing endless variations on a species' basic physical plan, it usually has a few alternatives when change (in the guise of a new predator, the disappearance of a food source, climatic shift, etc.) renders the standard model no longer functional. Most of these deviations from the genetic standard turn out to be "errors" that hinder rather than help the *individual* survive. But the fact of variance helps the *species* survive in changing environments because, once in a while, some deviant turns out to be exactly what's called for under new circumstances. The actual interaction of individuals with their predators and their prey determines which particular variant adds the most offspring to the next generation. That process is called "natural selection."

Differentiation into two sexes is very old in the history of life. It is widely encountered in every division of the plant and animal kingdoms, but it is not universal. Most microbes reproduce without sex. Under stressful environmental conditions, some female lizards can produce clones of themselves without males, although in favorable conditions their species reproduces sexually. In reproduction without sexuality, the DNA of the parent-individual is duplicated essentially without change from one generation to the next. For species in stable ecological niches, asexual reproduction has obviously worked well enough—so far.

But if the environment of such plants and animals changes enough to make their present form and functions ineffective, they have no alternative to extinction—they won't have time to mutate adaptively.

It takes two sexes to confer this constant genetic variability—and therefore adaptability. Thus what the evolution of sexuality involved, fundamentally, was the addition of males. So the original reason why males exist was to add variation to the gene pool.

Among vertebrates, males and females are distinguished by their primary sexual characteristics (the structure of the reproductive organs) and often by such secondary sexual characteristics as differences in coloration, size, or armament. For mammals, the female form is the standard model. Males are a specialized variant of the basic design.

€strus and Rut

Periodically—in many species only once per year—a mammalian female comes in heat (called "estrus"), the biological condition in which she is both fertile and willing to accept copulation. Her body advertises her readiness to mate by excreting pheromones, which are chemical signals, such as smells. These pheromones trigger sexual excitement, called "rut," in her species' males. Males have little or no choice about rutting; they are biologically programmed to respond to a female in heat, whatever the obstacles. That's one thing males are "for."

Because pheromones do not target a specific male but are carried by the wind (or occasionally in water), a female's advertisement causes every male within pheromonal range to go into rut. Since mature females achieve reproductive readiness only under certain physiological and environmental conditions, all those in the same area tend to go into heat around the same time, keeping every male in rut until the last female has completed estrus.

Males of many species will not share females. They are therefore forced to compete with each other for the opportunity to reproduce—and to do whatever is required to be "The One She Accepts." It's an exhausting business at best—and it takes a lot of time.

Sexual Dimorphism

Males and females do not always differ in ways that are casually apparent to human observers. Lizards, crows and cats, for example, do not. But baboons, pea fowl and lions do. Sexual dimorphism (di = 2, morph = form) means that each sex has a distinguishing shape or size or color as part of its secondary sexual characteristics. Dimorphism is high wherever males must compete for the right to reproduce. Among some herd animals, for instance, males fight for the right to become the stud for a harem of females. Natural selection (the tendency of advantageous physical traits to spread through a population because the individuals carrying them have a better chance of passing on their genes) thus favors those who are stronger and/or better armed, and there are many species in which the males are very much larger than the females. Many birds carry out elaborate mating dances or song contests; though these do not require size differentiation, their sexes can be told apart, at least during mating season, by the attention-catching plumage of the males. Well-armed solitary predators such as tigers or hunting spiders do not usually fight for females: that would be too dangerous. The male already risks death if his approach to the female is not adequately choreographed.

There are also circumstances in which males suffer a *dis*advantage if they are larger than the female; there are even some fish species in which the adult male is so much smaller than the female that he literally lives inside her reproductive tract, fertilizing her eggs on demand in exchange for living off her bloodstream.

Among many primates, especially the ground-dwelling or terrestrial apes and monkeys, a female in heat exhibits that fact with grossly swollen and luridly colored genitalia that fairly *scream* her accessibility. In many species the dominant males will try to keep the other males from mating with her at least until after her prime period of fertility is ended.

SEX AMONG HUMANS

You will have noticed that among people, even though we are primates, things are very different. What makes human females unique is the fact that human males cannot tell from a distance whether a woman is sexually approachable (some can't even tell up close, which is why there are sexual harassment laws).

The Absence of Estrus

Unlike other female primates, women do not appear obviously physically different when they are most fertile. Moreover, technically they are "continuously sexually receptive"—no matter how hilariously misleading men may have discovered that description to be. Because women do not go into heat, men are—again, technically—not triggered into rut. (You could argue that human males must always be in rut if human females are always sexually receptive, but that would overlook the fact that men can say, "Sorry, dear, I've got a headache," while animals in rut have little choice—

they must perform on demand. Teenage boys may find the distinction moot.)

Without estrus, there are no biologically determined breeding seasons for humans. But there are cultural ones: the probable reason for traditional June weddings in northern countries is that in times before the Pill, marriage was soon followed by pregnancy. For both mother and baby, the best time to give birth is in spring, before summer brings its heat and busy-ness. The least onerous time to be heavily gravid is when others have the most time to spend helping a mother-to-be: at the end of winter. And spring comes nine months after June. The fact that human females are capable of copulation even when they are not fertile provides one of the most obvious physiological foundations for human marriage and family—and thus for all of human sociality. But let's not get ahead of ourselves.

Human Sexual Dimorphism

Male and female plumbing obviously differs, but sexual dimorphism refers to secondary characteristics, and most of yours are acquired from local culture rather than being biologically given. To be sure, we remain a dimorphic species, more so than, say, tigers or turtles, but much less so than gorillas or peacocks. Among adult humans, males are generally larger than females and have deeper voices, beards and greater upper-body strength. Females are differentiated by their mammaries and more gracile features. Until the middle of the twentieth century, people assumed that men were "naturally" bigger than women. Today we are not so certain—size differences tend to be reduced once both sexes get the same adequate diet and exercise.

The cultural variation of the sexes is called "gender." Gender is about behavior rather than physiology; it grows and develops because people have ideas about what is "natural" for members of the two sexes to do. Sex is about the biological variations. The topic of gender has required books of its own.

Reproductive organs aside, it is thus culture, not biology, that most differentiates boys from girls. In the 1960s and 1970s, when "unisex" dress was fashionable and both men and women wore their hair long, it was occasionally difficult to tell the sexes apart from a distance. But fashion—even then—was never intended to confuse that issue. To underline their difference, some women wear eye shadow and lipstick and cover their facial skin with notions and lotions and magical potions designed to enhance their beauty and advertise their difference from males. That kind of advertisement by the female is another clear differentiation between humans and nonhumans.

"Scent of a Woman"

Our species may not be very dimorphic, but culture—at least, modern industrial culture—does what it can to make us appear more so than in fact we are. Culture encourages women to exaggerate their secondary sexual characteristics. It does not stop at harmless but pointless differences like hair length, what side your shirt buttons on, or whether you wear ineffective artificial pheromones. (Perfumes were invented many times in the history of the world. The ones we know were improved in France back in the days when Europeans did not bathe.) It is probably safe to say that, if anyone, only women believe perfumes attract men. Most human males, I'd wager, would rather have women smell like women or as if they had just stepped out of the shower; a few may prefer them to smell like barbecued pork or like a new car. But individual men can be conditioned to associate a specific scent with a specific woman, and apparently that's often good enough for her purpose: to be remembered and considered by enough men that she will be able to pick and choose among them if and when she wants a mate.

In any case, exaggerating dimorphism is not always so harmless to women. Breast implants can kill you. And acting stupid, so as not to frighten off some physically attractive but unintelligent male, can become a self-fulfilling prophecy—with devastating consequences for yourself and your offspring. ✺

In most societies women do not go to the lengths that North Americans do to advertise their sexual potential. In some, such as traditional Muslim nations, religion forbids women from enticing males. Such cultures limit sexual dimorphism to its "natural" parameters: beards on men, eye shadow on women. In the preindustrial world, our potential for elaborating dimorphism simply wasn't there—but people almost always differentiated the sexes with specific dress and hairstyles.

Note here that there is absolutely no agreement among cultures as to what specific traits constitute desirability in looks. In some societies women are required to wear long hair—in others, to have smoothly shaven heads. In some places men wear skirts and women pants; in others that is reversed. In Western culture, pants have become acceptable for women only very recently—remember that Joan of Arc was burned at the stake for wearing men's trousers: that "proved" her heresy. Dress can connote all sorts of cultural implications. Women in power seldom wear skintight, low-cut clothing and miniskirts. For some women who rank lower on the totem pole, such dress is almost a uniform. And we have known since 1919, when the anthropologist Alfred L. Kroeber pointed it out, hemlines rise and fall in regular patterns—and in contrast to the economy. He called it "style."

THE HUMAN SEXES

Still, in spite of the fact that most of our overt dimorphism is due to culture rather than biology, the fact remains that there are important differences between the sexes.

Women

At conception, everybody is female and will stay female unless testosterone bathes the blastula at precisely the right time, very early in its development. Each baby girl is born with over half a million oocytes (immature eggs), each with the potential, if ripened and fertilized, to be developed into a baby. Only about 400 of these oocytes actually do mature into ova; the rest degenerate.

When adolescence begins, a girl's body—like a boy's—has a 5:1 ratio of lean to fat tissue. Her metamorphosis into adulthood begins when estrogen encourages the deposit of fat into her breasts, thighs and buttocks. Menarche (first menstrual period) occurs two or three years later, when her lean-to-fat ratio has become 3:1. For the next year or two, depending on diet and exercise, menstruation remains irregular and ovulation usually cannot occur (but don't count on that). The threshold at which monthly ovulation takes place is apparently crossed when the body reaches 28 percent fat. At that point a woman is able to carry a fetus to term.

Theoretically, the average woman could give birth some twenty times during her lifetime. Fortunately that extreme isn't often achieved, because a human female must produce the next generation at the expense of her own energies. It will require some 50,000 calories beyond those needed for her own survival to bring her fetus to term. During much of that time she will need assistance in acquiring those extra calories—especially if she already has a child.

Unlike the females of other mammals, women can—and today more and more of them do—live beyond the age at which they can reproduce. That's called menopause, and we'll come back to it in chapter 5.

It is fair to ask why women "waste" 99.9 percent of the oocytes they are born with and why they go through menopause. There are no certain answers yet. Suffice it to point out that it takes time and energy to raise a child, and that any woman still has vastly more genetic potential than she or our species will ever need.

Men

A baby boy results when a Y-chromosome in the conception-causing spermatozoon triggers events that make the fetus grow into a male. Baby boys are born with one or two thousand primitive spermatogonia, the parent cells for sperm. Boys do not develop the capacity to produce viable spermatozoa until puberty—the time when their testicles begin secreting testosterone. Then the spermatogonia, now densely packed in the 1,000 or so 30-inch-long seminiferous tubules that make up each testicle, begin cranking out duplicates of themselves through repeated bifurcation. Each split results in a germinal sperm cell with 46 chromosomes. Meiosis eventually divides that into four spermatids each carrying 23 chromosomes. Then it takes about 74 days to nurture a spermatid into a mature spermatozoon capable of quickening an ovum.

Sperm can remain fertile for several weeks before it degenerates and is reabsorbed by the body, but once ejaculated, it dies in a couple of days. Spermatozoa are so small that if all human males in the world ejaculated at once, their total volume of actual sperm would be less than a tablespoon, though it might take a supertanker to hold all the associated seminal fluids. A ripe ovum, on the other hand, is typically 85,000 times as large as a sperm cell—the difference in size between a space ship and the planetoid it lands on, or more accurately, whose gravity well causes it to crash.

Males' production of genetic material is astonishingly profligate and redundant. A healthy male produces more than 3,000 sperm cells per second, 300 million per day, 100 billion per year. Over a lifetime, a typical man will produce from 6 to 12 trillion sperm—more than a trillion for every child he actually fathers. A healthy male averages between 20 million and 110 million per ejaculation, but single ejaculations of from 200 million to 500 million spermatozoa are not uncommon. Male sterility is defined as the inability to produce at least 10 million sperm per ejaculation. Unlike women, men do not experience menopause: it takes death to turn off their reproductive potential.

You

Anyway, here you are: proving through the fact of your existence that you had a biological mother and a biological father, even if you've never met either—indeed, even if your father was a sperm donor or your mother a surrogate. Somebody had to supply the egg that grew into you, somebody else the sperm. Only the combination of that one particular ovum and that one specific sperm could have resulted in you. Consider for a moment, from that point of view, the odds against your being here at all to ponder these things.

When you were conceived, your mother was one of at least 2 billion fertile females on the planet, and she theoretically had at least 2 billion fertile males to mate with (note that I use very conservative numbers). With each of those men producing 300,000,000 sperm cells on any given day for a potential total of 600,000 trillion, with another two weeks' worth already in the pipeline, and each of those women having one of 400 ova ready on any day she can conceive (totaling 800 billion possible eggs), and only one (1) of each involved in your beginning, the random odds against your specific conception were greater than 1 in 7,200,000,000,000,000,000,000,000,000,000,000. On any day. The zeroes go nuts if you insist on figuring in the odds against being born on your specific birthday.

Seen in that light, the fact of your existence is as miraculously improbable as the birth of any comic book superhero, or of any supernatural entity you may care to name.

But then, of course, in actuality your mother and father were not *randomly* mated, and the actual population they drew each other from was a whole lot more circumscribed than "any fertile human of the opposite sex."

In any case, yes, here you are. Against inconceivable odds, so to speak. Uniquely you, from DNA to fingerprints, from personal experiences to the web of relations whose center you form.

Yet in most physical ways you are just like me and everybody else. You and I share over 99 percent of our genes!

If being human meant only something purely biological, like being a virus or being a fish, think of how few of us there would be. Still, you have been a lot more than a merely physical being for quite some time now, haven't you? You have become a cultured creature—and *that* means that the zeroes on the formula have shot absolutely out of control.

For being human also means having a culture, and one of the primary effects of culture is that it negates some of the harsh realities of nature—at least in certain respects—while it creates some other (and often equally nasty) realities of its own.

Thinking It Through

1. Asexual reproduction works well enough for many ancient and widespread species. So what evolutionary advantage does sex offer?

2. What distinguishes rut from estrus, and why was that important for human evolution?
3. It's been said that women need a reason for sex, but men only need a place. With all those testosterone-driven men, do human females really need to go to such lengths to attract males? Why do they?
4. Why do human males produce so much sperm when it only takes one to fertilize an egg?
5. Could a difference in the sex drives of women and men be explained by the difference in the production numbers of spermatozoa versus ova?

The Other Double Helix

From Reflex to Culture

"Man is born a barbarian and only raises himself above the beast by culture."

—Baltasar Gracián (1601–1658)

"Just as a tree without roots is dead, a people without history or culture also becomes a dead people."

—Malcolm X (1925–1965)

The processes of cultural and biological evolution became entwined as the human species grew dependent on learning rather than on unconditioned reflex. Culture allowed people to accumulate what they had learned into a collective body of skills and lore.

*P*eople keep searching for ways to make definitive distinctions between themselves and other life forms—a sort of scavenger hunt for human uniqueness. You can tell yourself you are unique because of your opposable thumbs. Or because you walk on your hind legs, which leaves your hands free. By now a flood of other criteria has been suggested to "prove" the special qualities of humanity. The only thing wrong with this comes if you use these qualities to deny the fact that you are physically as much an animal as any porcupine or crayfish.

You may have been told that "only we" use language, use tools, modify our environment, practice agriculture, feel shame or need to, worship, have souls, use fire. But one after another these markers have turned out to be distinctions of scale rather than kind. For example, some rudimentary tool use has been observed in a number of species, from other primates to Galapagos woodpeckers. Many ant species grow fungi—that's agriculture. Many others "herd" aphids for their secretions. As far as language goes, lots of critters communicate even if they cannot tell each other what they did last weekend. For worship and shame I refer you to dogs. As for souls, there is no way to test for souls; there isn't even any agreement across humanity about what souls are and whether we (all) have them.

Anyway, you've probably found it hard to feel superior to animals about your anatomy when so many of them are faster and stronger than you.

That leaves fire. And yes, indeed, although you can teach a chimpanzee to smoke, no species of wild animals uses fire. But all human societies do and have since time immemorial. Indeed, it is obvious that all of the technology you take for granted today, from cars and computers to plastics and modern media, began with fire: how else to smelt copper for electric wires? But is fire using what made you different from animals, or was that ancestor who first picked up a burning brand *already* so different from the rest of nature that he *could* experiment with fire, something animals fear as people fear death itself?

It is the contention of anthropologists and related scientists that what differentiates humans from the rest of the world's creatures is no single biological or behavioral trait, but rather the way our species has specialized in culture. Culture—which a few other species do indeed sport in a primitive sort of way—evolved with us. That means that certain changes in our physiology enabled changes in our behavior, which in turn made possible still more changes in our physiology, and so on and so forth, until biology and culture formed two intertwining strands in human evolution: "the other double helix." Humanity's superior use of culture does set you apart; but it does not make you nonanimal. Culture now rewards—and curses—humanity with some degree of control over the evolution of other species as well as our own.

So how did all this come about? We may never have precise data, but we can make a rough outline of some of the steps that life and our species had to take to get to you reading this.

THE FIRST IMPERATIVES

You, like every other organism, are part of an ecosystem: a community of plants, animals and bacteria interacting in a particular physical and chemical environment. Ecosystems come in all sizes and overlap at many points. They are found everywhere we look (you even have a number of them on you and in you, but that's not the issue here), so you impact many of them as you live—and die. And, of course, they affect you at the same time.

In order to exist in any of these ecosystems, species adapt physically to different ways to make a living. Environments vary in the sort and range of opportunities they offer. Individuals and therefore species interact: at the very minimum, plants convert solar energy into substance, and animals survive by eating plants or each other. For animals at least, life for any individual requires the deaths of many other individuals: almost everything you ever ate was once alive. Consequently the success or failure of any particular lifeway affects the existence of other species and may create opportunities for still more adaptations.

From whales and giant redwoods to viruses and the creatures swimming in a drop of water, all individuals and all species must satisfy certain biophysical needs if they are to continue to survive. These are the original, the truly primordial motivators, and they are referred to as imperatives.

The metabolic or homeostatic imperative is to maintain homeostasis. That is to say, organisms, if they are to survive, have to be kept functioning within their design parameters. At the very least that means acquiring from the environment those energies and resources needed for sustenance and growth.

The reproductive imperative demands that life forms produce replacements for themselves.

Much imperative-satisfying behavior, at all levels of species complexity, is preprogrammed into organisms and demands no overt action on their part. Every cell and every body contains many built-in mechanisms that require little of the individual but maintenance. Vessels dilate, muscles contract and relax, sphincters control flows, hearts pump, kidneys strain, nerves transmit, all automatically, all without conscious volition. There is no sense of need, of pressure to perform, associated with this level of activity. But all life forms, even plants, require outside energies and substances to satisfy their homeostatic and reproductive imperatives. Together, these imperatives quite literally *drive* organisms into specific behaviors and are therefore called "primary drives."

PRIMARY DRIVES

Primary drives exist for every biophysical need and force animals (at certain times and under certain circumstances) to secure food, water, oxygen and other necessities; to eliminate carbon dioxide, heat, salts and other wastes; to rest and repair; to procreate (depending on physiology) through mitosis, parthenogenesis or sexuality; and generally to prolong their existence by whatever means they have, through fight or flight. Or, if they have enough brains, by being clever.

Organisms metabolize as long as they live. Therefore, metabolic drives cannot be permanently satisfied: even when just the thought of another bite of food is enough to make you gag, you know you'll be hungry again. But the need for energy, coolants, rest and exercise must be temporarily reduced often enough to enable an organism to avoid *becoming* dinner and to live long enough to express its reproductive imperative.

In fully functioning organisms, the urge to procreate is as strong as hunger—although usually not at the same time. But unlike metabolic drives, the reproductive drives will not kill the individual if they are never reduced (priests and nuns have proven that), and neutered mammals (including humans) confirm that some of the motivational power of these drives can be eliminated. Moreover, it is often highly beneficial to a population or a species that some of its members don't reproduce. Not only does this help keep the group from overexploiting its resource base, but childless aunts who help their sisters in rearing their children can be a deciding factor in the next generation's survival. Still, extinction waits if too many individuals in a population are kept from procreating.

Precisely that fate befell the Shakers, a religious community whose earliest American colony, in Watervliet, New York, dates to 1776. Half a century later they had 18 communities, as far west as Indiana. The doctrine of the United Society of Believers in Christ's Second Appearing (the Shakers' official name) included such modern ideas as the sexual duality of the deity, equality of the sexes, communal ownership of property and pacifism. Unfortunately their beliefs also demanded absolute celibacy, which means they did not reproduce but had to survive on converts. By 1860 their movement began to decline. Today, Shaker handicrafts and furniture are still admired for their innovative simplicity and superb craftsmanship, but a few old women at Sabbathday Lake are all that survive from this once-vital community.

All creatures have primary drives, but they differ greatly in the ways they can temporarily reduce them. If you draw a line representing the continuum from very simple, single-celled organisms to such a complex species as our own, that line will also trace the increase in their behavioral alternatives. As a general rule, the simpler the life form, the more its behavior is reflexive or "hard wired"—that is, programmed genetically. The more complex the creature, the more its behavior is acquired, that is, programmed by experience, learned.

Note here that most animals large enough to be seen by the naked eye can learn *some* things and that for the higher, more complex ones, learning is vital to survival. But for the smallest and shortest-lived, learning is not an important factor in survival; reflex is. On the other hand, even the most complex of creatures, like ourselves, continue to use reflexes for satisfying those primary drives whose reduction or temporary satisfaction would not improve through learned behavior. If you had to learn how to breathe, how to control your heart rate in response to oxygen demand or how to adjust the opening of your pupils in response to brightness, you would not be reading this.

Creatures respond to the metabolic and reproductive imperatives through unconditioned or through conditioned reflexes. That is to say, either a reflex takes place automatically, or else there is some control over the event. When there *is* control, it has been acquired—learned after the fact of the creature's existence. Learning is a way of conditioning reflexes that provides far more alternatives than mere genetic response tendencies can offer, but it is important to note that no creature can survive by learning alone.

Unconditioned Responses

Unconditioned responses are innate (inborn) drive-reduction mechanisms. All creatures great or small have them to deal with some or all of their primary drives.

Unconditioned Reflexes

For complex organisms, unconditioned reflexes—the simplest automatic behaviors—often remain the most efficient ways to handle *some* biophysical requirements. Examples are your involuntary eye blink or the way a sleeping cat flicks its ear when any hair growing from that ear is touched. Many species of simple organisms employ reflexes to deal with *all* of life's problems. Such creatures are capable at best of only a few responses to any stimulus: flight, fight, feed or breed. When a stimulus is novel or ambiguous, reflexes (being automatic) don't help in selecting the most appropriate response. Moreover, automatic behavior makes creatures predictable to predators. Consequently only the most rudimentary of life forms in the most stable of ecosystems can survive by unconditioned reflex alone. In such species, individual survival until reproduction is a matter of dumb luck.

Chained Reflexes

Less primitive organisms—those with greater capacity for discriminating between stimuli and possessing a greater repertoire of responses—are equipped with chained reflexes that enable them to survive through more flexible behavior based upon chains of response. In a chained reflex, such as suckling or breathing, the completion of a simple automatic behavior triggers its repetition until something else, like satiety, interrupts. Reflex chains such as ingestion or copulation or the walk of caterpillars are genetically "wired in" but often depend on specific conditions or changes in the environment before they can be triggered.

Species that depend solely on reflexes for their survival necessarily share a number of characteristics: they must be small and short-lived, mature rapidly without any "childhood" learning period and reproduce at prodigious rates to enable mutation to produce enough variant individuals that the species can adapt to changes in its ecosystem.

Instincts

In many speces, genes provide members with an entire schedule of different behaviors to achieve routine metabolic or reproductive drive reduction; these behaviors are known as instincts. In biological terms, *instincts are response programs that are species general* (meaning that they are common to all undamaged members of the species), *unconditioned* (the behavior is not learned but innate), *inflexible* (no adjustment to local conditions or individual limitations is possible), *hierarchic* (metabolic instincts outrank reproductive instincts whenever both are triggered), *specific* (they trigger predictable behavior and end in a distinctive consummatory activity) and *adaptive* (under the conditions for which it evolved, the program enhances the survival of the individual and its species.) Instincts are transmitted from parent to offspring in the same way as anatomical features, and vary and evolve by the same processes.

Insects are the most dependent on instinct. Among many species of hunting wasps, for example, after standard copulation has been completed, the female digs a small pit and fashions a mud-ball door to cover it. Thereafter she seeks a larva or caterpillar of the one or few insect species she is programmed to accept as appropriate prey for this purpose, paralyzes it by injecting venom into its neck, carries it to the pit, drops it in and injects some of her eggs into its body. She then "counts" her inventory, covers the pit with the "door" and flies off in search of another victim. When she finds one, she paralyzes it, flies it back to her pit, rolls back the door, dumps it in, injects eggs, counts inventory, covers the pit, flies off and repeats her maternal task once more. This time when she counts the larder there are three victims. According to her program, that's enough, so she closes the door for the last time. Her instinct satisfied, she can go on with her life.

But note that once this instinctive program is triggered, she cannot deviate from it: no substitute worm is acceptable even though what crawls from her eggs could dine on it just as well; hunger or thirst are not allowed to interrupt her schedule; and she'll keep hunting and injecting until there are three approved larvae in her pit. If each time after she puts in the second one, you remove it when she is gone, she'll bring a third, a fourth, a fifteenth, a two-hundredth—until she simply wears out. (That's been done, of course. In the name of science.)

Any entomology text can regale you with examples of unbelievably complex, truly improbable but scientifically verified instincts; for some species, the rules for ensuring the existence of a next generation seem to have been designed by Rube Goldberg on acid. Or by random chance. Clearly, therefore, survival for instinct-dependent species requires much the same anatomical parameters as those for reflex-dependent ones: brief lives, rudimentary capacities and prodigious reproduction.

It has become common in everyday speech to use the term "instinct" when what is really meant is drive, habit, training, intuition or some other behavior that is not a species-general, unconditioned, inflexible, hierarchic, specific and adaptive program of complex behavior designed to satisfy a primary drive. An athlete will train for years to be able to perform a certain feat automatically, yet on the evening news some person with hair will say he does it instinctively. In fact, the athlete's skill may be so practiced that it is automatic, but that does not make it instinctive. Similarly, a lawyer does not instinctively know how to interrogate a witness so that in her testimony a fact sounds like a lie and a lie sounds like a fact; he had to study and practice for years to acquire and perfect this technique. And there really is no such thing as an instinct for money, or for justice, or for neatness or dominance or a thousand other things now being bandied about as if the phrases meant something.

I know it does no good to decry this trend, but it does muddle your thinking and often falsely implies an automatism while willfulness is at fault. The incapacity or unwillingness to differentiate between drive and instinct—that is, between a need and its satisfaction—is the sort of confusion that keeps people from dealing with problems of inequality on the basis of sex, race and class. *To insist upon the confounding of drive and instinct is to insist upon mystification.*

It is also common to confuse all animal behavior with instinct. In fact, the simplest organisms lack the specialization of form and function without which instinct cannot operate or evolve. On the other end of the continuum, the most complex species, those possessing many information-gathering and -analyzing organs, take too long to reach reproductive maturity to be able to afford the vulnerability that total dependence on instinct bestows. Nevertheless, most visible creatures have at least *some* instincts in their behavioral repertory.

Conditioned Responses

As species evolve into greater complexity by adding anatomical structures and their resulting behavioral alternatives, reflexive and instinctive behaviors become increasingly costly. It takes much longer to grow a bear than a bird, and no bear would survive to reproductive maturity if as much of its behavior was as automatic and therefore as inflexible and predictable as a bird's. Nevertheless, advanced complex creatures like mammals cannot be expected to respond with originality to *every* stimulus: too many mistakes would be made, and survival chances would plummet. Nature therefore has evolved a mechanism by which successful nongenetic responses can be stored and accessed just like any unconditioned reflex. The term for such acquired reflexes is "habits."

Habits are not innate. They are learned behaviors that have been so practiced ("conditioned") that they have become automatic: when they are triggered they produce behavior for which no conscious thought is necessary, like the action of your right foot when a car in front of you suddenly stops. Habits are *learned* reflexes.

Secondary Drives

The most basic habits you have acquired are those that determine how and under what circumstances you will satisfy your primary drives. These are called acquired or secondary drives. They explain your values and attitudes, and therefore your motivations, while determining the habits of speech, thought and behavior which characterize you as a member of your social group, and as an individual. The next chapter will examine this idea; for now, let's consider the limits on learned adaptations as such.

Two Cautionary Tales

Two moths are sitting on a twig of a backyard bush, watching a third moth flit around the guttering flame of a gas light. Suddenly they hear his supersonic scream as he singes a wing on the flame. Horrified, they watch him draw ever tighter circles around the fire, protesting desperately all the while he is madly trying to flutter away but is always drawn back until finally his body ignites in a brief blaze of light and pain.

"Gorblimey," says one. "I sure hope I don't go like that!"

Just then a little lizard scurrying along the branch jostles their twig. Startled, they take off toward safety as their genes define that for them: straight for the brightest light around, which happens to be the gas flame.

"No!" they scream as they begin circling the light in ever tighter spirals. Moths can't learn from vicarious experience.

Sizzle! Pop-Pop!

Moral: Mother Nature cannot plan for every contingency.

Analysis: All three moths are victims of a type of chained reflex called a "tropism," which, when triggered, forces the creature to head for the brightest light. Startles and pain both trigger it, so each time the moth is hurt by the heat of the light, it is forced back into it by its own automatic behavior. Each wing of moths of such nocturnal species has a light-sensitive spot. When the escape reflex is triggered, the wing that receives the least light beats faster until it gets its share of brightness and the body shades the other wing, which then beats faster until . . . etc. This process aims the creature toward the brightest spot in its environment, which usually meant the moon when this go-for-the-light-if-you're-startled-in-the-dark behavior evolved. Light-seeking tropisms are common in insects, fish and other lower animals. So are light-shunning tropisms, but not, of course, in the same species.

Here's a story from the other end of the continuum.

It's 1970. Motorcycles are still a rarity and associated in the minds of young men with virility, daring and outlaw status. John is tooling along on his Harley-Davidson, hair blowing free, eyes squinting merrily, bugs in his teeth. A stranger, Jack, pulls his Honda alongside. Gallantly John picks up the pace; companionably Jack matches it. They grin at each other, duel with the white line for a while, then pull into a gas station for fuel and a chance to admire each other's bike.

"I'd like to try that Honda," John suggests.

"Hey, I'm game," Jack agrees. "But remember, the controls are on the other side!" (In those days, American motorcycles still had the clutch under the right foot and the brake under the left; Japanese bikes reversed that.)

They start carefully—neither wants to look stupid grinding gears—but soon hit their stride. They're opening 'em up: 70, 80. Sailing smoothly along the open road, slouched back, groovin' on the sunlight and the freedom. What a time to be alive and to be young and to be cool.

When they're doing an easy 100, some idiot begins backing a car across the road and then stalls it, blocking both lanes a hundred yards ahead. Barely enough time for a controlled stop.

They both die on impact.

Moral: Habits can kill you too.

Analysis: Seeing the danger, they'd sat up alertly, and the well-conditioned foot with which each always braked his bike automatically pressed what this time turned out to be the clutch. Before they had time to overcome the shock at what each momentarily perceived as "Brake Failure!" they both coasted into the car at 92 mph. Although it is true that habits can be broken while instincts cannot, crisis is not the time to do it. In a crisis, you are as likely to revert to old habits as moths are likely to be triggered into tropisms. ⊱

CREATURES OF HABIT

The further you go along the continuum from simple to complex organisms, the more you find behavior to be conditioned rather than innate. In other words, unconditioned reflexes are lost and supplanted by conditioned reflexes as species become more complex in form and function. Automatic behavior is as important as ever, but habit replaces instinct. Mammals—like cats and dogs, weasels and polar bears—have to teach their offspring how to catch and kill their food, but their reproductive drives are still fully handled by unconditioned behaviors.

When you reach the higher primates, however, it is difficult to prove *any* dependence on instinct, and when you look at people, it is clear that there are no societies, no races, no individual human beings who have *any* behavior that can properly be classified as instinctual. And that includes our supposed "maternal instinct" and "survival instinct." Drives, yes, certainly. Young women want babies—although not all do; young men want young women—although, again, not all do. But no woman innately, automatically, knows how to care for a child, and women do not all do that in the same way. Instead they learn how to deal with every stage of their child's maturation, and some of them give up and hand off, or desert, or even kill, their healthy offspring—all behaviors that instinct would preclude.

As for our vaunted instinct for self-preservation: we do not, as a species, use the same means to avoid death; we have no automatic escape reflexes or even fighting reflexes. What is the human way to fight? Boxing? Karate? Wrestling? The fact is, humans have to be taught what is dangerous and what to do about it. And that is the very opposite of an instinct at work. Show me an animal that commits suicide (and please don't trot out the poor lemming! It dies because those in back push those in front over the cliff or into the river; the lemming is a victim of population explosion and therein a lesson to us all, but it no more kills itself than does your dog), or one that will die for an idea, and I will show you an animal that has no instinctive way to satisfy its homeostatic imperative.

Instincts, you see, are a major improvement over mindless reflex, but they are not up to the task of keeping creatures alive in rapidly changing environments. And let's face it, yours is just that. So is every ecosystem after humankind enters it. Advanced species cannot afford a lot of instincts because instincts do not adapt (mutate, evolve) rapidly enough to stave off extinction.

A fair question here is: "So how is learning better than instinct?" And if you asked it, the answer you'd get from most people would be, "You can break a habit; you cannot break an instinct." That's true, but almost irrelevant; remember the motorcyclists? Habits can be as deeply ingrained as any instinct: surely you know someone who's tried for years to quit smoking or biting her fingernails or saying "you know" every few words. And do you know what an accent is? It's all those habits of what to do with your mouth parts, habits that you acquired and practiced with your first language, getting in the way of the habits required to speak the second language correctly.

No, what makes learning most adaptive, biologically speaking, is the fact that your human genes do not compel you to speak the same language your parents do, to share their beliefs and assumptions about life and yourself and the world around you, to make your living in the same fashion, to seek the same sort of mate, to be, in short, the same kind of person that they are or were. With habit instead of instinct, as immigrants everywhere prove every day, there is no necessary continuity in behavior between generations. Ultimately, that generational variability allows you to acquire and practice habits adapted precisely to local conditions, and *that* is the real advantage of habit over instinct.

Learning has other advantages over instinct. Among the most important is its ability to add habits to a creature's behavior repertory whenever that seems useful. For human creatures that means that learning makes possible the accumulation of coping techniques beyond the capacity of any single organism.

So how much do human beings learn, and how much of our behavior—like breathing and blinking and suckling—is still reflexive? For present purposes it is enough to know that learning is the primary human adaptive mechanism, that while simple internal functions like your heartbeat or your digestive processes continue to be efficiently controlled by reflex action, all human beings have to *learn* how to reduce their every primary drive.

But how did we get that way? What was there about our ancestors that made such heavy dependence on learned behavior possible, even necessary?

FETALIZING A PRIMATE

We are the only living mammals that normally walk erect, and so did all our ancestors for as far back as the archeological record can trace them. Creatures walking on their hind legs need heavier and more rigid pelvises than four-footers, because in true bipedalism there is nothing to help the pelvis bear all the weight of the head and torso.

If you, today, placed a series of humanoid skulls in a graduated row, with our most primitive known ancestor at one end and a modern human at the other, you'd see that cranial capacity—the size of the brain pan—has increased by jumps over the millennia (the only exception is that *Homo sapiens neanderthalensis*, a form of early man, had a larger skull capacity than today's humans; whether that was enough to make him much smarter is in doubt). Each new form of humanlike creatures usually had more brains than the one preceding it.

But if you placed complete skeletons in a similar row, you would *not* find a corresponding, clearly directional change in pelvises: from the neck down we don't look all that grossly different from our ancestors a million years ago. To be sure there have been changes in the angle of tilt of the pelvis, but the birth canal of the female has not widened appreciably over the millennia. In many women today, their baby's passage during the act of birth actually dislocates their pelvic bones. Yet even so there is a limit as to how big a child can be born without caesarean intervention.

The fact that our foremothers kept birthing ever larger-headed babies doomed ever more of them to death in childbirth. Large brains by themselves, in other words, had *negative* survival value. Our entire evolutionary line was at risk and would have died out—except for the fact that there were always some females who, for one reason or another, gave birth prematurely, that is, to babies whose skulls were still small and malleable enough to pass through the birth canal. Eventually these "mutant" females became the sole survivors of what can be called the Big-Head Plague—and they, in the evolutionary process, became the standard for our species. Their daughters unto the present generation have genetically inherited the tendency to give birth to fetalized infants. As I was, as you were even if you were carried "to term."

Of course such preemies needed a lot of care: there is no way for a human baby to survive without outside help. Humans are, as they always have been, among the most dependent of creatures at birth, and we stay dependent longer than any other life form. In fact, and in spite of belief and exhortation to the contrary, we never outgrow our dependency on other people.

Nevertheless, no organism or species can just shake off a reproductive parameter as important as length of gestation. Our ancestors lost not only the ability to carry a fetus to term; they also lost instinct. (Which does not, of course, prove that one event caused the other.)

But there was an upside, and it made us who and where we are today.

The brains of creatures born with complete skulls cannot grow much. But it takes quite a long time before the soft, open skulls of humanity's fetalized babies close after they are born, and their brains keep growing all the while—at least tripling in size. And as it turned out, large brains coupled to a long period of immaturity have *positive* survival value. That so-called developmental period is the time when infants and children play and experiment with the social and physical world around them and learn the skills and demands and rewards required of adults. We are surely not the only creatures who play, but we do it far longer than puppies and kittens, otters or monkeys. In many ways playtime, especially of the intellectual sort, never ends for some of us, and the point can be made that it *need* not end until death, that only inadequacies in our social support system make some of us lose our playfulness and our curiosity.

Ironically, the Big-Head Plague created behavioral possibilities that ultimately have made humanity responsible for its own evolution, if not for all life on Earth.

At some now-indeterminable point in our species' past, hindsight shows, your ancestors were using fire and surviving by satisfying all their primary drives through behaviors in which learning played an important part as it joined unconditioned reflex. They found skills and habits that they had to be taught or that they could teach with words to their fellows and their offspring. These were People, whatever their looks or lifeways. What that hindsight actually shows you is what you see in your own mirror: a creature dependent on words, habits, on habit writ so large that it is multi-dimensional and transferable across time and space. So that it is outside you as well as inside you.

The word for that is "culture."

Thinking It Through

1. What definitive characteristic differentiates humans from all other life forms?
2. What are humanity's "truly primordial motivators," and how are they important in human evolution?
3. Distinguish between drive and instinct. Is suckling an instinct? If so, why? If not, why not? Is self-preservation? Walking?
4. How did the "Big-Head Plague" affect human evolution?
5. When you learn a skill or a perspective, you are really acquiring a habit. Could it be that those of us who habituate easily are more teachable than those of us who do not acquire habits so readily? Would it follow that addicts are smart people trapped by their habit-forming facility?

How Your Culture Works on You

Perception and Behavior as Cultural Artifacts

"Culture consists of patterns, explicit and implicit, of and for behavior acquired and transmitted by symbols, constituting the distinctive achievements of human groups, including their embodiments in artifacts; the essential core of culture consists of traditional (i.e. historically derived and selected) ideas and especially their attached values; culture systems may, on the one hand, be considered as products of action, on the other as conditioning elements of further action."

—A. L. Kroeber (1876–1960) and
 C. Kluckhohn (1905–1960)

"Whenever I hear the word "culture" . . .
I release the safety catch on my pistol."

—Hermann Wilhelm Goering (1893–1946)

*It is culture that distinguishes
human beings from other creatures
and made you who you are
by having given you the capacity to
expand your possibilities. Culture is not
a biological function; it is a body of
knowledge and operations outside
yourself. But to be useful, it also has to
be inside your mind. Getting it from out
there into your head is called learning.
The more culture you learn, the better
armed you are in the struggle to survive,
and the fuller a life you can lead.*

Some concepts, once you understand them, affect the way you look at the universe so drastically that you are forever after unable to explain it without them. Mathematics is impossible without the concept zero; modern economies could not run without money; still others include the scientific method and evolution.

The idea of culture fits right in there.

The term "culture" is old. In the 1400s, it referred to both religious ritual and agriculture: Europeans in those days thought of culture as tilling the spirit and the soil. By the 1600s, the term had begun to mean "cultivated," which is to say, being carefully trained and sophisticated. Early anthropologists in the late 1800s adopted the term "culture" to explain behavioral differences among populations (which it does far better than climate or race or anything else that had been used until then to explain human variation). As anthropologists use the term today, culture covers that entire range of human conduct and capacities that is learned and shared within society but not biologically determined. Culture is what flavors our animal nature.

Charles Darwin and Alfred Russell Wallace are universally acknowledged for making us aware of evolution—but the names of most of the others who first imagined truly revolutionary concepts are lost to history. It is also difficult to establish who first named the class of phenomena and behaviors that brought humanity to its present position (halfway between beasts and angels, as some of our ancestors put it), who first imagined the modern version of the concept of culture.

In the flawed but brilliant focus of hindsight, one good candidate for that honor is Gustav Klemm (1802–1867), a German who had already been intrigued by the concept of evolution before Darwin showed how it worked. In the mid-nineteenth century Klemm offered a definition of culture that involved "customs, information, and skills, domestic and public life in peace and war, religion, science and art." He added that culture "is manifest in the transmission of past experience to the new generation." With that, he defined the essential difference between humans and other creatures.

31

In the English-speaking world, the adaptation of Darwin's insight to human behavior led to the near-simultaneous publication in 1871 of two books that made the culture concept part of every educated person's worldview and midwifed the birth of the discipline of cultural anthropology. In England, Edward Burnett Tylor (1832–1917) published *Primitive Culture*, and in the United States, Lewis Henry Morgan (1818–1881) published his *Systems of Consanguinity and Affinity*.

You may well wonder why it took until the nineteenth century before anyone came up with the anthropological idea of culture. I suppose the only answer is that we can't focus on things we don't notice. Someone once suggested that if fish had invented chemistry, the last major chemical compound they would have discovered would be water. And along that line, the last of the major elements that human scientists discovered was oxygen. It takes an unusual person to notice anything that is invisible. Like culture.

THE CULTURE CONCEPT

So what *is* culture? Suffice it for now to say that here "culture" means everything that human beings have created and transmitted socially across time and space. It therefore includes tools and weapons, computers and paper clips, airplanes and houses—everything that is artifactual, manufactured. Also chess clubs and armies, clans and oil companies, the IRS and NATO, families and labor unions—every sort of human organization. And ideas of every sort: meaning, values, ethics, religion, laws, politics, science, philosophy, art, novels, music, dance, games, and all the rules for making and using and performing all of the above.

There really ought to be two terms for culture: one with a capital C, Culture, for those qualities in the human condition that we all share, and another with a lowercase c, culture, to identify a specific society's lifeway with its characteristic customs and rituals, its technology, organizations, values and language. But there aren't, so the one term will have to cover everything about the human condition that is not genetic or "natural."

"Natural," by the way, is a greatly abused term. Cover girls and corpses, after makeup experts have toiled over their faces, are said to look natural, when the whole point of the effort was to make certain they don't. We use the term here only to distinguish some aspect of human existence from "cultural," meaning artificial, acquired or learned.

It is important for you to realize, however, that "cultural" and "natural" are *not* opposed categories. You don't have to choose between them. Almost all human behavior is "natural" (that is, biological) but has nevertheless been culturized. Bits of rudimentary culture are found among a few other species—particularly primitive tool making among chimpanzees and a few birds—but *human beings culturize **all** their "natural" behavior.* All bluebirds build the same kind of nests. All human beings do *not* build the same kind of houses. House building is as natural to human beings as nest building is to bluebirds. But some human beings build simple dwellings out of the natural materials at hand, while others build mansions using imported marble.

It is normal in every society to assume that what *we* do is natural and that what *they* do differently is strange or wrong or even wicked. Of course not everything is a value judgment, but often—and in every sphere of life—people operate according to unconscious cultural assumptions. (It is one of the purposes of anthropology and this book to look at assumptions consciously. That can be very uncomfortable, if not downright disturbing, and may be the reason why anthropology has been called "the subversive science.")

Although the terms are often used interchangeably, culture is not another word for society: society is people and the way they are organized; culture is behavior and artifacts and the meanings we attach to them. Culture is invisible: its existence is demonstrated through its effects. When you use culture to modify your environment, the result is "artifacts": anything created by human beings. In that sense, bricks and formulas, books and belief systems are artifacts just as much as weapons or songs, computers or the stock market.

HOW YOU GOT CULTURE

You, being human, have a biological predisposition for culture, for learning it and teaching it and for inventing or changing it as needed. Culture is the thing—and the *only* thing—that makes you fundamentally different from other life forms. People are said to "carry" culture, to bear it from one person or generation to another. All of us are culture bearers.

You acquired culture with your language, literally at your mother's knee. She defined the world and its important aspects for you. She taught you to pronounce words a certain way in a certain order; she explained why the sky is blue and why your pet died; she defined how and why things work the way she said they did. Father assisted but wasn't around as much, and it was only later that your peers, teachers, bosses and fellow workers helped you extend your cultural capacities.

You had no alternative to this conditioning when you were a child: culture was a given. But as you grew up, you noted inconsistencies and inadequacies in what you were taught. People beyond your immediate family told you things that conflicted with what you thought you knew. Sometimes that required you to unlearn things you had taken for granted: Santa Claus and the Tooth Fairy did not really bring gifts; people worked at jobs so they could buy them in a store for you. Around the time you realized that, you began to learn from more sources, often by yourself from books.

As you progressed from being a babbler to being a talker, you acquired and stored the labels for a plethora of things and acts and ideas. In that process, some of your unique observations and expressions became part of family lore, meaning that you began to influence the people around you, including the parents whose culture you were unconsciously emulating. Parents also learn from their children: how else can they become adequate child rearers without having an instinct for it? Successful education is always a two-way street.

"Mother Tongue"

My own English speech patterns were set in the U.S. Army, where my casual speaking vocabulary, like that of most soldiers, shrank to the F-word used as noun, adjective, verb, prefix, infix and suffix. When I came home after three years, I had lost the habits of thinking and dreaming in Dutch, and no matter what my parents spoke, I answered automatically in English liberally laced with the curses and obscenities I was no longer aware of using.

Regrettably, inevitably, two-way education took place.

My sainted immigrant mother never "took the Lord's name in vain." But when goaded beyond endurance, she could let loose a string of expletives that would make the eyes of any drill sergeant grow moist with admiration. She was a quick study.

"How can you swear like that, Mama?" I asked her once when we had both calmed down.

"It doesn't count," she assured me in Dutch, "I only said it in English."

"You mean God understands only Dutch?"

We both laughed, but as far as I remember that was the last time I heard her curse in *either* language.

I've noticed that sudden pain or intolerable frustration makes many (perhaps most) bilingual people swear in their first language. To this day, after half a century of being an American, I still bellow the guttural coarseties of my mother tongue if I hit my finger with a hammer or crunch a toe against furniture in the dark. It is simply more satisfying, more *real* than the trite ascriptions of sexual improprieties and species-crossing descent lines that categorize American invective. Besides, Dutch, like Russian, just *sounds* right for peeling the hide off people and things. (I've wondered, do all immigrants feel that way about their mother tongues?) ∽

Like many other foreign-born Americans, I still count in my first language. I do it because that was how I was drilled in the tables of multiplication and division, and true drill, as any ex-GI will tell you, does not wear off easily. I have been known to suddenly thunder "Tens-Hut!" in a lecture. More often than not, some ex-GI would snap straight up to attention. (You can try it yourself, if you don't mind a fat lip.) Which proves, as I always hurriedly explain, that well-practiced habits last far longer than people expect—even a decade or more after getting out of the service. Fashions in education theory aside, that is an important fact about drill. If we are to be creatures of *useful* habits, those habits need to be practiced until they're automatic, like driving. Or better yet, like speech.

Artifactually You

Whenever or wherever you were raised, as long as you are there, you can feel perfectly "natural." You may therefore find it hard to see yourself as an artifactual entity, as someone who resulted from innumerable cultural interventions and adjustments. But that, in fact, describes you accurately.

Let's inspect you quickly to prove the point:

- **Your hair:** Would it look this way if it weren't for shampoo, comb, and the ministrations of a barber or stylist? Would it look this way if you had been born in your grandparents' generation?
- **Your skin:** Compare your photograph to those of your ancestors a century ago when they were your age. Note how much more weather-beaten their skin looks. That is because they lived outdoors more than you, and without sunblock. Moreover, your soaps are milder than theirs and used more often because they didn't have showers and baths in their homes.
- **Your facial features:** Notice that in your picture you smile; they almost always look serious. They were being immortalized, and that was then a solemn occasion. When they do smile, their teeth are uneven and often stained: dentistry was in its infancy then and nobody had heard of braces on teeth. Do you wear glasses? You will if you live long enough. Surely you already use sunglasses, one reason you have

fewer squint lines than they. I've got to ask: is *anything* about your face natural?

• **Your body:** Odds are you are also taller than your ancestors and heavier: diet and exercise are different now and the difference tells on your physique. You are healthier and live longer. All because of culture.

Consider your clothes, your shoes, the chair you sit in, the floor it stands on, the building that houses you—all culture. The very air you breathe indoors has probably been heated or air-conditioned; the water you drink comes from pipes, not creeks. Outside there are planted, pruned and fertilized flora. You have to go very far indeed to get away from any evidence of culture: Antarctica has immortal beer cans, Mount Everest has been trashed, the oceans teem with garbage, and the detritus of civilization circles the space around our planet.

But back to you:

• Where would you have been without doctors and medicines, schools and families to carry you through difficulties?

• Did you know your grandfather? Only cultured beings can.

• Where did you get your ideas of right or wrong, your tastes in food and mates and politics, your goals and fears and hopes?

See? You yourself are a cultural artifact. If you think that's too strong a conclusion, will you argue the fact that everything about your behavior has been conditioned by culture?

Culture is the de facto human environment. It is therefore natural for human beings—an odd insight but an accurate one. Indeed, without culture one can only be potentially, not functionally, human. That is the way babies come into the world and into our societies. If you think babies are as human as you, then try to imagine one raised in a Skinner box or some similar artificial situation where it is fed and washed and kept healthy and active by machines, without human contact or exposure to culture through sound or sight until, say, age 21.

When you then enter into its space, it would not speak, of course. It would have no manners, no toilet training, no self-control, no pity, no conscience. Whatever it looked like, it would still be a baby, a completely self-centered being without a trace of consideration for others, for rules, for reciprocity. Now, full-grown, if this baby should want your nose or your eye—as babies often do—it would be able to rip it off and cram it into its mouth. You would find this creature, limited as it was to only the biological component of our bicultural double helix, a very scary monster indeed.

Playing with Food

You were not raised to be conscious of how much of your behavior is "culturized" and how much of your environment and existence is cultural rather than natural. Among the obvious examples are your basic bodily needs and the ways in which you express them. As a living organism, you must ingest (eat, drink, inhale) parts of your environment; digest (break down) what you ingest; and egest (defecate, urinate, exhale) what is unusable. Our species is technically omnivorous, meaning that you can subsist on almost everything that occurs naturally if it is small enough to pass through your gullet and doesn't have a foul taste. As a baby and toddler, you used to swallow coins and bugs and hairballs and everything else on the carpet like some self-propelled vacuum cleaner, and most of that bothered your parents a lot more than you. But as an adult, you eat only "food."

"Bon Appétit"

So what is food? Well, that depends on where and when you grew up. I grew up in Holland during World War II. Just before that ended, the Americans parachuted canned food into our starving cities. We loved the meat and the butter and the bread; I had never eaten peaches before. But we were all greatly puzzled about the canned pig slop which, even though 22,000 of us starved to death that winter, most of us could not eat. We wondered why the Americans would insult us that way? We had theories, of course: maybe the slop was meant for our beasts; the Americans may not have known that we had already eaten all our farm animals, our horses and cattle, swine and goats, chickens and sheep. Those were food. We had also even eaten every cat and dog we could catch, and many people ate tulip bulbs, tree leaves, rats, and other things that definitely were *not* food. There were even recorded cases of cannibalism in Amsterdam. My mother kept us alive for a year on sugar beets and wild plants. The Canadians and Americans saved our lives, for which we remain eternally grateful. But we could not eat their pig slop. ⌇

As an anthropologist I pride myself on being able to eat whatever the natives cook their way, and I've cut a gustatory swath through a veritable zoo of life-forms from land and ocean. I've eaten cat, dog, snake, monkey, anteater, capybara, iguana, piranha, and grotesque-looking ocean dwellers for which I have no names—all with genuine, lip-smacking appreciation. But to this day I have trouble downing a spoonful of creamed corn. Oh, I know that it's irrational, that creamed corn is perfectly good food, and I don't even mind the taste (though I vastly prefer corn on the cob). But old ways of looking at things die hard, and you and I both know what that stuff really is.

On the other hand, Hollanders eat some things that most Americans wouldn't even touch with somebody else's mouth. Raw herring and smoked eel are traditional delicacies. Unlike Americans, we don't like only sweets, we also have a taste for bitter confections, and our sour pickles will suck the fillings right out of your teeth. We have a candy, *zoute drop* (salt licorice), which is made with sal ammoniac. As far as I have been able to determine, only Hollanders love it. It's available here and there in the States; you owe it to yourself to try it as a harmless test of your gustatory flexibility.

In short, our species may be omnivorous, but you are not. You define something as "food" because your society says it is, not because it is digestible. Your food preferences as well as your food taboos are thus purely cultural in origin. Children are often horrified to learn that lamb chops do not grow in those plastic wrappers in butcher shops but are hacked from the cadavers of cute little animals. Perhaps a billion people are revolted by the thought of eating the flesh of *any* animal, usually because of religious or ethical considerations. But there are also societies where people eat almost nothing else, usually because their environments offer few alternatives. Others refuse to eat specific meats or fish species because of religious prohibitions that have nothing whatever to do with taste or nutrition.

But even something socially defined as food may not be "edible." Social contexts matter. If you are forced to share a table with a stranger, and he leaves something on his plate that you are fond of, would you fork that tidbit into your own mouth? No, you say: that would be eating his garbage. But if your mother left that something on her plate, you wouldn't let it go to waste, would you? Doesn't that mean that "garbage" is not the same as "leftover," and that "food" is situationally defined? When, and by what social alchemy, does "food" become "garbage?" Dumpster divers prove that your answer must be relative.

How do we eat? All you really need is your hands and your mouth: even soup can be slurped without benefit of spoons. But almost every society expects its adults to eat with tools of some sort: knife and fork, chopsticks, whatever. And it doesn't stop there: there are rules for how and by which hand the tools are to be used, and some of them can truly amaze an outsider. Until just a couple of decades ago, using your eating tools the way North Americans do, switching them from hand to hand as needed and laying them down between uses, marked you as hopelessly lower class in western Europe. "Respectable people"—including the bourgeoisie and the striving poor—"ate with knife and fork." That involved never putting down the fork in your left hand until you had completely finished with it, and only letting go of the knife in your right (parking its tip on the edge of your plate) to pick up your glass.

Among the bourgeoisie in my hometown during the 'forties, *deftig eten* (dignified eating) meant always holding the fork upside down ("because it is a stabbing instrument, not a shovel"), so that bites of food had to be loaded onto its curving bridge of tines against the force of gravity. The knife was used not only to cut the food, but to push it onto the back of the fork. Eating peas in that fashion was the ultimate test of table manners. Everything from Jell-O to drumsticks was eaten with fork and knife. I have watched a mother teach her child how to eat a wrapped candy bar that way. The use of spoons was less counter-intuitive, but even today it is worth the price of admission to see a waiter in a good restaurant serve salad from a bowl, using only a pair of spoons in one hand; it's a triumph of skill over function. Like professional basketball.

In almost all societies, the family meal assumes a central position in the concept "home." But all over the urbanized world, the Fast Food Phenomenon is encroaching upon that custom. People get their dinners from drive-through windows, eat in their cars, or in barely camouflaged mess halls geared to narrow menu choices and rapid service and turnover. Eating remains a necessity, but its contexts evolve as culture marches on.

Other Culturized Drive Reductions

It is obvious upon inspection that the *way* you deal with your basic needs, like *how* you eat and *what* you cat, are as important and as culturally determined as *when* you eat—and, under some circumstances, as *that* you eat. This principle holds true for the satisfactions of your every primary drive. In other words, your secondary drives are able to contradict or even trump your primary drives.

Elimination

For example, you must egest waste products from your body, that is, urinate and defecate. Babies do that at will; you do it only in culturally specified ways.

In all the classes I've taken and taught, there must have been thousands of times that someone had a painful urgency to go to the bathroom. But never in all those years have I seen a student walk to the corner of the classroom to relieve himself. Not even in all-male classes. Yet in the field, whether camping with Americans or

living with natives, in forest, desert, or tundra, I've seen people simply walk a few paces away from the group to answer nature's call.
In Western societies, the bathroom in the family home is used
by both sexes, but rarely is a public toilet. As a nineteen-year-old
soldier in Korea, full of beer and *kimchee*, I once walked into a
movie house's restroom through a door labeled MEN. I found a
group of people of both sexes companionably squatting over porce-
lain trenches in the floor. Some were actually holding hands. A
child of the West, I instantly developed constipation and fled. Men
alone I could have handled: life in the army had already forced me
to suppress my first culture's repugnance of doing one's ablutions
in public. But peeing with girls was too much.

You may recognize that my cultural conditioning (learned
expectations) caused my youthful distress in this case, but culture
can influence behavior even in areas that most people think are
beyond learning.

Sleeping and Dreaming

In various societies people are taught "the correct" way to sleep: in
some, women cannot sleep on their backs, or men cannot sleep on
their sides. Or elsewhere, vice versa.

Even dreams are not always free. Dreaming—which is a physiological necessity because dream deprivation leads to psychosis—is
culturally controlled in some places. Among some hill tribes of
Southeast Asia, children are asked each morning what they
dreamed last night. If the dream was scary, the parents analyze
how it could be improved next time: "You dreamed you fell out of a
tall tree? Next time wake up before you hit the ground, so you will
not die." Elsewhere, people are trained to dream for specific purposes or about specific events or entities, and they can do so on
demand. (The concept of "lucid dreaming" has now come into vogue
in America, so these examples may no longer raise your eyebrows.)

Some dreams can be functional. Isaac Singer, the inventor of
the sewing machine, insisted that he dreamed the idea of how a
continuous-stitching machine could work and that his 1851
patent application was based on this dreamed design. More often,
the function is not technological, but psychological, as in making
up the dreamer's mind. In shamanistic societies, dreams are seen
as sources of legitimate information and spiritual guidance. In
many Native American tribes, individuals recognize their calling as
healers and spiritual curers through dreams.

Every culture appears to incorporate some way to interpret
dreams but, not surprisingly, different societies give them greater or
lesser credence. Dreams have been judged important enough to
base whole new religions on—the dreams of Jacob and Joseph and

their interpretations are a biblical case in point. Aboriginal Australians conceive of life as part of the Eternal Dreaming, a continuum in which the past, the present, and the future coexist simultaneously. In Western societies, dreams are usually considered irrelevant to everyday life, but do have important psychological implications.

So What about Sex?

That's a topic we'll keep coming back to, but let me point out here that there is absolutely nothing inevitable or natural about what you do when in the throes of passion: it's all learned, and that's easy to prove. To begin with, try to remember where and how you first heard about sexual intercourse. Didn't you exclaim in horror: "My mommy and daddy don't do that!"? So much for instinct. Second, how do you "do intercourse?" Yes, yes, I accept that you know how the various parts couple together. But if no one had told you they went like that, would you ever have figured it out? Regardless of what you believe yourself capable of in the pride and vigor of your youth, odds are that you simply don't remember when you first received the information. Zoo literature is full of examples of gorillas and chimpanzees raised in isolation who, when brought together for mating purposes with a similarly deprived member of the opposite sex, couldn't figure out what came next and wound up expressing their sexual urgency in fighting and killing each other. Which is no way to start a meaningful relationship. Do you think you are more instinctual and primitive than an ape? If so, the literature of psychology offers examples of human beings who were never told and never saw and thus never figured it out.

The point is, sex is a cultural phenomenon as much as a biological one. Years ago it was noted that the spread of oral sex coincided with the spread of modern plumbing—especially the shower. Although that makes perfectly good sense, it doesn't prove a cause-and-effect relationship—and I feel compelled to remind you that it also coincided with the spread of the idea of people as consumers.

Seeing Is Believing

In any case, the influence of culture is not limited to your biological drives and their expression; it extends into the very ways you experience life. Culture determines every aspect of your perception.

Consider, for example, something as mundane as the color green. "Green" identifies a range of wavelengths in visible light. All persons with normal vision can perceive a continuum of those wavelengths; we call it "the visible spectrum." The waves themselves are a physical phenomenon, and the proper province of physics. Your ability to see them as colors, however, is biological.

The retinae of your eyes contain rods and cones, specialized cells that allow you to respond to light to distinguish the form, shape, and color of objects. The cones give you color vision. The shortest wavelengths you can see are called violet in English; the longest are called red.

But *what* colors you see is a cultural phenomenon.

Every human group has found it useful to indicate objects by their color, meaning that every language has a color vocabulary. But because there are no breaks in the continuum of wavelengths, any division of the spectrum into useful segments must be purely arbitrary. All languages have labeled such arbitrary segments. In English, the major or elementary colors are red, orange, yellow, green, blue, indigo, and violet. It should no longer surprise you that what we consider a perfectly self-evident way of partitioning the visible spectrum is not universally accepted. Some languages have names for as few as three colors, which translate roughly as dark, light, and red—in those, green simply is not a category. Others designate fewer or more than seven primary colors, and these designations do not necessarily cut the spectrum in the same places that English does—that is, color names may not translate.

When I was a graduate student in psychology—before I switched to anthropology—I once admired a painting by a Navaho artist. It was a very realistic and skillfully crafted representation of Monument Valley—pastel sands, red rock formations, light blue grass and a pale green sky. I asked the artist why he painted the grass blue and the sky green, instead of the other way around. I assumed, of course, that he was colorblind. He asked me if I had never heard of blue grass, and had I never seen the sky turn turquoise and green for a few moments just as the sun sets? Well, yes, I had, but blue grass made me think of Kentucky, not the Navaho Reservation, and the shadows of the monoliths in his picture did not indicate sundown.

In the shadows, he answered, grass can take on many colors. And weather and the seasons often make the sky not-blue. And besides, he smiled, in Navaho there are no words to distinguish what Anglos call blue and green, for all that they see it as clearly as anybody else.

Back home, like a good budding experimentalist, I devised a simple test that you can run yourself. I cut one-inch squares out of color photographs in magazines that showed sky, grass or snow and marked the back of each square with its source. In their original setting, every one of these squares appeared to be obviously blue, green, or white. Then I asked students in introductory psychology courses to classify the (shuffled) squares according to color. I found general agreement among my subjects about where most of the squares fell on the color continuum. But when I tallied up the results, only a minority of the squares turned out to be classed with the expected hues for sky, grass, or snow. Yet when I put the squares back into their holes in the pictures, many subjects would change their minds, "seeing" them now as blue, green, or white again. Some, perhaps suspecting me of sleight of hand, demanded to know how I managed to change the squares' colors.

There are several ways to look at these results, but the point is that you see what you expect to see, and what you expect to see is what culture has taught you to expect. Grass is green, the sky is blue, snow is white. As for what you label any particular segment of that seamless continuum called "the visible spectrum," that depends on what your culture has taught you. ("Is that red too, Mommy?" "No, that is pink.") In other words: even something as profoundly basic as *seeing*—the vaunted "evidence of your eyes"—is influenced if not determined by culture, which means that *there are alternatives to the ways you experience the universe and yourself, and they are not necessarily worse or better than the ones you know.*

What you perceive depends on your perspective, and changing your perspective expands your perception. There is real danger in being stuck with a single point of view, because it may convince you that you already understand the world and your place in it. The world is undergoing rapid and drastic change in all of its major aspects, and there is no hope that this turbulence will slow during your lifetime. So even if you did understand it, that would only be a temporary condition. Sooner or later, whatever you take as a given now will turn out not to be, and then the efforts that worked for you in the past will work no longer. Take it from science: *no matter how complex things seem to you now, they were never as simple as that!*

"Okay," I hear you mutter, "so what?"

So this: When things are not working out, for you or your society, the tendency (because of perceptual habits) is to repeat the approach. As the playwright Samuel Beckett advised: when you fail, you should "Try again. Fail again. Fail better."

Although this advice may help you persevere and perfect your technique, it also means that if things fail to go right even when you try harder *and smarter*, you (or your society) have only two choices left: giving up or becoming fanatic. The writer Brooks Atkinson made a more useful observation: "The most fatal illusion is the settled point of view. Since life is growth and motion, a fixed point of view kills anybody who has one."

Whether you flourish or perish in your personal future will turn out to be not merely a matter of hard work and study, but of the flexibility of your perspectives. And this rule holds just as much for corporations and societies as for individuals.

It's true even for humanity as a whole. Slavery, smallpox, space travel and every other longtime human problem that has ever been worked out was solved not by running into the brick wall one more time a little harder, but by looking at the obstacle from a new point of view. Obviously the hunt must be on for new perspectives. So where do you find those?

One excellent source of fresh perspectives is the record of other cultures. Every society that ever existed has had to deal with the same basic problems which you face: food, shelter, reproduction, strife. Each of them developed means (their cultures) to satisfy these needs, means which were effective—for a while. All of them had to adapt to changes in their environments, including their own and their neighbors' behaviors. All those that failed to adapt have disappeared as social units. This is as true for Western ghost towns as for the Roman Empire or the Soviet Union, for Angkor Wat as for the Maya or the Indians of the Great Plains. And it will be true for American life as you now know it unless our nations and peoples and cultures respond successfully to the lethal challenge of the race between resources and population.

ONE WORLD, ONE CULTURE

Cultures are organic: they are born and they die. Mostly, in between, they change. Depending on where their bearers, their culture-bearing individuals, live, and when, cultures mature and survive at different rates. In its earlier stages, change was glacially slow. At present, cultures' component elements are moving away from each other like the seeds in a growing watermelon, like galaxies in the universe itself. Some change noticeably slower than others, and those, the archaeological record seems to imply, are doomed. Still, in this particular version of the turtle-racing-the-hare story, societies that change cultures fastest may win the sprints only to burn out on the long haul. Consider. . . .

At the beginning of the Third Millennium we are witnessing the disappearance of an ever-increasing number of species. Animal extinctions you're aware of, but do you know that worldwide one out of every two species of plants is threatened and that one out of every eight is becoming extinct? And that these include many of the ancestors of the foods we are most dependent on? Scientists warn that it is statistically a near-inevitability that sooner or later a plague will wipe out some major staple, as it almost did the potato more than a century ago. In that event we will need to breed new and resistant strains from the parent stock. If that stock is extinct, massive starvation will occur in all the nations that today depend on that staple. The others will run out of surplus food to sell them, and the Final War will begin. If that sounds fanciful, consider rice and the fact that China is a nuclear power. There are no scenarios for civilization's survival in that contest. It is therefore undeniably imperative that humanity continue to cultivate viable stocks of every wild ancestral food species, to ensure against its extinction and our own. It does not matter that some of them are barely edible; what counts is their further genetic potential.

We are also witnessing the difficult and dangerous birth of a world culture, sired by the twentieth century's Big Bang explosion of people and technology, and forced on us for the profit and convenience of multinational corporations. Having already lost most of the ancestral lifeways of our species, we are converting the rest into variants of the First World's high-tech, high-density, high-stress, high-alienation, profit-for-the-few-is-the-bottom-line lifestyles; building a hive with a thousand queens. The danger in the homogenization of cultures is analogous to the threat in losing genetic variety in food staples: Every culture, whether "primitive" or "world," inculcates only its own perspective on the human condition, and a world with a single one-size-fits-all way of addressing problems maximizes its vulnerabilities.

It is, of course, inconceivable to us—as it was to Pharaonic Egypt, Rome, and all succeeding empires including, more recently, those of Great Britain and the Soviet Union—that our culture could end. But it will, because it is vulnerable in more ways than any of its predecessors. For example, today's America depends for its survival on the flow of foreign oil and steel and many manufactured goods, as well as the continuous immigration of a variety of skilled professionals (e.g., math and engineering profs, nurses and doctors), none of which our own culture any longer produces in sufficient quantities. This flow could be cut off through war, economic depression, or even through some not-yet-gene-spliced biological weapon that would render oil unusable. In this sense the U.S. economy resembles that of the major colonial powers of a century ago: its wealth and power derive from the flow of resources from overseas to the motherland, but when that flow stops . . .

You can tell that culture change has taken place when you cannot go back to the way things were. We can no longer exist without cars. We can already no longer go back to the way things were before computers, or before civil rights, or birth control. But what if (or when!) our present high-tech lifeway grinds to a halt? With what sort of culture would you replace it? It is too late to return to the agrarian yeomanry that Jefferson espoused: there are too many of us, but not enough who know how to wrest surpluses from the land without petroleum-based technologies. In replacing all cultural alternatives that once existed in America (and every other mass society), we have lost them.

Imagine a cataclysmic end to modern, technology-based culture (this is a popular theme in fiction). It would bring death to almost all of us—do you see why? The few who survived would have to make do without the communications technology you take for granted, without petroleum or the internal combustion engine, and without the copper and other irreplaceable resources that have been exhausted in creating our present culture. Unthinkable though such an eventuality is, it is nevertheless becoming increasingly likely. It is, in fact, the pious hope of many—here as well as abroad—who would eagerly bring about the collapse of civilization through the sort of interventions we now call terrorism.

What you need therefore, now, before it is too late, are viable alternative perspectives and values, indeed viable alternatives for everything you take for granted. And again, the seeds for these can be found in other cultures past and present.

Fortunately, the benefit of alien cultures and their perspectives does not necessarily end with their demise. Thanks to ethnography (the anthropological study and description of individual living cultures), archeology (the study and reconstruction of extinct cultures), and history (the study and interpretation of recorded societies), you have access to records of a vast number of different ways of being human. Naturally these are incomplete: there are no complete descriptions of *any* culture, certainly not of your own. But the gist of many of these societal experiments has been saved for you to refer to and to build upon. Ethnographies will show you how major areas of interest have been approached differently from the way things are done where you come from. Inequality, marriage, work. Medicine, scarcity, war. The record indicates how virtually everything that's important to human existence has been handled successfully in other times and climes. Moreover, you can read *why* people did things that way, which is the most instructive of all.

You might ask: But what good is the record of losers? What can we learn from failed cultures except not to be like them?

The fact that a culture has vanished does not indicate any general inferiority on its part. Nor does its persistence over time indicate the opposite. Cultures are adaptations of societies, and societies, it appears, are mortal. Moreover, of the ones still with us, none still has the culture it had just one lifetime ago. It is as true for societies as for individuals that longevity says more about luck than about merit. Albert Einstein, William Shakespeare, and Thomas Jefferson are dead, but their recorded thought lives to guide us. It is that way with the cultures that ethnographers and archeologists have recorded. It doesn't matter that you wouldn't want to live in some of them; what counts is their further cultural potential.

A RAY OF HOPE

So what about *your* odds on the good life?

You're a culture bearer, but you carry only an infinitesimal portion of the whole. Some of that is essentially predetermined: which language you speak; where you were born and to whom; that you share their etiquettes and religious values. In our species that's a starter kit for life. But it's not enough for a decent living, so here you are, as the bumper stickers used to say, on the very first day of the rest of your life, with a growing awareness that you may need a Plan B.

The prime prerequisite for a functional Plan B is flexibility: your goal must be adaptiveness, *not* resistance until death. The longer you survive, the greater the number of times you can expect to change careers, to relocate in physical and social space. When inevitable change presents you with threats and opportunities, choice demands not only that you recognize your alternatives but that you distinguish their immediate from their long-range implications. Therefore you need to understand how your cultural environment works. But learning that will require some work, and you may well ask, "Is it worth it?"

Let's review the bidding: both biologically and behaviorally you are a product of culture; you are who and what you are because of what you have experienced. Surely you see the implication? *You can reinvent yourself by managing your cultural input!* I'm not suggesting that you can become anything you can imagine: you do have biological, social, and psychological limits. But even within those (and we all have them; you are not unfairly handicapped here), you are already no longer the person you were as an infant or a 15-year-old. Not just your body, but also your identity and your capacity to affect your environment have grown.

For much of this transformation you were a passive recipient: growing taller and older without much conscious thought. But now volition has become a factor: you are able to determine major aspects of the culture you live by and in. Indeed, you can actually design and direct many of the most important changes you will experience as a member of society, as a bearer of culture. And if your innovation works for you, it may extend to others, even to the next generation(s). Isn't that why you sought an education in the first place? If ever the world handed you an invitation for personal responsibility, this is it.

But how can you be sure that whatever you commit yourself to, in terms of careers or beliefs or relationships, will last in this Age of Impermanence?

Well, you can't. That's the point! Nothing lasts. You won't either. But between now and the grave there are a lot of better things to be than poor, dumb and lonely. And you now know that it's up to you to maximize your odds.

So which way to go? What should you become?

The study of alternatives is a necessary foundation for a lifetime of change. Here an anthropological perspective can work as a sort of Netserver in your effort to cruise the web of existence. At the very least it will make you aware of your own cultural baggage, enabling you to decide how much and what part of it you will continue to backpack through life, what you'd be better off without and what else it will take to make you a happier camper on your pilgrimage.

MAKING THE CULTURE CONCEPT MANAGEABLE

You now know that "culture" involves everything that human beings have made or thought and transmitted across time and space, that is, everything about the human condition that's not genetically ordained or "natural." That makes culture the trademark of our species. No other animal has anything remotely like it, even though there are many other species whose behavior is largely learned. Chimps may occasionally make primitive tools, but they don't depend on them for their survival. Only humans use fire, only humans can lie about politics or being in love, only humans read, only humans profess.

If that's opened your eyes, you're probably sputtering, "Then *everything* is culture!" And you'd be right: it largely is, for humans. What's worse, there is no single, all-encompassing, universally accepted definition of culture for you to memorize and test your observations against. In 1952 two anthropologists, Alfred Kroeber and Clyde Kluckhohn, listed and analyzed some 300 definitions of culture that were then in use. Now the number is vastly greater, but we will get to the problem of definitions in a few pages.

The problem with any concept *that* encompassing is that it's unwieldy. Culture—like "life"—needs to be divided into manageable chunks if it is to be useful. But how to go about that? Which chunks? And why those?

Like the similarly continuous spectrums of color and sound, culture has no natural or preordained places to indicate "here starts a new segment," so the only way you can break up its seamless continuum is arbitrarily. And consequently there is a large number of perfectly satisfactory ways to partition this unwieldy concept. Happily, each different approach offers new insights into how it and you work.

Levels of Culture

In one approach culture is differentiated according to the level of organization it serves.

Species Culture

If you look at culture as the behavioral equivalent to the gene pool, then all members of our species share certain habits and customs of thought and behavior—you can say that we share the gene for culture. Every undamaged infant—wherever born— learns to speak the local language, to walk, and to acquire the local habits of thought and behavior. We are all carriers of culture at this level.

Societal Culture

Physically, human populations can be told apart because they have different gene frequencies: every interbreeding population has a characteristic *gene profile* (defined as the percentages of people with specific genetic features in such variables as blood type, skin color, ratio of femur length to tibia length, fat storage pattern, resistance to specific diseases, etc.). Far more conspicuous, every society has some identifying *culture profile*, meaning that its people behave in characteristic fashions because of their conditioning and consequent habits, which in turn are based upon their assumptions about themselves, about the nature of society and the universe around them. When we talk of Aztec culture, Viking culture, or Zulu culture, we acknowledge that these societies exhibit(ed) unique and characteristic combinations of values, language, kinship patterns, artifacts, and other traits in their specific applications of species culture. A society—an interacting collectivity of people who see themselves as a social unit— may have more than one culture, and under some circumstances a culture may expand beyond its society's borders.

All of us carry a societal culture in this sense; some of us (immigrants and ethnographers) may carry two or more, though usually only one is kept current.

Familial Culture

But the partitioning of culture doesn't stop there: within every society, each family raises its children in a slightly different manner from every other. You grew up in a milieu whose specific profile of culture traits—from food preferences to vocabulary—was unique to your parents, your siblings, and you. It is easy to spot family culture in jokes and expressions and memories that mean something only to you and yours and in the way you all share a taste for food the way your mother cooked it. But family culture can extend indefinitely beyond that homey basis.

The manner in which children are punished, for example, tends to be carried on even by those who most resented the way it was done to them: if your father was a fanny beater, odds are you'll be one with your kids; if he was a face slapper or locked you in the closet, you're likely to punish that way too. On a still more visceral level, there are family-specific superstitions. Long past the time we have learned the scientific rationales for things our parents did not understand, some of us persist in believing the "explanations" they gave. If that seems disingenuous now, remember that for all of human history until the last century or so, family culture was the only culture that ever mattered to most people, and that for many its continuity remains their highest value.

Associational Culture

Most societies also harbor organizations that are *not* kinship based. From churches and states to armies and corporations, from support groups, Cub Scout troops and service clubs to chat rooms on the Internet, all enduring associations have cultural aspects that are separate from (though dependent on) family culture for their survival and continuity and that similarly impose upon their members a host of expectations, definitions of reality, and demands for consent and performance. In modern complex societies, the impact of associational culture can be just as marking as that of family culture. As in: "Never ask a man if he is a Texan (or a Marine). If he is, he'll tell you. If he ain't, you don't want to embarrass him."

Individual Culture

Finally, undeniably and inescapably, there *you* are, with your characteristic assemblage of habits and your unique integration of all you value and can do and believe and will put up with. Your biological aspect is heavily influenced by your life experiences. Your individual—or idio—culture is that compendium of traits that you acquired and adapted from your familial and associational cultures, as well as from your unique life experiences, your interpretations of the whole mess, and whatever substantial decisions you have made along the way. Oh yes, and your biological limits.

In short, culturally, as much as biologically, you are like no other persons, like some other persons, and like all other persons. Just like the rest of us.

Though this way of cutting culture into manageable pieces serves a variety of functions, it gets us no closer to understanding how the process operates and evolves. The trick is to perceive culture as a whole while distinguishing a connection between its different aspects and those of the social group and yourself.

The Wheel Analogy

One common method visualizes culture as a wheel wobbling from the past to the future.

In this diagram you are the X, the person surrounded by culture; imagine that you are the axle around which culture spins. The thickness of the disc or wheel is language, that which underlies the other aspects and makes them possible. T stands for technology, O for organization, and I for ideation. Note that each of these three is connected to the others with arrows that point both ways, indicating two-way flow and feedback.

Note especially that there are no borders between the aspects: this is a *not* a pie diagram; you are *not* to assume that there are places where one aspect stops and another begins. For although it may often seem that way, in fact the wheel's spin blurs any borders you may think you perceive.

Take, for example, a Christmas card. Which cultural aspect does it belong to? Well, cards don't grow on trees; they are manufactured.

That makes them *technological* items. But the reason for sending them is to maintain bonds of kinship and friendship, and surely that's an aspect of sociality and therefore *organization*. However, the reason for the season in which Christmas cards are sent is (or originally was) a religious one, and therefore this bit of folded paper is clearly *ideational*; and the card is to remind its recipient of that, too. And of course its messages, both the printed one and the one you write by hand, communicate meaning through words, so the card is obviously *language.*

The difficulty here is that you and I, raised in a culture that makes a fetish of deconstructing everything for analysis and cataloguing, are intolerant of the idea that anything can belong to more than one category. But that is not a universal human bias, merely one from modern Western culture. Being aware of the interrelationship of cultural elements allows us to see how each one functions to contribute to the continuity and survival of the culture as a whole.

Functional Cross-Currents

The aboriginal hunter spears a seal coming up for air, drags it onto the ice, clubs it to death with a single blow and then, before proceeding to butcher it, sucks water from the fish-bladder flask he carries under his fur parka to keep it from freezing. Opening the beast's jaws, he carefully squirts his mouthful into the dead seal's maw.

"Thank you, oh excellent seal," he prays, "for granting me your flesh and your fat. I give you sweet water for your final journey. Now that I have kept the covenant between our people and yours, she whom I desire can move into my hut without shame, for I am a Man now. Tell the seal people not to shun me when I hunt them, because I treated you respectfully and gave you a good death."

Then he inserts his knife into the beast's belly and commences to disembowel it.

"So what am I seeing?" inquires the watching ethnographer. "Is this hunting? Marriage? Religion? A manhood ceremony?"

"Exactly!" answers the hunter, pleased that He Who Keeps Asking is finally beginning to understand. ᷧ

On Definitions

Before we can begin discussing the implications of each of the aspects of culture, we must agree what we mean by terms, so that we can agree what it is we are talking about. That means definitions. Now there are two things to remember about definitions, no matter who makes them or why.

1. *Complete definitions are functionally impossible.* Say that the proverbial Alien from Another Planet holds up a piece of chalk and asks you to define it. Just answering "That's chalk!" won't do: a label is not a definition. So you might

mention that this object is used for writing on a blackboard, but then you would have to explain "writing" and "blackboard." If you note its cylindrical shape or its color, you would also have to indicate whether those are attributes of the entire category "chalk" or merely of this particular example. Any attempt at a complete definition would also have to deal with chalk's atomic weight, specific gravity, hardness, frangibility, electrical resistance, organic origins, evolutionary implications, and so forth. By the time you finish a complete definition of a simple piece of chalk, you will have written a five-foot shelf on everything from physics to economics. And obviously things get even more complicated when you try to define human behavior.

2. *All definitions are relativistic: they can only be judged by their usefulness to the purpose for which they were coined.* When rocketry was in its infancy after World War II, there was some interest in the possibility of using rockets to send mail and passengers from coast to coast. Engineers writing on the subject defined a person or passenger as "a liquid-filled bag with two air bubbles." For their purposes that was fine: if they could manage to have such a sack arrive without the liquids leaking out or the two bubbles becoming one, their job was done. But for a surgeon or a psychiatrist, "a liquid-filled bag with two air bubbles" does not usefully define a patient. Does that mean the engineers' definition was no good? No, it only means it is of no use to surgeons and psychiatrists.

The definitions that open the chapters on language, organization, ideation, and technology are thus limited and situational.

Thinking It Through

1. Consider the second double helix (of biology and culture), and the fact that without culture you cannot survive. From that perspective, are preculturized persons (like babies and infants) really fully human? Why or why not?
2. Demonstrate that the colors you see are arbitrary points on a continuum. Can you identify other such continua in human perception?
3. Can you define culture and distinguish between natural and cultural phenomena?
4. Draw the TOIL model of culture. Don't forget the arrows. Why are its component areas not clearly separated?
5. Can you explain the levels of culture, and offer an example of a typical trait for each?

In the Beginning Was the Word

Language

"The symbol is the universe of humanity . . . It is the symbol which has transformed man from a mere animal to a human animal."

—Leslie A. White (1900–1975)

"Language is not simply a reporting device for experience but a defining framework for it."

—Benjamin Lee Whorf (1897–1941)

*Language is the system of shared
utterances (sounds) with their meanings
(vocabulary) and rules for usage (grammar)
through which human beings
communicate. Language use requires
the creation, learning, manipulation,
and teaching of meanings that are
arbitrarily attached to utterances. As such,
language is that aspect of culture that
most immediately conditions the
perception, storage, and transmission
of information.*

*Y*ou were born with the capacity to learn whatever language was spoken around you, and that imitative ability evidenced itself long before you made your first voluntary utterances. Within an hour of your birth, your flailing of arms and legs began to assume the rhythm of the language you heard your mother speak. Long before you mumbled your first "Mama!" you had the music of her speech down cold.

The physiological equipment you use in producing speech is essentially identical to that of all other members of our species, regardless of race, culture, or even sex—at least until males' voices change in puberty. Of course there are individual variations: basses and tenors, sopranos and altos; no two people are identical and all that. But the bulk of the differences in speech patterns between communities is due to conditioning—that is, to culture, not to biology. For an obvious proof, look around any classroom: regardless of what their last names sound like, students who were born to U. S. citizens can usually speak the local variety of English without accent or other ethnic giveaways.

But not so their immigrant ancestors, who may all speak mutually unintelligible tongues. One reason for that incomprehensibility is that languages not only use different words for the same concept or thing, but also that they almost all make some sounds that simply do not occur in the repertories of other languages. And they do so with the standard human vocal equipment.

YOUR SOUND SYSTEM

The range of vocalizations human beings use in communication is astonishing. Speakers of almost every language employ vowels and consonants that speakers of some other language find impossible to imitate without considerable practice—if ever. This is true even of closely related languages such as Danish and Dutch, two Germanic tongues spoken in countries bordering on Germany but not each other, although the Netherlands and Denmark lie less than 250 km (160 miles) apart. Yet Danes make some sounds that Dutch people cannot duplicate, and vice versa. When you start comparing languages more widely separated in space and history, you run into noises that your oral habits simply will not allow. These "impossibilities" are not limited to such truly unusual ones as the various clicks in the Khoisian (Bushman and Hottentot) languages of South Africa but include some of the vowels and consonants used in languages not that far removed from yours. One irritatingly wonderful thing about this infinitude of utterances is that any baby can learn to make them, yet you and I cannot—or rather, can no longer.

Vowels

You were probably taught that the sounds we use in speech come in two flavors: vowels, the noises you make with your air stream and vocal cords, and consonants, the noises you produce by interfering with that flow. In fact, vowels come in a bewildering variety, depending on where you place your tongue and whether you keep it flat or raise its back (e.g., for the *oo* in *look*), its tip (e.g., for the *i* in *tip*), or its middle (e.g., for the *uh* in *rubber*). Technically, there are also deep vowels, high vowels, low vowels, abnormal vowels, retroflex vowels, and a slew of even more esoteric categorical distinctions.

Just as colors are arbitrarily selected but culturally standardized points on a seamless continuum of light, so vowels are arbitrary but regularized points on a continuum of human-produced sound. Try this demonstration: Hum with your mouth open. Keep it open, still giving voice, but purse your lips. The noise you make now will sound more or less like the *oo* in *you*; minor adjustment of your jaw will make it come out right. Open your mouth wider, lips still pursed, and you'll arrive at the *o* in *hope*; open further and relax your lips: you'll have the *a* in *father;* stretch your lips in a grin and there's the *i* of *fit;* raise your tongue slightly to the roof of your mouth and hear the *ee* in *feet*. From there, if you pucker up again, you'll do the *u* in the French *tu* (= you) or in the German *tür* (= door)—and you'll have produced a sound that English-speakers usually cannot make.

Your vocal apparatus is habituated to stopping at certain places on this continuum; from lifelong habit it "jumps" there automatically, bypassing all the intermediate stages that your language doesn't recognize as "correct" sounds, very much like an express train passes by numerous stations to stop only at the scheduled major ones. But other cultures slice the vowel continuum differently, and some of the stations that your express train ignores turn out to be major stops for *their* language's express train—which hears *your* habituated utterances as unacceptable variants or even as "impossible" noises.

Try the vowel experiment again, but this time listen closely to all the in-between stations. Somewhere between *o* and *a* you should experience the sound of the *au* in *caught*. Then pucker your lips with your mid-tongue reaching for the front of the roof of your mouth, and you'll produce a sound like the French and Dutch *eu* or the Scandinavian and German varieties of *ö*—which all sound slightly different from each other in a way that every native speaker will notice but that you will not hear. When you learn a foreign language, this is what you must teach your tongue to do: to arrive automatically at different vowels by stopping at different places on the sound continuum.

Notice, in this exercise, that the definition of "vowel" is not absolute, because you reach different vowels by affecting the sound flow with the shape of your mouth, and technically that's consonant behavior. Okay, so perhaps the definitions of vowel and consonant are themselves merely customary stops on a seamless continuum and, like any other definition, no better than their usefulness. You've heard that before.

Consonants

Vocalizations can be created and affected not just by vocal cords, tongue and lips, but by throat constriction, nasalization, teeth, cheeks, the arytenoids (two cartilaginous hinges at the rear of the larynx), and so forth. To get an idea of the immense variety of sounds a literally uncultured person can make, spend half an hour listening to an infant at the babbling stage of its development, as it exercises its vocal equipment in happy solitude.

Technically, consonants are sounds made by closing off the airflow in the vocal tract completely (e.g., the *g* in *gone* or the *d* in *dog*) or partially (e.g., the *v* in *very*, the *z* in *buzz*). Plosive consonants momentarily plug the airstream in the nasal and oral airways to make an explosive sound (e.g., the *b* and *k* in *buck*). Many consonants can be either voiced (*b, d, g, m, v, z*) or unvoiced (*p, t, k, n, f, s*); some are aspirated (meaning that they are pronounced with a puff of air, an *h* sound) in some contexts, in others not (e.g., the first *t* in *total* is aspirated, the second *t* is not).

Tongue-produced consonants are fairly easy to imitate. For example, you can vibrate the tongue tip while producing voiced or unvoiced air, and get the "rolling" *r* used in Spanish, Dutch, Scottish and a host of other languages; you can curl the tip and hold it steady to produce the English varieties of *r* in *roaring*, you can vibrate the back of the tongue or the uvula and wind up with the throaty Parisian *r*, which sounds very much like the *ch* in the German *Ich* or the *x* in the Spanish *Mexico*, all of which are similar to but softer than the Dutch *g* as in the name (Vincent van) *Gogh*, which I defy any non-Hollander to pronounce like a native. (This example also illustrates the fact that the letters of the alphabet do not necessarily describe the same sound in different languages.)

What complicates things is that most speakers are not aware of their own oral activities, and in some languages certain sound-distinctions make a difference in meaning while in others they do not. I had lived in the United States for almost three decades before I was made aware that the *th* in *they* is different from the *th* in *thigh*: the first is voiced, the second is not. Since I had never voiced *th* at all, my pronunciation improved once I understood that principle. I've also endured the humbling experience of listening to a native speaker of some foreign tongue patiently repeat a minimum pair (two words that sound identical except for one sound, e.g., *b*atch and *p*atch, *th*y and *th*igh, or ser*v*ice and sur*f*ace) without my ever hearing the distinction or being able to imitate it: "No no, it is not *loro*, it is *loro*. Hear the difference? *Loro, loro; loro, loro; loro, loro!*"

Accents

Foreigners learning English will have greater or lesser difficulty with pronunciation depending on how similar their mother tongue's vowels and consonants are to those of English. Dutch uses the so-called "Italianate" vowel system, which means that there are only two or three ways to pronounce each of the vowels in the alphabet. For instance, the letter *i* is pronounced either like the *i* in b*i*t or like the *ee* in f*ee*t, there are no alternatives. (Netherlanders call theirs "pure" vowels; you see where that leaves yours.) In Dutch you cannot voice consonants at the end of a word, regardless of how that word is written. So *Bud* is pronounced the same way as *butt* (which can have unfortunate consequences) and *hard* sounds the same as *heart*. Furthermore, there is no *th* sound in Dutch: the name *Theo* is pronounced *tay'yo*.

The effect of such a primary conditioning on the acquisition of English as a second language is that many immigrants cannot at first distinguish or pronounce the difference between *bat, bad, bet, bed, bath,* or *Beth*: they are all perceived as *bet*. "On a bet Beth batted the bad bat from the bed into the bath" becomes "On a bet Bet betted de bet bet from de bet into de bet."

Nonverbal Communication

Making sounds is not the only way that communication can take place: think of a shrug, a wink and gestures. Like words, gestures are not universally understood, although with the spread of such American culture traits by such means as Hollywood movies, some are becoming very widely recognized indeed! All gestures, whether rude or not, come under the rubric of learned symbolizing behavior. Moreover, things we call signs in human communication also turn out to have symbols attached to them: there is no other reason but arbitrary cultural convention why stop signs should be octagonal.

Rules and Meaning

Semantics is the study of the meaning of words.

All languages and dialects have built-in rules to determine whether an utterance has meaning. These rules may differ as much from one language to the next as their sound systems do and can be as rigid, arbitrary, and enduring as those governing any other aspect of culture. In practical terms, this means that merely being able to make the noises and knowing some words of another language does not mean you can speak it. For that, you also need to know the order in which words are to be presented, that is, the rules governing the formation of words and their relations in a sentence.

Grammar

There is evidence that all human languages share some universal structural underpinning, implying—among other things—that some sort of template for communicating is hardwired into our brains. Nevertheless, languages differ not only in the sounds they make, but also in the way they organize them.

"Grammar" refers to the rules that govern how the elements of a language—its sounds, its morphemes (the smallest identifiable sound units with a specific function and meaning, such as the *s* at the end of a word that signifies "there is more than one"), its words, and its sentences—are to be presented in order for their meaning to be generally understood. Every dialect and language has a grammar, but just as there are no complete definitions of any thing, there is no such thing as a complete grammar for any language.

That's so in part because languages live and evolve. Just as your culture loses technological traits as they are supplanted by later (New and Improved!) hardware and techniques, so once-hard-and-fast rules for speech become relaxed and are forgotten. For example, recently an announcer on National Public Radio said that "Fortunately for you and I . . ." Until recently such a grammatical blunder marked you as semiliterate, because this variant is illogical as well as ungrammatical (Would you say "Fortunately for I and you?"). But now even some college professors use *I* where *me* is correct. Obviously this rule of grammar is weakening. Call it debasement of the language if you will but recognize that language use changes over time.

Of course, not all deviations from traditional grammar are so objectionable. For example, knowing the rule for when to use "whom" versus "who" was long a class-marker in American society, but dropping the "m" does not affect clarity. A case can even be made that anything that reduces grammatical eccentricity in English should be welcomed, and that the who/whom distinction, which almost no one can handle anymore, therefore *should* be dropped.

Syntax

Syntax refers to the rules for ordering or combining words into broader utterances such as sentences. In some languages, such as English, the order that words take in a sentence is crucial to its meaning: *man bites dog* is not the same thing as *dog bites man.* In others, such as Latin, you may present those three words in any order you like—as long as you indicate what meaning you intend through your choice of the five declensions and six cases in the inflection of each noun. In English, you make an effort to minimize the distance between a verb and its object: *I have gone to the store to buy some bread.* In Germanic languages, verbs tend to pile up at the end of the sentence: *I am to the store for some bread gone to buy.* Long, complex written sentences may momentarily puzzle even native speakers about which verb refers to which action.

Languages also differ in their rules for combining words. In Inuit (Eskimo), parts of different words are combined (more often in infixes rather than suffixes or prefixes) into sometimes very long terms for which English would require separate sentences. Germanic languages can add entire words together to make new terms: the recently coined Dutch noun *Europrijsstijgingen* compounds three words: *Euro* (the new monetary unit of the European Union), *prijs* (price; "ij" is how the letter "y" is written in Dutch), and *stijgingen* (advances, increases). Thus it means "Euro(-based) price increases."

In many other languages, such combinations are simply not allowed or are impossible, because the combining of words would interfere with meaning.

Stress, Pitch and Intonation

In some languages, including English, stress—the energetic emphasis laid on a particular word or part of a word through extra loudness or intensity—is capable of changing the meaning of the utterance. The classic example linguists use compares:

"What are we having for dinner, Daddy?"

"What are we having for dinner—*Daddy?*"

The first inquires what's going to be eaten, the second, who.

Native English-speakers tend to carry their habit of using stress as a distinguishing characteristic of speech (and *writing*) into every other language they know, which marks them as non-natives to people (like the French) whose languages do not indicate emphasis in this way.

Pitch is a related concept. It refers to the fundamental or conventional frequency of the tone of someone's voice. Generally, your voice gets higher as you become excited, lower as you calm down. In most European languages (Swedish is an exception), pitch is not usually phonemic, beyond the idea of using rising pitch to turn an utterance into a question: *This is coffee?* Falling pitch indicates a statement: *This is coffee.*

Intonation is the conventional melody or pitch accent of speech. Because of culture, class and other social categories as well as physical condition, individuals differ characteristically and from time to time on how much intonation they use. When you are very tired, your intonation will be much "flatter" than when you are not.

In some languages, however, intonation is phonemic, meaning that tonality is structured into every word. In such *tonal languages*, the sound *tsyk* (to use an imaginary example) may mean "cat" if pronounced in the speaker's flat tone, but "welcome" if pronounced with a rising tone, and "modern" with a falling tone.

The best-known tonal language is Chinese. There are actually many mutually incomprehensible languages spoken by the billion Han Chinese, of which Mandarin, Cantonese, Fukienese, and Shanghai are the most prevalent. These differ not only in vocabulary, but also in the number of tones they use. There are 3-tone, 4-tone, 6-tone, and so on, forms, and among the tribal mountain dwellers in the southwest, 12-tone languages are spoken. Naturally these are all difficult to learn for someone raised to speak a nontonal language, but the warble of 12-tone Chinese must be almost impossible to acquire even for a 3-tone speaker. (One marvels at the musician's ear it must require to converse in such a tongue!) What unites all the Chinese into a single linguistic unit is the fact that they all use the same characters in writing, so that a

6-tone speaker can communicate with a 3-tone speaker on paper. This, more than ideology or organization, explains the unequaled persistence of Chinese ethnicity over the millennia.

Many African tongues incorporate some tonality; that explains how "drum-language" is used to transmit messages over great distances. The rhythm and pitch of the drumbeats can mimic the intonation of a simple standard vocabulary, thereby communicating meaning even in the absence of vowels and consonants.

Gender

Gender, linguistically, is a set of categories into which all nouns are classed. It is most evident in Indo-European and Semitic languages, but it is also encountered in many other tongues. At its simplest, gender tends to correspond somewhat with sex and animateness, but gender is seldom simple. Typically, gender is indicated by the form of the noun itself, or by the terms that indicate or modify it. In English, where gender is so rudimentary as to be almost unnoticed by its speakers, *he* replaces *the man*, *she* replaces *the woman*, and *it* replaces *the relationship*. (Note that in English the article in every case is the same: *the*. You will soon become very grateful for that.) But gender does not simply indicate sex or its absence: *the ship* is also *she*. In other languages, gender can get much more complicated.

In Latin and in German, there are three classes: masculine, feminine, and neuter. In Spanish and French—though both descended from Latin—there are only two: all nouns are either masculine or feminine. In Dutch (which is Germanic) there are also two (indicated by the articles *de* and *het*), but they do not cover the same terrain: Dutch nouns are either common (sexed) or neuter. In French, nouns are always either masculine or feminine, designated by le or la; *the man* is *le homme* (always contracted to *l'homme*) and *the woman* is *la femme*, *the house* is *la maison*, *the heart* is *le cœur*, and *the table* is *la table*. While the definite articles *le* and *la* indicate the noun's masculine and feminine gender, this is obviously not the same thing as the sex of the subject of the noun: houses and hearts and tables presumably have no sexual characteristics.

As if to rub in the arbitrariness of language, gender does not necessarily translate: what is one gender in this language may be a different gender in that. In Dutch, *the man* is *de man*, *the woman* is *de vrouw*, and *the child* is *het kind*. Linguistically, in other words, Dutch children are sexless. *The house* is *het huis*, *the heart* is *het hart*, but *the table* is *de tafel*: houses and hearts are sexless, but tables are not.

If gender seems confusing to an English speaker, imagine a language with even more genders. There are living examples of languages using four, others use five, and still others exist at every level up to more than twenty. Obviously these cannot all deal with variations in sexuality. Linguistic gender does not equate with behavioral gender.

Nevertheless, gender as we talked about it in previous chapters, that is, gender as the behavior of the sexes, is always a factor in how language is used. All known languages express differences between males and females in vocabulary, word choice, sentence construction and even in tones and stresses. Although subtler and less formal than the inflexible linguistic genders, these sex-specific ways of using a language can be important.

In a few societies (mostly in New Guinea) they are so exaggerated that women insist they cannot understand men, and vice versa, even though the women raise both sons and daughters. In North American English, masculine speech patterns include far more active verbs and aggressive terms than feminine speech does. Such habits as ending every sentence with a tonal rise—making it sound like a question—are far more typical of women than men. This particular trait, by the way, is likely to handicap any woman professionally. Because it makes everything she says sound uncertain and apologetic, the men she works with will automatically judge her inconsequential or question her competence. Whether male or female, if you have this habit, break it!

COMMUNICATING

For creatures like our remotest ancestors, forced to replace instincts with learned adaptations, speech was one specific set of habits that made all the difference in the world. Language dramatically increases the efficiency of teaching, and therefore of learning. Many other animals learn, but language gives us the capacity to turn individual experience into group knowledge and group capacities. Your successful new coping technique, or the novel experience that you survived, need not be lost to those of us who did not share it. Language makes the accumulation of knowledge possible by storing it outside ourselves beyond the genes or the brains.

That was already true for Oma and Opa Backpacker, your ancestors in the distant Pedestrian Past. They had language and brains with more memory capacity than they needed, and they turned anything that worked (and much that didn't) into their intellectual legacy—knowledge and advice to be tapped when necessary.

Humanity's earliest reference libraries were the minds of those who had survived the most experiences. It was the elderly who most likely knew what *this* was, what *that* meant, and how to make *those* things work. They knew because they had lived through similar situations. Which is why, in preliterate societies everywhere, the elderly are respected, even revered: they have survival value!

Because language lets us share experience, any human population, then or now, has accumulated an astonishingly large collection of facts and interpretations to help it survive. Even the simplest cultures contain far more information than any one person can use or even remember.

But your capacity to use language lets you do far more than store and transfer knowledge; it allows you to create it. Language makes possible that capacity for purposeful dreaming, planning, and inventing, which many hold to be the most singular characteristic of human existence. You may have assumed your capacity for ideas to be a purely biological phenomenon, believing your ability to handle ideas to be a given, like intelligence, or even that it is an indication of aptitude. But again, things are not that simple. There is a lot of feedback between the capacity for imagining alternatives and the abilities to recognize and to solve problems. Culture influences them all.

Language, moreover, allows the creation of alternatives without the risks involved in actual experimentation. The word for that is "thought," but language also makes it possible to create alternatives that exist only in the words themselves. I'm thinking here of fiction, of lying, of theorizing—and also of fanciful "explanations" for such observed facts as death and disease, bad luck and good, and for the way an environment changes once people have been living there for a while. Without language there could be no religion and no science.

Language lies at the foundation of culture. Without its aid in thinking, learning and teaching, technologies and organizations could never have evolved much beyond those of the chimpanzees, and your intellectual life, your ideation, would be little better. Language, in other words, is the triggering factor behind everything that makes you more than a mere animal.

Animals do communicate, of course, and people often confuse that with language, thinking that the difference is merely one of degree, not of kind. There are indeed a number of points that animal and human communication have in common. But the crucial distinction is that animals use only signs, and humans use symbols as well as signs.

Signs are signals, usually genetically determined signals. The calls of birds, the throat-baring surrender pose that ends fights among individuals in many mammalian species, the flash of white tail with which a fleeing deer warns others of danger, these are all innate signals. During its lifetime an individual animal does not add to its vocabulary, its store of signs. Signs form a closed system of behaviors whose meaning is fixed, with only minimal adaptability to the environment from one generation to the next. Signs are shared by all normal members of the species.

Human signs in that biological sense have been covered, and perhaps hidden, by language. Almost no human communicative behavior is both unlearned and universally understood or automatic. The closest you can come to some remnant of protohuman signaling is to smile; that is a sign that all babies respond to innately.

Symbols, on the other hand, involve the arbitrary attachment of meanings to behaviors and to artifacts. You have to learn those meanings: they are not part of your genetic code the way a territorial-defense song is for a bird. As new things and ideas enter your environment, you have to keep enlarging your vocabulary. Moreover, the communication that symboling allows is purely abstract: consider $(2 \times 2) = (2 + 2)$. A dog or porpoise cannot do that, but in humans the capacity to learn symbolic communication is innate even in persons who were born without the ability to speak, or hear, or both.

Because the sound symbols that language uses are abstract and arbitrary, there is no reason why the communication of one group of people should be comprehensible to another that evolved its language in a different place. In every locality, language is the conventional way of associating certain sounds with certain meanings according to certain rules. If your rules and sounds are different from your neighbors', you will not understand each other. If there remain great similarities between related languages, there may be some one-way intelligibility. Speakers of Netherlands Dutch can usually understand quite a bit of German, but not the other way around, possibly because Dutch uses a few sounds that German lacks, which throws the listener off. On the other hand it is usually easier for a German to read Dutch than vice versa because Dutch grammar is somewhat simpler. But neither can make sense out of French without specifically being taught that language, nor, as any Belgian will attest, can Francophones "naturally" understand Dutch.

Dialects and Language Evolution

A dialect is a distinct version of a language, specific to some region or social category. All languages have dialects. Since everybody speaks locally and belongs to some recognizable group, even the "standard" or preferred version of a language is but one of its many dialects. Typically, dialects differ in pronunciation, vocabulary, and idiom (common expressions), and may therefore not always be completely mutually comprehensible. That could explain, for example, the occasional misunderstanding between native English-speakers from New England and those from the deep South.

Dialects, like any other local deviation from the wider culture's norms, originate in individual variation. Idiosyncratic expressions, pronunciations, and labels may gain popular acceptance, and soon "everybody" talks that way. Geographically and socially separated groups therefore offer the ideal breeding grounds for the evolution of dialects. Over time, the speech patterns of any isolated population will become somewhat unintelligible to other speakers of the same linguistic background, and eventually a new language is born.

Although this evolutionary process operates randomly, statistical analysis nevertheless makes it possible to measure the relationship between languages. Linguists have established that basic vocabularies—the universally necessary terms for fire, water, mother, death, sky, earth, etc.—remain fairly stable. Comparing a list of such terms for two societies gives a measure of how far their languages have diverged over time. This method for tracing the antiquity of and relationships among languages is called *glottochronology*, or *lexicostatistics*. Though hardly a precision instrument, it is exceedingly useful in establishing where a specific language—and therefore its speakers—originated, and roughly when. Glottochronology cannot, however, establish what importance such other factors as diffusion and conquest have had on the evolution of distinct languages.

Dialects can indicate any of numerous social factors such as the speakers' geographic origin, social status, profession, and age. The distinction between dialect and separate language is not always easy to draw, but the fact that dialects can turn into separate languages is obvious. Afrikaans, for example, descended from the language of seventeenth-century Dutch settlers in South Africa. Over centuries of isolation and separate evolutionary paths, that dialect turned into a language that obviously has its roots in the Netherlands but has a uniquely characteristic vocabulary, pronunciation and grammar. A similar process has been at work in the Anglophone nations: neither U. S. Americans, Canadians nor Australians speak English the way Britons do, but the unbroken communication plus the standardizing effect of the broadcast media have kept mutual intelligibility largely intact. The same broadcast media are ironing out the regional dialects in Britain itself as all Brits learn to speak RP ("received pronunciation").

Of all the languages ever spoken and written, English—which is certainly not the simplest to learn, even for native speakers, because its spelling is maddeningly illogical and inconsistent with its pronunciation—has the largest vocabulary. That's due to two probably unrelated historical events. The first began in A.D. 1066, when, with the conquest of England by French-speaking Vikings, virtually the entire language of the conquerors was laid over the speech of the stubborn Anglo-Saxon locals without replacing it. Over time, as the two tongues melted together, words with originally more or less identical meanings in the two languages drifted into distinct shadings of those meanings, thereby swelling the shared vocabulary. The second event was the English colonization of North America, which gave the English language the opportunity to become the vehicle of expression for the technological and scientific explosion of the nineteenth and twentieth centuries, set off there by immigrants from all over the world. That's what turned English into today's international *lingua franca*.

But even though English often has separate words for shades of meaning, opening any dictionary will convince you that it is equally often as true in English as in other languages that one word can have several different meanings. So the meaning of a word is often situationally defined.

A crucial point about language is that *if you don't have words for something, you cannot communicate it or even store it in your memory.* That is why most introductory courses revolve around vocabulary; before you can understand what a discipline is about, you need to understand the way it labels experience and gives meaning to phenomena you may have never noticed—as this book is trying to do. Every discipline whose basic language you learn gives you a new perspective on your surroundings. And usually it is not the facts but your view of them that determines your understanding. There is even a term for that: *linguistic relativity*. It means that every language incorporates a worldview, a built-in bias; that since language determines perception, the speakers of different languages experience the universe differently. We'll return to that idea in a few pages.

Pidgins and Creoles

There are, by the way, no "primitive" languages. Every human tongue is capable of all the coding, storing and transmitting of experience that every other language can manage, however it is done locally. That's why translation is always possible. But that doesn't mean that all languages handle experience in the same way, and that's why translating poetry is almost *im*possible. Language does, indeed, encode your perception.

Translation is a crucial problem whenever cultures with mutually incomprehensible languages meet in trade or in conquest (as in
colonialism). The need to communicate then often results in the creation of a mutually pronounceable vocabulary (which usually bor-
rows most heavily from the speech of the dominant or richest side)
and a rudimentary grammar. Such a trade language is called a *pidgin*. Some pidgins, like Africa's Swahili, make it possible for dozens
of societies with different languages and cultures to trade peacefully,
to make treaties, and interact in other ways. Similar pidgin-based
lingua francas are used among tribes in New Guinea. Occasionally a
pidgin becomes a people's only language, its native tongue. It is then
technically a *creole*. And a creole, like any other language, will
develop dialects that may evolve into separate languages.

The Difficult Birth of a Language

The Kwinti (among whom I did my fieldwork) are one of six tribes of
Maroons (descendants of eighteenth- and nineteenth-century runaway
plantation slaves) in the tropical rain forest of Suriname (formerly called
Dutch Guiana), the country between Guyana and French Guiana on the
shoulder of South America.

Ancestors of the Kwinti were among the many African tribesmen who
came to the New World during the time Holland dominated the slave trade
in the eighteenth century. The Africans bound for the colonies in the New
World thus were from many different tribes and did not all speak the same
language. They were first brought to Curaçao, where they were taught a
pidgin that would render them useful to planters in the American, British,
Dutch, French, and Portuguese colonies.

Unlike planters in the southern United States, those in Suriname preferred to staff their plantations with slaves from as many different African
tribal areas as possible. The reason was to make it as difficult as possible
for their slaves to communicate with each other and cooperate in revolts
and escapes. This tactic of ensuring that any slave in Suriname would not
encounter people from his own ethnic background was successful
enough that plantation slavery endured there until 1867, and without the
massive uprisings that occurred in Guyana.

Nevertheless there *were* a few successful mass-escapes from outlying
plantations. Because no single tribal language was dominant among these
runaways, the Maroons continued using the pidgin their masters had
taught them, evolving it over the centuries into the creoles they speak to this
day. Each is based on (now often almost unrecognizable) Dutch, English,
Portuguese and French terms, but has been immeasurably enriched with
words and idioms derived from the many West African languages that the

individual runaways spoke and which mothers taught their children wherever the vocabulary of the colonials' pidgin proved inadequate.

The six tribes lived along different rivers in this vast expanse of tropical rain forest, and some individual African terms became generally accepted throughout the entire culture area while others did not. Over the centuries these creole languages have become sufficiently differentiated that at least one, Saramakka or Saamaca Tongo, spoken by the second largest of the tribes, whose origin was more heavily influenced by Portuguese than the other five (because their slave masters were Brazilian Portuguese-speaking Jews who fled to Suriname during the Inquisition), is no longer intelligible to the others. Intertribal politics and economics have caused two of the three smaller tribes, the Boni or Aluku and the Paramakka or Paamaca, to emigrate into French-speaking Guiana, where their speech is undoubtedly similarly evolving. ⌇

LOSING BABEL'S BENEFITS

Like people and cultures, languages die, but nowadays they're dying a lot faster than they're being born. Extinction came to perhaps four thousand of them during the nineteenth and twentieth centuries, and to unguessable numbers before that. It is safe to say that those that have disappeared vastly outnumber those still being used: the Babel effect is being reversed. Today there are—by most measures—still some six thousand mutually unintelligible languages being spoken in the world (over eight hundred of them in Africa alone), but the rate of extinction is increasing, and many are in danger of being lost because so few people still use them. They are being replaced by the languages of mass societies. This is particularly likely to happen to the unwritten languages of small, preindustrial societies that have been made part of nation-states.

The Sapir-Whorf Hypothesis

Why should that be important to you?

Because, as Edward Sapir and Benjamin Lee Whorf realized more than half a century ago, and described in what has become known as the "Sapir-Whorf hypothesis," *language structures the reality you perceive, and each language structures a reality that's somewhat different from every other language's.* As originally formulated, the hypothesis implies both a deterministic and a relativistic view of language, because it maintains that language determines thought processes and, also, that every different language incorporates a different worldview. Specialists still argue these positions, but for our purposes it is sufficient to understand that language influences perception.

For example, a speaker of English perceives and experiences a different social universe than a speaker of, say, Chinese. The English-speaker uses only one term—cousin—to refer to all the sons and daughters of his father's brother as well as his father's sister's, his mother's brother's, and his mother's sister's sons and daughters. Consequently all these people are defined as being his relatives in the same way: as socially equidistant relatives of his own generation, and therefore they are all sexually taboo.

The Chinese-speaker, on the other hand, has no word for cousin. But he does have a term for mother's brother's son, another term for mother's brother's daughter, a different set of terms for mother's sister's son and daughter, still another set for father's brother's kids, and so forth. What is important is that because of this labeling the Chinese-speaker does not see his "cousins" as all having the same relationship to himself. Although all these people are of his own generation, *some* of the females may properly be considered (even preferred) for marriage. Furthermore, the males on his father's brother's side are necessarily more important to him than any of the others because they belong to his father's (thus to his own) lineal descent line.

Adaptation through Linguistic Diversity

Language shapes perception. Different languages incorporate different worldviews. Different worldviews lead to different human experiences and to different cultural solutions to the same problem. In a world that is creating problems faster than people and science can recognize them, it is good to have as many ways to approach problems as possible. That's true even on the personal level.

It is certainly not news that there are opportunities in knowing another language, but the range of these benefits may not be obvious, nor their import understood. For example, the longest war in America's history was lost, at least in part, because neither our political leaders nor our armed forces bothered to understand the values or the language of the Vietnamese. Proving once again that those who do not learn from history are condemned to repeat it, we have now entered the war in Afghanistan with intelligence provided by agents who spoke none of the local languages, and with troops who knew nothing of the local cultures—even though thousands of Afghans live in the United States and still speak their mother tongues.

Addressing this topic in mid-2002, the American Council on Education concluded that "On the whole, the quantity, level of expertise and availability of U.S. personnel with required skills do not now match the national strategic needs at home or abroad, as recently evidenced by the shortage of language experts in the war against terrorism." The council warned that without an adequate supply of people who understand exotic cultures and are fluent in their languages, America risks "serious costs in terms of potential foreign-policy failures, military blunders, terrorism and a decline in U.S. competitiveness in the global marketplace."

There are also personal reasons to overcome monolingualism. Because every language incorporates a unique worldview, truly bi- or multilingual individuals enjoy an advantage over monolinguists: they automatically perceive, and can therefore deal with, their personal world in more than one way. Logically, that edge should be sharper the more unrelated their languages are. From that perspective, you could expect "exotic" immigrants, such as Southeast Asia's Hmong (who are now going to college and combining their ancestral worldviews with the West's), to become an important source of innovation and original thought for tomorrow's America. If you are contemplating studying another language, you should consider learning Russian or Chinese instead of another Western European tongue.

In an ideal world every college student would learn one truly alien language well enough to dream in it, with special rewards for mastering a nearly extinct or truly obscure tongue. But this is not that world, and the economics of student life may not encourage such goals. Our nation would be well served, however, if the children of immigrants would keep speaking and reading their parents' tongue, while at the same time learning English so thoroughly that they would require no interpreters to participate in the workings of our economic, educational, governmental and legal institutions. This advice runs counter to American culture's customary efforts to squash the native tongues of Amerindians and immigrants—efforts that are misguided and maladaptive.

Every two weeks on average, another language disappears. Languages are lost when their speakers die out. When this happens, especially to an unwritten language, the intellectual culture that this native tongue once made possible also disappears. Archeological ingenuity and efforts notwithstanding, that loss is irreversible. The argument favoring the widest possible biological and cultural diversity must therefore be extended to emphasize the need for saving the world's remaining languages. You'd think that a world so desperate for alternative perspectives that it amuses itself with role-playing games and the invention of imaginary languages such as Klingon would be able to offer space and a subsistence to speakers of exotic living languages, so that we could all continue to benefit from non-Western cultural logics and viewpoints! But not so far. So if you are looking for a way to "make a difference," you could do worse than to help change this.

A Thought on the Origin of Diversity

According to the Judeo-Christian Bible, linguistic diversity was a punishment for humanity's hubris. Apparently using the same reasoning as Suriname's planters, God prevented people from completing an objectionable project (building a tower that would reach heaven) by making the builders incomprehensible to each other, and therefore unable to cooperate.

By now you should be able to consider at least one different interpretation of the story of the Tower of Babel. Obviously the Creator of the Universe was a good enough engineer to realize that the tower would fail in its mission, and that if mankind were ever to reach heaven and become a welcome neighbor to Him, humanity would need far more sophisticated approaches than people then were capable of imagining. So, in giving them different languages, each with its own built-in perspectives, He gave the tower builders a leg up. Babel caused an explosion in cultural evolution that led to mankind's dominion over the Earth, opening the path to human perfectibility—and all its alternatives.

Be that as it may.

Thinking It Through

1. Assume the Sapir-Whorf hypothesis reflects reality. What does this say about the role of language in the evolution of culture?
2. Why haven't tonal languages been replaced by ones that are easier to learn to write?
3. Would a society of deaf-mute people have culture? Would it survive?
4. How did English evolve into the dominant language on Earth?
5. What is meant by "the cost of losing the Babel Effect?"

The Marrying Kind
Kinship I—Affiliation

"It is so far from being natural for a man and woman to live in a state of marriage that we find all the motives which they have for remaining in that connection, and the restraints which civilized society imposes to prevent separation, are hardly sufficient to keep them together."

—Samuel Johnson (1709–1784)

"The family in today's Europe and North America is unusual in many ways. To repeat—it can't be said too often—your unusualness limits your experience, and with it your views about what a family is."

—Paul Bohannan (1920–)

*The recognition of paternity is a
uniquely human capacity, and the source
of all human kinship patterns. Kinship
everywhere involves two interrelated
principles: marriage and descent. Both are
expressed cross-culturally in a multitude
of forms, all of which have attributes and
implications that go beyond the mere
mating-for-life of some other species.*

*O*n land as in the primordial oceans, life forms differ in how much they normally seek the company of their own kind. Among those species of animals called "solitary," the only time adults associate with others of their kind is for reproduction. After their sexual encounter, they go their separate ways. The female raises the young; she leaves them to fend for themselves as soon as they can. Survival means staking out a private resource area and defending it against your fellows. Some solitaries, not all, can even ignore one another when they are brought together around a plentiful food source.

THE BIOLOGY OF SOCIALITY

"Social" species aggregate for safety if they are prey, for cooperation if they are predators, or for companionship if they are large enough to fear few. Fish such as herring travel in schools so that a predator cannot focus on any individual; wolves and hyenas run in packs for group hunting and shared baby-sitting. Many herd animals, such as deer or cattle, group together only during breeding season. Others, such as horses, keep company for life. Individual members of social species can survive on their own, but usually not as well as in their typical associations.

Organization is a tool in the struggle for survival. Baboons trek across the open plains in highly organized groups, with the most vulnerable members in the center of the formation and the toughest males on the perimeter where they can deal with trouble. While even the strongest baboon is no match for a leopard, cooperatively they can best this solitary hunter. But the whole troop will flee from a lion, because lions are social hunters: if you see one, others are around. Since baboons have a minimal division of labor in their defense system and a hierarchic organization, they qualify as having true societies.

The social insects (the ants and termites, some bees and wasps) beat humanity to the idea of social organization—by at least 150 million years. They divided labor for both production and defense, which they managed by getting rid of their excess males and raising physically specialized members.

Our own species' males are more costly than females (think of crime and violence and vandalism as well as appetites and dominance games), but humans have never figured out how to thin out our males without harming females and children. Culture makes morphological specialization unnecessary.

With their castes (the various ranks of differently shaped specialists like workers and soldiers) and with economies that can involve agriculture, slave holding and raiding, the organization of some social insect societies can actually appear more complicated than that of the simplest human ones. But insect societies are instinct driven and behaviorally inflexible, while even the most rudimentary human lifeway is cultural and therefore adjustable. Moreover, kin relationships in all human societies, especially in the less "developed" ones, are orders of magnitude more complex than those of creatures that behave as if each individual were but an interchangeable mobile cell of the hive.

SEXUALITY REVISITED

You are a member of the societally most differentiated species known. Your sociality is rooted in the unique sexuality and the infantile dependency of your Stone Age ancestors. It is based, as it is in all mammals, on the primary dyad (two-person relationship) in human existence: the mother–child bond. However, biology and culture have produced at least two other dyads from which people build social structures. The first and most crucial of these is the durable male–female pair bond. The second, the father–child bond, grows from the idea of paternity.

The *fact* of paternity is present in all mammals. The *idea* is not. Males of some other species would seem to grasp the fact— some kill the young of the females they take up with, ensuring that the "replacement" offspring are theirs. This has led some people to believe that these animals understand the link between sexuality and reproduction. I remain unconvinced. But in all human societies males know, right up front, about paternity (although the Trobriand Islanders and some Australian aborigines a century ago denied it to early ethnographers). Such knowledge makes it possible to create social structures that go far beyond those of creatures limited to living by biology alone.

The Second Dyad—and the Third

Child rearing among apes and monkeys is strictly a female occupation. Presumably this was also true for our earliest ancestors. In those species of ground-dwelling primates (like chimpanzees and baboons) whose males are large enough that their collaboration can deter a predator, males defend the troop's females and young. But these animals lack a second characteristic of human sociality: their adults do not routinely share food. Only rarely will males offer unusual tidbits—like meat—to females, and then only in exchange for sex. Dinner dates, it would seem, are an ancient tradition among primates.

Burdened with utterly dependent and vulnerable infants, your foremothers needed to convince your forefathers to help them take care of the kids, to share food with them and defend them—not just occasionally, but all the time. They offered males *continuous* sexual access in exchange. But before the males would accept the responsibilities of long-term bonding, they had to be convinced not only that the females were as constantly horny as they themselves, but also that the children those females bore were in fact begotten by themselves.

Concealed Ovulation

To keep their males sexually interested enough to accept responsibility for their offspring, your ancient foremothers had to evolve not just their behavior but also their anatomy: one thing that makes us unique among primates is the fact that men cannot tell when a woman is fertile. Ovulation is hidden from men, and until less than a century ago, most women were not aware of when they ovulated, and before that no one even knew what ovulation was. Information about human sexuality is very recent and still not widely understood.

The result of the absence of estrus is that human beings can have sex anytime, and that sex is about a lot more than babies—it has become its own reward. Bonobos (the species of pygmy chimpanzees that shares more DNA with humans than any other life form—meaning they are your closest nonhuman relatives) are the only other primates that can have sex anytime for fun and sociality. People who study chimpanzees and bonobos have said that chimps settle sexual problems with power, but bonobos settle power problems with sex. Dolphins can have intercourse at any time too, but we don't yet know enough about them to say how their hypersexuality factors into their social organization. In any case, neither they nor bonobos nor any other creatures have anything like the human family.

That uniquely human institution depends on the loss of seasonal sexuality and the recognition of paternity. For your ancestors, the relatively permanent attachment of a male to the mother–child dyad proved immensely successful. Recognition of the father–child dyad converted the old male–female dyad into something new: the father–mother dyad.

Menopause

Concealed ovulation obviously worked to the benefit of the species, but it is not the only biological oddity about women. Unlike the females of other mammalian species, women lose their capacity to reproduce long before they die of old age. Men don't. This makes humans even more unusual than fun-sex does; though menopause reputedly occurs among small whales like the orca and the pilot, it has not been reported for any terrestrial animal. Women are the only females on dry land who can enjoy sex after their reproductive lives have ended.

There are no convincing biological explanations for menopause. A cultural explanation must focus on the role of the elderly, the valued repositories of knowledge in every preindustrial society. Consider:

- Before the twentieth century, the *average* age at death (for those who survived childhood) was between 45 and 50, everywhere.
- The risk of dying in childbirth increases as women age, so without menopause, precious few women would have survived into old age.
- Since men without women generally die younger, there would also have been few old men.
- Without the memories and wisdom of the elderly, much of culture would have had to be reinvented in every generation, perhaps at prohibitive cost. (Imagine a world without grandmas!)
- The older the mother, the more likely her baby will be handicapped physically and/or mentally to become a burden on her survivors.
- The immature children of an old woman will be orphaned when she dies, and the odds are against orphans in even the best of cultures.

Clearly then, menopause has been of inestimable value in perpetuating and evolving culture—and the species.

The Sexual Division of Labor

When your ancestors were still backpacking through life, there were perfectly good reasons why sex (physiology) should determine gender (cultural behavior). Women took the mortal risk of child-bearing; men took the risks of hunting and defense—first against animal predators, then against other men. In the process, men and women developed overlapping but distinct lifeways: the culture of men is nowhere the same as the culture of women, but both are necessary for either to live well.

Pragmatically speaking (and ignoring for a moment the immense cost of sexual inequality), it is not important which sex does what in maintaining the family and society—as long as everything gets done. The most important thing about the sexual division of labor is that it maintains a reciprocal dependency between husband and wife, thereby ensuring that both will be around to help their kids survive.

Traditional gender roles were assigned as soon as it was determined whether the baby was a girl or a boy. Girls were taught to cook, sew, and take care of children. Boys learned to hunt, fight, and do whatever brute-strength manhandling was required. Inevitably, this pounded some square pegs into round holes, but most of the time it worked well enough: you're here, aren't you?

When people took to raising food instead of hunting and gathering it, culture burgeoned in areas that had nothing to do with functional divisions of labor. Decisions had to be made about whether any new trait was to be added to the male or the female sphere of life.

Because most innovations were not survival-basic, the personal charisma of individuals could determine where a new trait was assigned. Nevertheless, for any such decision to become part of Reality for future generations, its intrinsic arbitrariness had to be repressed—or argued away. So we find to this day that tribe A still explains the making of blankets and pottery as "naturally" women's work, because pots and blankets are household items, and women rule and maintain the household. But to their neighbors in tribe B, weaving and pottery are "naturally" men's work, because they are artistic expressions, and only men have the time and talent to be artistic. In tribe C, both sexes make pots and blankets because such items are neither weapons nor magic, so they can be made by anyone. And tribe D maintains that blankets are women's work because women's domain includes the bedroom, but pots are men's work because they are made of the earth, which is men's domain.

Every basic task other than breast-feeding is somewhere the traditional gender behavior for either sex. Which means that: (1) *the division of labor in any society is based on what people once believed the differences between the sexes to mean;* and that (2) *all such beliefs are based on cultural, not biological, considerations.*

When machines were designed to replace muscle, either sex could perform any task. That and the development of the nursing bottle in the nineteenth century weakened traditional concepts of the sexual division of labor. The essential unfairness of the status quo wasn't widely admitted until the middle of the twentieth century (first in North America, then gradually in more and more places). Once acknowledged, it led to rapid and drastic changes, but this particular revolution is far from complete.

WORKING THE REPRODUCTIVE DRIVES

Because the female animal is the one whose body produces the next generation, one of her most important tasks in reproduction is choosing the best available father for her offspring. If she picks a winner, her brood will probably make her a grandmother; if she accepts a loser, her young may not survive that long. Since estrus triggers rut in every male in her vicinity, her only problem may be an embarrassment of riches: sometimes so many mallards pile on the same duck in a pond that the object of their frenzy literally risks drowning under them—which may help explain why so many species have evolved selection rituals that limit many males' chances to mate.

One of the most arresting differences between human and animal sexuality is that it is the female, not the male, who "dresses to kill." Men wear suits—essentially a drab uniform—while women celebrate their diversity and uniqueness in eye-popping fashions and colors designed to maximize their desirability. Women spend more time and money on their appearance than men do. European mothers used to tell their daughters, you have to suffer to be beautiful.

You also have to pay. American teenaged girls—a category of human beings that probably least needs to gild the lily—have been culturally programmed (by advertisers) to believe they are inadequate "as is." They spend between $90 and $100 *billion* on beauty products and services per year—far more than is spent on their education and health care combined.

But, you may now ask, if men are so testosterone driven, why do women need beauty shops? Why, as in the rest of the animal kingdom, is it not the male who must attract the female's attention?

Again, part of that is culture. The inequality of women has grown immensely since Oma and Opa Backpacker, and history records few societies where female sexuality was as ruthlessly exploited for profit as in the United States. Nevertheless, or as a result, many young males everywhere do suffer indignity, pain and mortal danger to attract the attention of the girl of their dreams.

Still, the rest is your human biology—it's that first double helix again. To begin with, the absence of estrus means that when the reproductive urge strikes a woman, her body cannot automatically summon a lineup of candidate men to choose from. Second, among most of our fellow creatures the male's part of the reproductive task is completed when he has bathed her ovum in his semen. Baboons, badgers, bats, and bears have no division of labor; their females don't really have any use for males beyond that random encounter that resulted in impregnation. Women, on the other hand, are handicapped (at least economically) once they have children, and they and their offspring—in fact, all of society— are threatened whenever they have to raise the kids alone. (And *that*, unfortunately, is *not* becoming less true in the Third Millennium. Witness how unmarried mothers and their progeny make out in life as compared to women and children with a father on the premises.) The human female needs not just a male, but a male who will invest himself in her. Most women consequently feel a need to be noticed by enough men to give them a reasonable selection to choose from.

MARRIAGE

Marriage, a uniquely human institution, facilitates child rearing. No other organisms are as helpless and as dependent on adults for anywhere near as long as human babies are. Nor has that dependency lessened or grown shorter because of culture. On the contrary: the more complex a culture becomes, the more its children need support and protection. Just since the Industrial Revolution we have evolved a new maturational stage, "adolescence," during which individuals who are already biologically capable of begetting and bearing offspring are still inadequately prepared culturally (meaning ethically, economically and educationally) to make sound decisions about doing so. This is demonstrated most graphically by all the hopelessly trapped teenaged single mothers whose children disproportionally crowd our prisons and walk our streets.

The brunt of the costs of raising a child still falls on women, and with childhood in modern societies so greatly prolonged, it is as clear today as in our ancestors' time why women should want to marry: they need a husband to share the burdens of raising their child. But what's in it for men? The obvious answer is sexual access: supposedly a married man doesn't have to risk being turned down for a date. But there are many societies, including your own, in which nonmarital sex is accepted without debate. Moreover, it's been true at least since the Pill that attractive males have more sexual exposure while single than after they are married—especially after the baby is born. (There seems to be some sort of conspiracy to keep you ignorant about this fact, and young people vehemently deny it when they're in love: "Not us! Twice a day, forever!" Sure; dream on.)

Almost every society recognizes the difference between mating and marriage. Mating implies sex with no further obligations or permanent responsibilities on the part of the male. Marriage, almost everywhere, implies a man's contractual commitment to a mother and her child. In many societies, for sound and logical reasons, mating outside of marriage is forbidden. In many others, with different but equally compelling arguments, nonmarital sex is tolerated, expected, or even encouraged.

It is impossible to make a single, universally applicable definition of marriage. The reason is simple: marriage has many separate functions, so different societies can emphasize different aspects—and hence not mean quite the same thing by the term. Nevertheless, "marriage," however ill defined, is a characteristic of (almost) all human societies. *Usually* it defines and controls the sexual activity of the people involved, provides for where they live, legitimates their procreation and verifies the children's membership in at least one of the couple's two kinship groups. *Usually* marriage establishes the couple's place in the community; defines each party's rights in the sexuality, domestic labor, and property of the other; and establishes a joint responsibility for the children. But none of the other things marriage can be used for (politics, economics, status striving, love) is applicable or possible everywhere. *The only universally recognized purpose of marriage is to create a safe environment in which to raise children.*

During the twentieth century in the "developed" nations, some of the support a woman traditionally expected of her children's father and his kin was shifted to a tax-based welfare system. This is unlikely to become a permanent aspect of world culture, because it can too easily be argued that welfare requires the competent to support the incompetent and forces reproductively responsible people to pay for the children of the reproductively irresponsible.

Nowhere has institutionalized child rearing worked as well as marriage: without the latter we now have children no one is raising—kids who turn out to be a major problem in your schools and on your streets. Modern illegitimacy *proves* that, second only to birth, marriage is the most important step in a person's life—at least to society, that is, to the rest of us.

Marriage can also symbolize other commitments, and many societies celebrate special kinds of marriage for nonreproductive purposes. The ethnographic record describes such oddities as a Kwakiutl Indian who was married to his tribal chief's knee to symbolize his vassalage. (That was a metaphor, not a perversion.) More commonly, a culture will push the reproductive implication of marriage to its logical limits.

Husbands and Wives

Among peoples of Sudan and in some West African societies where business is women's work, older women gained access to strategic information through their trade connections—and sometimes got rich. In order to make their political counsel available to the men running their society (who could not seek such advice from a woman), occasionally such a female would be formally declared to be male. This meant that she was allowed to marry other women (her own position as a man's wife would not be affected by this). Girls often saw such a union as a better deal than accepting marriage to the much older men their fathers picked out for them. When they married this female man, the girls continued to see their boyfriends. The children they bore belonged, of course, to their legal husband, the old woman. (It is a near-universal rule, even in Western legal systems, that for purposes of custody and affiliation, "the husband of the mother is the father of her child" unless and until proven otherwise.) Their husband's reason for accepting the "honor" of becoming a man was the opportunity to start her own descent line, something otherwise possible only for males. ⤳

Shopping for a Spouse

Whatever category of person is culturally defined as sexually permitted, there will be competition for its members. If your society prefers for you to marry someone who has no genetic ties to you at all, that means you'll have to shop for a mate among strangers whose interest in you may be limited. Consequently much of female culture in "developed" societies, especially among the newly nubile, revolves around becoming irresistible to heterosexual males. The competition for men is unrelenting and no-holds-barred; that's why there's all that makeup and mammary enhancement, the shaved legs and that tippy-toe walk on high heels, the padding or binding to look as un-boy as possible.

Many women resent this, and with good reason: it is neither inevitable nor necessary that women should measure their self-worth so critically in terms of their effect on men. None of this is a matter of instinct after all; it is only culture—and not even *species* culture, but *societal* culture. Any look at the world's remaining small-scale ("primitive") societies will show you that the insecurity of Westernized women is not universal, that in other times and cultures young women have not become bulimics or anorexics or smokers to fit some impossible-to-attain ideal of feminine beauty.

It is not surprising that some young women, thinking they lack alternatives (or simply gambling on the Big Pay-Off), respond to sexual inequality by trying to attract a male with demonstrated assets who'll support them, instead of competing with hungry young men for a place in the sun. Your culture encourages female predation on males. Just glance at the covers of the women's magazines lining your supermarket's check-out stand, and ask yourself if their advice will improve a woman's chances of snaring a *dependable* helpmate, or whether (temporarily) being sexually irresistible is just another social trap. Most women realize sooner or later that the pursuit of glamour is a fool's game and—if it is not yet too late—focus on developing more durable and less limiting competencies than the ability to trigger the sexual interests of male strangers.

So what *does* determine a woman's choice for the father of her offspring? Who *can* she marry?

Essentially: availability determines selection. For the thousands of generations before teenagers got cars, most people in most places married some sort of cousin who was culturally defined as "eligible." Billions of people continue to do so.

Marry Whom?

Consider, for example, China, which constitutes one-fifth of the human population in the world's most enduring society. Until the Communists took over, persons with the same surname could not marry—under severe penalties, including execution. Then as now, every Han Chinese carried one of the nation's roughly 100 clan names as a surname. Technically therefore, everyone with the same surname belonged to the same clan. Their culture forbade marriage with any member of one's own clan. It did not matter how many miles and generations separated your family and your love's: if you were a Hsu and your love was a Hsu, your marriage would be incestuous.

On the other hand, a boy's parents hoped he would marry his father's sister's daughter. We in the West call that "inbreeding," and inbreeding has a bad name because everybody "knows" that it produces mentally defective children with lots of physical problems.

Humans are mammals and, ideological convictions aside, the rules that govern genetics in mammals apply equally to us. How do you breed new types of dog or sheep or cattle? You select individuals with the characteristic you want and breed them to each other. Then you pick out the offspring that most strongly exhibit your desired trait(s) and breed them together. Repeat until you have your new "breed."

What happens if your breeding animals carry harmful traits?

In the wild, the healthy ones will out-reproduce and outlast the genetically flawed ones and simply replace them. In domestication, however, the disappointing specimen is eaten or neutered; only the favored one gets to reproduce. Therefore, everywhere and always, isolated breeding populations grow to differ from each other in any number of anatomic ways and characteristic behaviors. (Which is how we got St. Bernards, Shar-Peis and Yorkshire terriers out of ancestral wolves.)

It's even more true for people. Our species complicates the reproductive picture by adding culture. For humans, local breeding patterns result in an ever-branching diversity in everything from blood types to nose forms and skeletal dimensions, from skin color to tooth shape and disease resistance and a range of other variables that grows as we speak. Plus, of course, the infinite differentiation of "characteristic behaviors" through culture. All that from cousin marriage, without weakening the stock.

"But . . . Incest!" you sputter.

Yes, but what does "incest" mean? There is no cross-cultural agreement on what constitutes incest, because all societies need to reproduce within the gene pool at hand, following rules specifically designed to enable unique forms of social organization to perform their local functions.

To a typical American, the word conjures up the sexual exploitation of children within a nuclear family. To the Kwinti it means that all opposite-sexed members of your clan, no matter how far removed from your own line of descent, are sexually taboo. The definition of incest varies from society to society and from one age to the next, depending on how their definitions of "kin" evolve.

The fact remains, however, that your ancestors, since time immemorial, have mated with close biological relatives, and did so without shame or guilt. Whom else could the children of Adam and Eve have married?

Every society defines and outlaws incest, but few agree on what categories of people are involved. *"Incest" thus refers to marriage or sexual relations between prohibited categories of kin; it is a cultural, sometimes a legal proscription, but not a biological imperative.*

"But what about all the horrible results of inbreeding we hear about?" you ask, queasily recalling the movie *Deliverance*.

Okay, let's look at that.

Genetic Degradation

Puppy mills often breed and sell dogs with dysplasia, a hereditary condition that dislocates the animal's hind legs at its hips. Some people spend great sums to have the condition surgically corrected. But unless such an animal is then sterilized, its genes—including the one for dysplasia—will spread throughout dogdom. Had such an animal been born in the wild, it wouldn't live to reproduce: unable to catch prey and to keep up, it would die very young. Natural selection weeds out any genetic variant that is less than adaptive, and replaces it with the genes of variants with a proven advantage. So it is culture, and nothing else, that keeps dysplasia genes in the canine breeding pool.

Culture can thus overcome natural selection.

If you marry a close relative, you increase the chances that your children will possess some particular gene—good, bad, or indifferent—that you and your spouse-relative share, and that it will spread throughout the coming generations. Mind you, it makes no difference whether your people habitually marry first cousins or second cousins: either way, a specific set of genes will become characteristic of your population.

Any family, any person, can suddenly acquire "bad" genes. Mutations are random variations in the genetic code of an individual. They occur all the time and everywhere and will never be preventable because the cosmic rays that cause them are inescapable. In nature, and in human societies without modern medicine, deleterious mutations usually die with their unfortunate carrier or disappear within a few generations: those who exhibit them are unable to find mates, or those who do are unable to raise their offspring to reproductive age. But modern medical intervention can correct or compensate for the disadvantages of hip dysplasia, spina bifida, achondroplastic dwarfism, hemophilia and a very long and rapidly growing list of other genetic disorders. Their carriers can lead more or less normal lives—and add their troubles to the gene pool like so many randomly placed mines. For example, progressive myopia (increasing nearsightedness) is most common in populations that, like the Dutch and the Japanese, were among the earliest to enjoy the benefits of lens grinding.

Inbreeding in humans can also lead to physically and intellectually *superior* types. Take Cleopatra, the evidently brilliant and admirably endowed Egyptian queen who, after her younger brother-husband, Ptolemy XII, died, bewitched and bewildered first Julius Caesar and then Marc Antony—two of the most powerful men in the world. At the time, she was still married to her second husband, Ptolemy XIII, her next-younger brother. She and her brothers were children of a brother-sister marriage, as were their parents, and theirs, and theirs, and theirs, and so forth in accordance with family custom and the culture of their time and place. The rulers of Egypt were divine, after all, and gods cannot marry humans without watering down their divinity. The point is that all that inbreeding produced a truly exceptional specimen of humanity.

Genetic degradation can be *very* real. During the Great Depression of the 1930s, the U.S. government underwrote huge public works projects to create employment. These weren't all blue-collar enterprises either; efforts to engage out-of-work academicians included the earliest really large-scale archeological investigations in the New World, and the collecting of slave narratives— the systematic recording of the memories of the last surviving Americans to have lived as slaves. In the Appalachian mountains, psychologists tested the IQs of populations that had long been geographically isolated from each other and mainstream culture. Not surprisingly, considerable inbreeding had occurred in many of these remote "hollows." The Jukes (a pseudonym the reports used), an extensive family, had bred entire generations of feeble-minded social misfits. The Kallikaks (another pseudonym) had two lines of descendants, one of which was stocked almost exclusively by mental deficients, criminals, and social misfits. But the other line boasted respectable citizens of far better than average intelligence, whose descendants have since moved into the upper reaches of their states' professional and political circles.

It is thus culture, in the form of medicine and value assumptions, that is directly responsible for the spread of human birth defects. It is not "inbreeding," the mating of individuals from the same stock, but the prevalence of deleterious genes in that stock that leads to genetic degradation.

Since the beginning of the twentieth century, every successive generation of North Americans and Western Europeans has been born with greater percentages of genetic flaws. This is less true for societies that have only recently acquired the benefits of Western medical science. Our increasing genetic load (the proportion of harmful genes in a population) means that the percentage of children born with birth defects must keep increasing unless and until science achieves complete control over human reproduction. And whatever else *that* may imply, at least expect it to be expensive.

Paradoxically, then, although never before have so many people had sexual access to strangers, it has never before been so important to avoid inbreeding.

The Universality of the Incest Taboo

So yes, *now*, because culture has pulled nature's stopper out of the bottle in which birth defects were kept since life began, *now* we understand why mating with biologically close relatives is something devoutly to be avoided. But that doesn't illuminate one of the oldest and most enduring mysteries in anthropology: the question why, as far back in time as we can peer, people have always avoided nuclear-family incest.

There are clues and theories aplenty.

- Item: the universal human prohibition on sexual intercourse between a mother and her son may well be the only example of the incest taboo for which no exceptions have ever been published.
- Item: studies on wild primates have shown that, pheromones or no pheromones, males typically will not mate with their own mothers even though they will do so with other females her age.

The root of humanity's incest prohibitions may thus lie in our pre-human past.

But this does not explain why sex between human fathers and daughters, or brothers and sisters, is similarly prohibited, except to gods. Other primate females will as readily mate with their own fathers and brothers as with any other available male. But alone among all life-forms, human females can point out to their children who their fathers and grandfathers are. There is no evidence that this ability is based in biology. Its cultural origin dates from our primordial hunting-and-gathering past, for otherwise not every culture would have carried the taboo forward to the present. Even when no one could possibly have foreseen or understood the link between certain matings and physiological disaster (genetics is only a century old after all), even when its effects were least malignant, your ancestors prohibited mating and marriage between and among parents and their children.

Naturally there is a spate of hypotheses attempting to explain the universality of the incest taboo, each focusing on a different issue. They range from an assumed innate horror or revulsion at the idea of incest, through the economic and political advantages of marrying out, to the breakdown in authority that would result if parents had sex with their children. All explain *some* aspect of the problem, but all suffer from serious inadequacies.

Naturally I have my own thesis. Humans have always learned culture at mother's knee—usually within a family setting. When our mobility was restricted to how far we could walk, and our economy required us to live off very large territories, different groups of people evolved different adaptations to their terrain and its resources. As populations grew, as humans spread into new areas and developed different languages and ways of doing things, nothing was more precious than knowledge (read "culture"). But in that age before writing there was no way to share information except through personal contact. So when two bands encountered each other, each group, even if wary, was eager to learn what the other knew, because knowledge enhanced the capacity to survive. Knowledge came wrapped in layers of magic and ritual. It took a long time to share it. The best and easiest way to transfer culture from one society to another was to exchange members. The safest and most direct way to do that is to marry into the other group. Then each would have a resident expert in each other's culture. But who to send over?

In all hunting and gathering societies, men's work—hunting and fighting—required teamwork. The division of labor among men sorted them typically into leaders, experts, competents and novices. A man knew his hunting partners, which means he understood their individual capabilities and exactly what he could expect from each of them if things went wrong—if the bear turned, or the herd stampeded, or someone got hurt and needed rescuing. You grew up into your role on your team; lifelong shared experience was the key to survival. Removing a man from his own team and assigning him to a strange one endangered both: one team lost a known performer, the other "gained" an unpredictable one. A transferred male must have faced much the same welcome as a rookie replacement to a front-line infantry squad.

Women's roles, however, did not demand this kind of division of labor or this kind of teamwork. A woman and her children constituted the household whose economy she ran. Women were companionable and helped one another, but they were almost never part of a team. That made them the ideal medium for the spread of culture. They were no threat to their host society because they did not weaken its vitally necessary teams. Incoming wives were quite adequate replacements for daughters who left to go to *their* husbands. Besides, when women spread culture they taught a far wider variety of useful traits than men could—botany, midwifery, medicine, cooking.

Wife exchange did not occur only among strangers. Hunting bands were necessarily small; you cannot feed masses with what you pick up along the trail. To improve the odds of survival for everyone, bands in many regions split into still smaller family groups when winter came. Many families spent most of each year in isolation. Under such circumstances, the exchange of women could be a necessity for *maintaining* culture, enhancing the ties between families and updating their cultural preparedness. And of course men gained importance through their control over the exchange of women; this may have been the origin of all politics.

As counters in their fathers' political games—which they still are in many societies—daughters' exchange-value diminished if they already had children. (You do see why?) Politics and the diffusion of knowledge both demanded that daughters be kept from pregnancy—which, in isolated hunting bands, meant from their own male relatives. Those traditions proved to be enduring: the incest taboo remains a universal. Today, determining whether it came before or because of bride exchange is a chicken-or-egg sort of question.

Societies that encouraged the exchange of culture through women accrued not just in-laws but allies and trading partners. When a group's traditional resource base was temporarily unavailable (as happened occasionally because of drought, flood or fire), having female relatives in neighboring bands meant having access to alternate hunting and gathering areas without having to fight for them. If there ever were peoples who did not marry out, they became culturally and economically disadvantaged in any competition for resources with those who did, and eventually they either converted or died out.

Nobody can prove to everyone else's satisfaction why nuclear-family sexuality should "always" have been prohibited everywhere. Suffice it to say that without that prohibition, the human species would not have been able to develop the principles of kinship, which are the basis for all organized life and the culture you take for granted. You could even say that the incest taboo made us human.

MARRIAGE TYPES AND FAMILY SYSTEMS

Although technically the term "family" remains difficult to distinguish from "household," for our purposes several types of "immediate" families can be distinguished.

The *nuclear family* (also called biological family, conjugal family, or family of procreation) is formed when Ego marries and has children. A typical nuclear family's household thus composes only two generations: the husband and wife, and their children. Adding other people such as a surviving grandparent to this small unit is difficult.

There are many kinds of *extended families*. Normally each is composed of close relatives—usually only along male lines or female lines but not both—who share a household, rights, and property. Unlike in nuclear families, Ego in an extended family does not necessarily need to leave at marriage. One way to establish an extended family is to maintain a household composed of at least two nuclear families, usually of brothers or sisters, with their spouses and offspring. (Technically these are *composite* families.) Another is for a man and his sons' families to live in a single household, or for a woman and her daughters and their husbands and kids to dwell in the same place. In *consanguineal* (literally, shared-blood) families, nuclear family bonds are minimized in favor of father–son or mother–daughter bonds, depending on which sex is the focus of lineality.

In yours as in almost all "developed" societies today, marriage is a legally defined relationship. Legal language identifies only three marital conditions: monogamy, bigamy, and polygamy. Bigamy literally means "two marriages," polygamy means "multiple marriages." Bigamy is thus a species of polygamy, and both are illegal in Western societies. For any but legal purposes, these definitions are less than useful because they do not illuminate the qualities of the relationships involved, nor do they acknowledge that in other times and places various forms of polygamy have been and still are not only legal but are the preferred forms of marriage.

There are four possible (but not equally probable) ways in which men and women can be united in matrimony:

- Group Marriage (2 or more men married to 2 or more women).
- Polygyny (1 man married to 2 or more women)
- Monogamy (1 man married to 1 woman)
- Polyandry (2 or more men married to 1 woman)

Each of these leads to a distinct type of family. Monogamous societies always produce nuclear families (also called natural or biological family types) composed of a wife-mother and a husband-father with their children living in a single household.

In polygyny, two or more family-households, each composed of a co-wife with her children, share one male as the father and husband.

In polyandry, the family consists of a woman with her children, and two or more co-husbands.

Because there are no indisputable examples of group marriage, it is impossible to determine how it would structure the household and the family.

Group Marriage

This is never the cultural preference in human societies because here paternity, and therefore one specific male's responsibility for the offspring, is always deniable. Without specific male–female ties, only a woman's sexual attractiveness determines what men she spends time with. But her allure largely disappears when she is heavy with child and first begins to really *need* support. Worse, when her baby (which may not be his) is born and does its screaming to terrorize all within hearing into taking care of it, it would be a rare man indeed who'd stick around when he has access to childless women.

In the absence of a sexual contract, both men and women necessarily tend to satisfy their own needs at the cost of others. In other words, without a binding commitment from a specific man, a mother will be severely handicapped in competing for males' support, and her child will have less chance to grow up. Favoritism and orphans result. This violates the dictum that marriage exists to provide a safe place in which to raise the next generation. It also explains why every experiment in group marriage has failed to last two generations. What happens is that once enough women are burdened with children, they can and will establish special relationships with an individual male. Group marriage is thus necessarily unstable; it breaks down into polygyny and monogamy, and sometimes polyandry. Eventually, depending on economic and other factors, one of those becomes the dominant form.

Polygyny

"Many wives" married to one man was the most commonly preferred form of marriage in some 70 percent of recorded cultures, making it the norm in the world's societies until the twentieth century. Polygyny formalizes two often-denied but enduring observations: that men's interest in sex is more constant than women's; and that women do not, in general, need or want a man around all the time.

Of course not every man in any polygynous society has more than one wife. Even among those who have reached the right age, most will remain single or marry only one woman. There may be all sorts of explanations for that: not every man is successful or attractive enough to merit the interest of a woman and the trust of her parents; sexual preference or romantic exclusivity also come to mind. But the primary reason for monogamy, wherever it occurs, is always the same: the demands of responsibility for the welfare of more than one woman and her child(ren) is too great for most men. Those demands are not limited to economics: marriage involves not just responsibilities to the spouse, but also obligations to the spouse's family—which may be very extensive.

In the traditional polygyny of preindustrial societies, a man (over time) marries a number of women, or they marry him, but his relationship to them is essentially limited. He performs for them the necessary labor that requires brute force or that their culture has determined to be men's work, and is a male role model. They, in turn, cook for him, sleep with him, clean for him,

and so forth. As long as the co-wives all get along, this is a mutually satisfactory and rewarding arrangement. In traditional polygyny, women are not a man's dependents.

Polygyny still works best (meaning kids survive and people are
happy enough) in societies where women provide most of the subsistence. If they weren't economically self-supporting, that is, able
to produce the food and basic necessities they and their children
need, their husband would have to feed them and their children,
and even in the best of environments that soon becomes an overwhelming responsibility for one man.

Typically, the first woman a man marries becomes his boss-
wife, and she has a strong voice in who her co-wives are going to
be. Typically also, a woman may encourage her husband to take a
second wife so that she will have somebody with whom to share
the chores. Often both husband and wives see the team of co-
wives as a cooperative of specialists who share the father of their
children. The first wife, for example, may be economically astute,
the second one have political connections, the third be an ambi-
tious healer, teacher or religious specialist, and so forth. That way,
the cooperative gains with each additional wife. That, of course, is
a "best-case" scenario. Polygynous marriages can also become
complicated hells if co-wives do not get along, or must compete for
the husband's attention, or for their children's inheritance rights.
Worst of all, in some societies, rich and powerful men can accumulate women, like so many heads of cattle, and confine them.
But harems are not a meaningful indictment of polygyny: like so
many other social perversions, they are not characteristic of small-
scale societies but of certain civilizations.

Polygyny is *not* multiple monogamy: the societies that practice
it do not generally regard romantic love as a reason for getting
married. Indeed, in a lot of languages there aren't any words for
romantic love! There is only one society on record that ever
encouraged men to marry for love, then meet another pretty girl
and fall in love again and marry that one, too. That was the Mormons of the nineteenth century who, as Euro-Americans, had
zero experience with the actual workings of polygyny and very
much *did* hope to turn it into multiple monogamy. They were
driven to this by their religious beliefs (which had grown out of an
ancient monogamism) and the undeniable insight that surplus
males—unmarried men—are a scourge on the rest of society.
Remarkably, the Mormons made their brand of polygyny endure
for half a century before the poison of sexual favoritism and
threats by the U.S. Government scuttled the experiment. It can be
stated categorically: polygyny never works well in societies based
on the nuclear family.

But in societies where it does fit, the polygynous lifestyle offers security to the elderly of both sexes and makes it possible for women to wrest a great deal of collective power from men.

Normally every woman has her own domicile—at least her own kitchen and sleeping space. Marital relations are not orgies: the husband usually spends time with each of his wives in turn, and woe to him who seems partial to one at the cost of the others! Relationships among co-wives can be heavily politicized by the rules of inheritance: when the old man dies, whose child will inherit what? Even a woman who has managed to share a husband amicably may have great difficulty with the idea that her co-wife's son will get all the good stuff! Still, co-wives more typically see the value in cooperation and neighborly relations, and the ethnographic literature is full of examples of co-wives acting as a united front against their boss-male, even of co-wives collectively beating up a wayward or brutal husband.

Quite distinct organizational potentials derive from the three ways to marry women: if you wed only sisters (*sororal polygyny*) you develop a redundant and therefore very strong relationship with one other family, and you will be a valuable man in its councils. Even if your (first?) wife dies, the in-law bond remains unbroken. All your children, regardless of who their mothers are, belong to the same clan or family. In matrilineal matrilocal societies (those wherein family membership goes through the female, and husbands join their wife's matrilineage), the sisterly co-wives form a core group that has far more power than their husband, a power that is enforced by their brothers. Such a kinship and residence system offers the best possible environment in which to raise children.

If you are polygynous in a society that specifically bans a man from marrying sisters (*nonsororal polygyny*), then you will have equally valid relationships with as many different families as you have wives, but the children of different mothers will have different kinship loyalties, even though they are all yours. Some very interesting difficulties arise with nonsororal polygyny in matrilineal societies (that is, where the rules of descent state that your children belong to your wives' families and not to your own). At least three of Suriname's Maroon tribes practice nonsororal polygyny, and all six tribes are matrilineal. Since clans have their own villages, and all the women of a clan are considered sisters for marital purposes, a polygynous husband must travel from village to village to visit his different wives, there to chop their subsistence gardens out of the tropical rain forest, to build and maintain their houses and canoes, etc., and then to move on to the next wife. Of course his position at the nexus of interacting families means he has the opportunity to mediate among them, which may confer status and power as a go-between or peacemaker.

If you marry several women in a society that practices *general polygyny*, thus making any unmarried human female not of your own line eligible, then your political potential is more directly due to your personal choices than to the social structure of your culture, and your children will have different family ties.

"But," you probably want to know now, "how is polygyny even possible, without massive male-infanticide or somehow dooming most men to celibacy, when there are usually between 105 and 115 boys born for every 100 girls?"

You probably already know that, beginning with conception, boys die off more rapidly of almost every cause than girls: males are stronger but not as durable.

"But surely," you protest, "not enough males die to create the surpluses of females needed for polygyny to work?"

The answer may disappoint you with its simplicity: to create a female surplus, all that a society has to do is to set the age at which men can get married much higher than the age for women. There are always good and rational reasons for that decision, not least that it takes a while to convince the average young man that he ought to settle down and accept responsibility for a family. Every society has a lot more young women than old men. Try any population pyramid you like; make women marriageable at 15 and men at 30; keep the under-30 males out of the competition somehow, and Presto! There'll be, if not a clamor, then at least the surpluses of females necessary for polygyny.

One reason the Mormons got such a bad press, a century ago, was that their men were skimming brides from the American West, which had notoriously few women to begin with. Given a few more generations of practice, and the wisdom and humility to study other societies instead of trying to convert them, the Mormons might conceivably have evolved a polygynous system that actually worked. But given the outrage in the monogamist rest of the nation, it is not likely.

Monogamy

The (relatively) permanent bonding of one male to one female is a monagamous form of marriage. Even where polygyny was the ideal, its economic realities and often burdensome social implications always made monogamy the commonest form of marriage actually practiced. Until the twentieth century, monogamy was the mandated marital arrangement for only 25 to 30 percent of human cultures, and it was most often encountered in societies undergoing prolonged economic stress. It may therefore well be the original way to form a family: wherever our pedestrian ancestors neared the limits of their resource base, or colonized new and therefore dangerous ecozones, they experienced prolonged economic pressure. Still, the hunter-gatherer societies that survived long enough to be recorded by ethnographers generally did not compel their members to be monogamous: the most successful and powerful men often had more than one wife.

As a general rule in small-scale societies, monogamy works best where each spouse has only limited interaction with the other and derives his or her major psychological satisfactions from "blood" relatives. Otherwise, as with us Westerners, each person has to learn to become all things to a spouse, and marriages become "brittle."

Nevertheless, as human numbers increase and our resource base shrinks, we must expect monogamy to become the *de facto* norm for humanity, even in societies that officially prefer polygyny. The reason, still, is economic: wives get pregnant, and as the world becomes urbanized and industrialized, children become economic liabilities. In rural and preindustrial lifeways, kids did "chores," but there are vanishingly few ways in today's cities for children to contribute meaningfully to their family's larder or bank account. Also, it costs more than ever to feed, house, exercise, socialize, and educate a child. It is therefore almost impossible for the mother–child dyad to thrive in urban societies without far more economic and parental input from the father–husband (or his limited surrogate, the welfare office) than was required in the preurban or premonogamous past.

When a polygynous society's men can no longer support multiple families they become monogamous, and its culture will eventually evolve the ideology necessary for them to believe that this is the only decent way to live. Unfortunately, in many societies the recent rise of monogamy has come at the cost of diminished life chances for women. While overpopulation everywhere makes resources ever scarcer and requires families to have a full-time father, mothers are no longer able to share with their co-wives the burdens of maintaining a man. Meanwhile, traditional attitudes of "obligatory natality" (mandatory childbearing), which made some sense when infant mortality was high, persist long after they can no longer be rationally defended—if only to prove the potency and enhance the status of men. This example of culture-lag turns polygyny's once quite independent women into vulnerable dependents: when a woman desperately *needs* a man, not merely to give her a child but to keep her and that child from destitution, she can usually be turned into his house-slave—or worse. Once a society's female sex has been made dependent, whether by economics or custom (and custom, in the form of law and religion, routinely backs the male), women find themselves unable to escape abuse because they have no other alternative but the street. So a responsible mother can be turned into a chattel, exploited, and brutalized by a man who believes that such is his right and God's will. Remember the Taliban? Then also remember that spousal abuse and child abuse are the commonest forms of violence in violent America.

Polyandry

"Many husbands" married to one woman is rare; it apparently has occurred as the preferred form of marriage in less than 1 percent of the world's cultures. It seems to originate spontaneously wherever economic conditions are so harsh that even a full-time monogamous husband is not enough to guarantee the survival of children. Then, sometimes, men (usually brothers) will band together to collectively support one woman and her offspring. The best-known cases of polyandry occur in the Himalayas: it is still practiced in Tibet, and still for the old economic reasons. When economic conditions improve, polyandry usually gives way to monogamy or even polygyny. However, anything as fundamental as marriage patterns is slow to change—there are examples of persistent polyandry among people who could well afford monogamy or even polygyny. Consider the polyandrous Toda of India.

Where the Boys Are

Traditionally the Toda practiced 100 percent female infanticide. No, that's *not* impossible! Since there were no female Toda, all the women in a Toda village were in-laws. The way it usually worked was that, as soon as the youngest brother was old enough to be interested in girls, the most presentable brother was sent out among the neighboring tribes to scout for a wife. His arrival was, of course, anticipated. Unmarried women lined his path. *(Question: do you think they lined up to throw rocks, or kisses?)*

Once he had made his choice and gotten approval from his would-be bride's family and his brothers, she moved to Toda territory, where she had a great pomp-and-circumstance wedding, after which her husbands would spend quality time with her on rotation. She expected to be pregnant or nursing the rest of her life and to have no daughters. But she had unparalleled opportunities to play off one guy against another, and she would never have to worry about money, because the Toda were the richest tribe in the region—and all the brothers had contracted to support her. *(Answer: Remember that female infanticide is common in societies with population problems. The Toda could be a very good catch for any woman who knew how to handle men.)*

But then the British colonized India and imprisoned Toda men for killing girl babies. Eventually something occurred that was entirely unnatural to Toda society: the first Toda girls became women. ("Girls can't be Toda! It's a guy thing! There are no female bulls by definition!") Toda culture has not dealt well with this basic denial of its charter. Who can a Toda girl marry? Male–female relations there remain . . . unusual. ✎

During the Great Depression of the 1930s, when millions of men in the industrialized world discovered that they could not support their wives and children, something like polyandry occurred in the most destitute neighborhoods—only it was never called that. Here and there, a family with an unemployed husband would take in a boarder who not only paid rent but who had unspoken though uncontested sexual access to the wife. As soon as the economy improved and the husband found work, the boarder was kicked out and virtuous monogamy became the rule again. There is precious little information on the extent of this connubial oddity in our culture, but that this adaptation has been with us for a while was suggested by the musical *Paint Your Wagon*, in which three pioneers lived a polyandrous arrangement on the woman-poor Western frontier.

WHAT'S LOVE GOT TO DO WITH IT?

Well you may ask.

Let's begin by distinguishing two sorts of romantic love: one, that hormone-dominated, frantically obsessive interest that seems to be the subject of most popular music and the aspiration of every teenager; and two, the emotion happily married people feel for their spouses. Let's call the first one "being in love," and the second "loving."

Millions of sailors and prostitutes have demonstrated by now that neither being in love nor loving is a prerequisite for sex, and thousands of cultures have proven that it is not required for a successful marriage, either. Indeed, many cultures—even those whose language does have a word for "love"—have noted that it is an irrational basis for marriage.

When you are in love you are quite mad; everybody who has ever been in love knows that. Temporary insanity is not the best condition in which to make decisions that will so greatly affect the rest of your own life and that of future generations. In most of the world, therefore, marriages used to be arranged by parents or by matchmakers, and in many places they still are—sometimes involving nuptials between very young children, not to be consummated until the kids are adult—however that maturational stage may be defined locally.

Even though many spouses in arranged marriages may come to be genuinely loving toward each other, the idea horrifies people raised to believe that being in love is a necessary and sufficient cause for a wedding. But when you compare arranged and romantic marriages, the former have lower divorce and abuse rates. These are meaningful measures, because it remains as true for yours as for any other society that, *as a rule, divorce reduces the socioeconomic well-being of the woman and her children, while it improves that of the man.* Certainly there are spectacular exceptions to that rule: some clever beauty will manage to marry and divorce the local Donald Trump and receive a settlement so bountiful that she never has to worry about money again. But spectacular exceptions do not affect probabilities.

Sleeping with the Enemy

Had you been born among the many peoples whose languages include no terms for friends or strangers but only words for kin and enemies, then, since the incest taboo keeps you from marrying kin, you must marry an enemy. Among the Dobu of New Guinea, a famous example, the wedding is a day of armistice between warring villages. The newlyweds retreat to either the bride's or the groom's village, where the terrified stranger suffers the rage and suspicions of his or her hostile hosts for one year. Then the couple moves to the other spouse's people, where abuse and persecution are now heaped on the other enemy. In this institutionalization of the dysfunctional family, all parties resent marriage as a duty whose only purpose is to create children, and once a contracted number of those has been produced, there is no need to live together any longer. Love is never even imagined under such circumstances: affection is reserved for one's own relatives, not for enemies.

Extreme cases like the Dobu are rare, of course: most people are sensible and tolerant in-laws. ✎

But back to romantic love of both kinds. When you've achieved it or "found" it, nothing is more rewarding and enabling; so if or when you lose it, nothing is more devastating. It makes you wonder how so many different societies have gotten along without it! The fact is that romantic love as Westerners experience it becomes a possibility only under certain cultural conditions. But a case can be made that it has become a necessity for you, in today's world.

You live in a society where the only constancy is change, where you cannot reasonably expect your environment and your relationships to stay what they are. For several generations now, Americans have been moving on an average of once every seven years. Each time you pack up, you leave behind people who have been important to you: relatives, friends, colleagues, lovers. You move to new places with new opportunities, new stresses, new work and social environments—new occasions to stretch and to succeed, new chances to fail. Even your parents and siblings are only temporary relations: you remember them fondly from your youth, you visit them when you can, but you do not live with them anymore. In fact, *the only people you can take along when the movers come are your spouse and your underage kids.* In the process, the idea of "spouse" has become loaded with far more expectations than it used to have.

So what *is* the primary prerequisite for an adequate spouse in your era? Rationally: the ability to offer you that tolerant and supportive familiarity that has been called "the perfected psychological response" and that the rest of us usually call "loving." The ideal spouse is one who not merely complements you by being strong where you are weak in areas your partnership requires, but who somehow boosts you to be better than you thought you could be, and whose face still lights up when you enter the room. That's a hell of a lot to expect from another human being, and statistics indicate that half of all marriages end in divorce.

But then, half don't.

DIVORCE

You do not stop growing, evolving, maturing—pick a term—just because you marry. Why should you expect yourself and your spouse to change in the same ways? A century ago, when divorce meant personal failure, but you could reasonably expect to dance on an intolerable spouse's grave soon after the kids left home, today's marital statistics would have been proof that society had broken down. But the average human life span then was about 45 years. Today, life expectancy is over 70 for both sexes. Today, also, safe and effective birth control can prevent children until the stability of your union and its economic basis have been demonstrated; your expected postwedding lifespan is several times as long as your grandparents' allotment. And divorce, we are beginning to see, is no longer proof of your failure so much as part of your learning process. Be grateful that your culture evolved in that way!

Societies vary greatly in the ease with which their members can initiate divorce. Suriname's Maroons occupy one end of the continuum; a woman there signals that she's had enough of her man by simply tossing all his clothes out of the door. That is an irreversible act: once the breach has been so indicated, she can never pick up with him again. Of course the children stay with her. Because a husband has made a commitment to his wife's matrilineage and invested into her house and canoe, it is somewhat more difficult and expensive for men to get out of an intolerable marriage, but certainly not prohibitively so. Among the Kwinti, the smallest of these tribes, the very ease of divorce may be a problem: there are so few potential spouses to go around that many people wind up married to Maroons in other tribes.

On the other end of the continuum are societies such as the many Catholic countries in which until recently divorce was simply not possible; or perhaps even worse, where, as in most Islamic countries today, divorce is impossible for women but easy for men. And because women's inequality is always legitimated on religious grounds, it follows that any society that denies women the right to dissolve an intolerable relationship will also denigrate them if they do not marry. *Wherever divorce is made very difficult for women, they are always vulnerable to exploitation and abuse, and they typically lead unenviable lives.*

This does not imply that easy divorce guarantees female equality.

Anyway, what keeps marriage on the books in our sort of society is that a man can become so habituated (imprinted?) to a particular woman that he believes his life with her will be more endurable than life without her. And that a woman can feel that way about a man. And that sometimes they are both right.

Even when they aren't, even when Being Madly In Love hasn't adequately metamorphosed into Loving Each Other Realistically, culture usually succeeds in programming a man to love his kids. Most men experience genuine loss when divorce forces them to part from their children. The fact that this loss has its roots in culture rather than in biology doesn't make it any less painful. Many a marriage has survived alienation between husband and wife simply because the man could not face losing his kids.

And some of those families have proven that there can be worse things for kids to live with than their parents' divorce.

Thinking It Through

1. Women are generally turned off by the idea of sharing a man, but would that be true if marriage was not based on love? Does your reasoning hold for polyandry?
2. "It is culture, and nothing else, that keeps dysplasia genes in the canine breeding pool." With that in mind, can you demolish the argument that human inbreeding necessarily leads to mental and physiological deterioration?
3. What are five popular reasons for the universality of the incest taboo? What is wrong with them?
4. Why is group marriage never the preferred form in any society? And why is romantic love not a universal ideal in human societies?
5. If you understand what males contribute to the species, and recognize that males are far more costly than females, what do you think of the idea of artificially limiting the percentage of males being born? How would that affect the war between the sexes, the economic and political position of women, and sexual opportunities for men? Once everybody got used to the new sex ratio (which might take two generations), wouldn't life be better?

Bloodline Logics
Kinship II—Reckoning

"When an African chief says he knows his ancestry for forty generations, he is stating a fact within the sociological conventions of his society. He need command a knowledge of only forty names, in contrast to the 1,048,576 ancestors the stickler for biological accuracy would be compelled to know."

—Melville J. Herskovits (1895–1963)

"As part of language, kin term systems reflect unconscious logic and conceptual patterning as well as social institutions."

—Alfred L. Kroeber (1876–1960)

*The possibility for kinship to evolve
is rooted in our biology. In all societies
until recently the rules of kinship
determined an individual's rights and
obligations. They continue to define how
one must act toward specific others, and
what to expect from them. Kinship
classifies not only the categories of
your relatives, but determines the
organizational parameters of your society.
Cultures differ in what they emphasize
through kinship, so the only way to reckon
an exotic kinship system is from its
structural assumptions.*

*Y*ou may never have considered kinship a big deal, because you were born in an age and place in which the roles and powers of the family are minuscule, compared with those of government, the legal system, the educational system, multinational corporations, the stock market, et cetera. Sure, you love your parents most days; you get along with your siblings well enough; you may have a favorite cousin or two. But odds are that you don't know the names of the brothers and sisters of your grandparents. You have probably never met *their* grandchildren, who are nevertheless blood relatives in your own generation, and probably a lot like you in some ways. Some will have the same last name as you, yet you may not even consider them relatives.

It may indeed be wiser not to.

On the other hand, you may belong to that minority for whom kinship is still extremely relevant. In the United States, that depends largely on your ethnicity. Americans with African ancestry can usually name more kin than Americans of European descent; recent immigrants from Asia can probably name more than either. But do you fully appreciate that for your ancestors it meant "money in the bank" to have relatives?

Since forever, in every society, "family" used to do everything it took to keep human existence going. You and your relatives performed enough of every task necessary to feed and house and clothe yourselves, maintain order, defend yourself against predators, relate to your dead and supernaturals, socialize and educate your young for survival, maintain the grandparents, practice healing, wage war, govern . . .

As societies urbanized, kinship could no longer do what was needed. Other kinds of associations—based on contract, community, citizenship, religious affiliation, or other criteria—took over the functions once performed by kin groups. Every form of organization you now take for granted, from bureaucracies and school dance committees to labor unions and terrorist cells, finds its roots in kinship. The rules and customs that determine who *does* what and who *gets* what all began in the customary face-to-face-relationships of Neolithic hunting bands. Every institution today fulfills a set of roles originally developed by the family; every agency carries out some function of the family. All except one, that is. Nothing ever tried has worked half as well as parents for turning babies into decent and useful adults. Moreover, even today in this most complex of modern societies, the family remains the fallback agency for every institution. When disaster strikes, when all else fails, whom can you turn to but family?

When kinship is important (and at some point in your life it definitely *will* be, regardless of your sex, age, race, creed or country of national origin), you will assuredly need to know who is family and who is not. In other words, to whom are you affiliated and how is that determined?

RECKONING AFFILIATION

A human being *needs* to belong to some sort of family.

There are only three ways in which you can be a member of a family unit. You are born into it, you are adopted into it, or you marry into it. There are also three ways to be born to a family: you can be a member because your mother is, or because your father is, or because your birth made you a member of both your father's and your mother's kinship groups. Family is nowhere an inclusive concept.

At a minimum, all societies have *rules of endogamy* to *specify the group or categories of persons within which you must marry,* and *rules of exogamy* to *specify the group you must marry out of.* For Americans, the minimum rule of exogamy is to marry out of the nuclear family; the minimum rule of endogamy is less clear, but may include your race, class, and educational level. In the kinship systems of most other societies, the rules of exogamy are more complex, and the rules of endogamy more specific.

Necessarily, therefore, every society has taken steps to ensure that only *some* of the people related to you genetically will be considered "kin." Different cultures have arrived at dividing lines that are perfectly logical but, once again, based on arbitrary standards. And each of them may have a different way of categorizing relatives for specific purposes.

KINSHIP NOMENCLATURES

There was a time when every intro anthro text sported a chapter or two about the many ways in which non-Westerners reckoned kinship, that is, determined who was family. That's now less common for a variety of reasons—some of them intellectually defensible.

So why am I going to bother you with it here?

Because it is an effective, safe way for you to experience an alien logic.

Although other cultures reason as rigorously and rationally as yours does, they start from different assumptions than yours. Cross-cultural misunderstanding is rooted in that fact. Each side will appear incomprehensible until one can reason from the other's premises. It is easy enough to memorize that the Hoojies do X, the Veeblefritzes do Y, and the Bongobongo do Z. But internalizing these differences, being actually able to look at some part of the universe the way the Hoojies do, requires a lot more than "tolerance for differences."

Perhaps the ideal test of your intellectual flexibility would be to immerse yourself in some exotic population's theology, then to argue some important point from their perspective, giving all the whys and wherefores, and see if the native believers agree that you have represented their position accurately. That's something ethnographers are expected to do. But again, ours is not an ideal world, you're not an ethnographer, and the subject of religion is far too inflammatory for casual use here.

However, kinship reckoning, which (I promise you) can be almost as mind-bending as creed, lacks the explosive implications of religious belief and can be discussed with almost mathematical objectivity. The intent of this exercise, then, is twofold: to get you to think about something familiar using an alien logic, and to let you appreciate how such logic affects the structure of other societies.

The Need for Classification

Biologically you are similarly related to all of your kinfolk in any generation, and therefore to all the people they gave rise to. If you had a record of all your ancestors and their siblings and *their* descendants, you would find that we are, as so many religions insist, if not all brothers and sisters then at least all relatives.

That sounds nice at first, but remember that you have obligations to everyone who is kin. And those responsibilities go beyond the need to find a birthday card or buying a Christmas present for every relative. Would you let an uncle starve, a cousin go without shelter, a sister do without medicine?

Socially, economically, politically—even psychologically—you cannot possibly afford all the responsibilities and obligations involved in counting all those people as kin. Human societies everywhere, everywhen, have therefore limited the "Us–ness" of kinship to one descent line (or at most two) out of all the possible ones that genetics could justify. And once again, the way to arrive at the dividing lines is perfectly logical, but based on utterly arbitrary standards.

Consciously or not, and in spite of fashions of political correctness, all human beings classify continuously. They must! You cannot survive if you treat all events or persons as uniquely relevant. We have special terms for what is important (hence professional vocabularies), and general terms for what (we think) is not.

The rules of kinship determine an individual's rights and obligations to others and to self. They define how s/he must act toward specific others, and what s/he can expect of them. Moreover, kinship classifies not only the categories of your relatives, but the sort of organizations and of collective effort your society will be able to field. In doing all that, kinship embodies and determines some of the most fundamental value assumptions of cultural life.

What makes someone kin? Shared descent. But how far away that sharing is reckoned or acknowledged will depend on the type of kinship assumptions a system makes. *"Descent" technically means that certain kinship lines are divided off from others and used to form larger groups than would be possible if all lines were considered equally.*

Within the nuclear family, every separate relationship warrants its own specific term: brother, sister, mother, father, and so forth. Beyond the household, however, there may be multitudes related to you in some kinship fashion: the male and female siblings of each of your parents, their parents and their respective siblings with their children and children's children, your own and your siblings' are out there, one generation away in every direction. It would soon prove impractical to give each separate relationship a distinct term. Every language therefore "lumps" some different kinds of relationship under categories to which they give a single term. But they don't all do it in the same way: the lumping always reflects the particular principles of kinship in terms of which a society is (or was originally) organized.

The English term "cousin," for example, indicates both males and females on both your father's and your mother's side, who descend from either parent's brothers or sisters. The term does not indicate whether these individuals are younger or older than you; whether their parents are younger or older than your parents; whether or not they are alive, or whether you are male or female. The term "cousin" can thus indicate some 32 relationships, 152 if you include "second cousins." In many cultures, some or all of those distinctions are indicated with their own terms.

Terminology and Diagramming

A kinship nomenclature is not the same thing as a kinship chart. The latter is a list of family members' names, the former a list of relationship terms. A nomenclature identifies the set of terms used to indicate the parts of a system. In kinship analysis it refers to what an individual calls people who are related to him or her. You are related to your father in a different way than to your mother: both are your parents, but they treat you differently (as you do them). The differences are symbolized in the words you use for the relationships. In English, the woman who bore you is your mother; the man who sired you is your father. You can have siblings—that is, brother(s) and sister(s) who share both your mother and your father, or half-siblings who share only one of your parents with you. Together you are organized into a family.

This is how you diagram that. The triangles indicate males, the circles, females, the square "either sex." The = sign signifies marriage; everyone below a horizontal line shares a consanguineal or blood tie, the vertical line is descent. "Ego" is the "you" in "What do *you* call this kind of relative?"

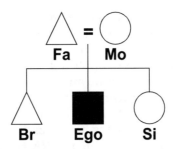

Figure 1.   The Nuclear Family

Note that every term indicates this relative's generational relationship to Ego, whether the relative is related by blood or marriage, and whether s/he is in the same line of descent. Also note that the sex of each of Ego's relatives is indicated by a geometric symbol.

If you need to indicate more brothers and/or sisters, simply add them to the horizontal display. Kinship terminology charts remind some people of electric circuit diagrams, and you may find it useful to think of them as blueprints of kinship circuitry, mapping a power flow not for electricity but for "blood."

Figure 2 shows what happens when you shift Ego to another position on the chart: all the terms of reference change. Don't do this accidentally.

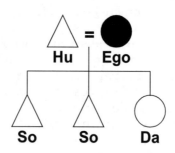

Figure 2. Shifting Ego

For analyzing alien kinship systems, the terms you have learned at your mother's knee are less than useful. The reason is that each carries specific meanings and implications that are not universally shared. For example, you cannot translate "cousin" into many languages without specifying the kinship links between Ego and the cousin in question. Every kinship term, yours or theirs, defines a unique set of local expectations.

Consider "father." This term may refer to the actual biological male parent of a child, in which case the technical term "genitor" is more precise and universally applicable: all of us have a genitor. But "father" can as accurately mean the societally recognized male individual responsible for raising that child even though he may not be its genitor, as with a stepfather. Then the precise term is "pater."

"It is a wise child that knows its father," says a now almost forgotten proverb. Until the advent of DNA testing it was virtually impossible to establish paternity. It is still something you normally take your mother's word for, but what if your sire denies it? In most human societies it is important to know who your father is, and it makes a big difference whether or not he contracted with your mother to be responsible for you. In some kinship systems that is crucial to your very survival; in others it is not.

There have been societies (the Trobriand Islanders, for example) whose cultures did not acknowledge the male's role in pregnancy. For them, paternity began when the mother married, regardless of genetics. In polyandrous societies the assignment of "fatherhood" was, necessarily, arbitrary. The Toda male who last performed "the ceremony of the bow and arrow" for his and his brothers' wife remains the official father of her next-to-be-born children until and unless another brother performs that ritual. Consider also adopted children and the male who raises them.

Similar confusions surround the term "mother" with its meanings of "genitrix" and "mater." To keep things simple, kinship charts depict only biological descent.

Often, relationships carry such labels as "father–child" even when no such biological tie exists. That does not mean that there are whole societies of people without a clue who their biological fathers are, but that for certain purposes the relationship between these classes of individuals is deemed equivalent to that which operates between a father and his child.

Among the matrilineal Kwinti, for example, my assistant—an intelligent illiterate who spoke at least four languages and understood perfectly well what I was asking him—quickly named six or seven women as his mother. When I raised my eyebrows at that, Sempi laughed. "You did not ask the question right," he said. "You mean to ask who is the woman who made me." Indeed I did. So he told me who that one was. In his language, all female fellow clan-members in his mother's generation are thought of, and addressed as, "M'ma."

So does M'ma mean "Mother?"

No, it means "clanswoman of my mother's generation."

This is a crucial distinction. If you translate alien kinship terms into your own, you will never be able to make sense of them.

Anthropologists use a precise, analytical vocabulary with a two-letter shorthand for each core term involved:

Fa	Father	**So**	Son
Mo	Mother	**Da**	Daughter
Ch	Child(ren)	**Hu**	Husband
Br	Brother	**Wi**	Wife
Si	Sister		

So your FaSi is one specific kind of aunt; your MoBrWi is another, as are your MoSi and FaBrWi. The English term "aunt" covers all four of these relationships.

Like any other major cultural variable, kinship nomenclature can be studied from a great many perspectives. Here, because we are interested in who can marry whom, we will focus on the most common analysis, that of cousin terminologies. There are two kinds of cousins:

Parallel cousins (//-Co) are the children of Ego's FaBr and MoSi. Because from a lineal perspective these cousins "parallel" the way you are related to your own Fa and Mo (like you, FaBrCh are related to your father's descent line through a male in that line; like you, MoSiCh are related to your mother's descent line through a female in that line), parallel cousins are usually addressed by the same terms as siblings.

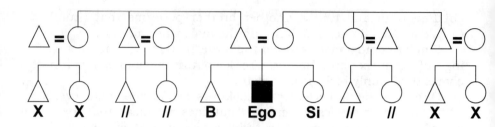

Figure 3.   Cousin Types

Cross-cousins (X-Co) are the children of Ego's FaSi and MoBr. The connecting relatives "cross" the divide between the sexes. In most unilineal societies these are terminologically distinct from Ego's siblings.

The Principles of Relationship

In 1909, young anthropologist A. L. Kroeber demonstrated that there are eight principles or premises of relationship that can be used to determine the kinship distinctions in any society. These are:

- *Generation:* (grand) parental, Ego's own, children's, etc.
- *Blood or affine:* direct or "married on"
- *Lineal or collateral:* in own line of descent or not
- *Sex of relative:* male or female
- *Sex of speaker:* indicates Ego's sex
- *Sex of connecting relative = bifurcation:* male or female links
- *Age in generation:* older or younger
- *Life or death of connecting relative*

Kinship systems can usefully be classified by the particular combination of these eight principles that they use to distinguish and lump Ego's relatives. No culture known uses all eight principles; all cultures lump.

Languages differ greatly in the actual number of kinship terms they have. English has 21, all of which indicate generation, blood or affine, lineal or collateral and (except cousin) sex of relative. But English has no terminological indicators for the other four principles.

Compare Lakota (Sioux Indian). It has 31 kinship terms, all of which indicate generation and blood or affine, but only 20 indicate lineal or collateral, while 18 indicate sex of speaker, and 6 sex of connecting relative. Lakota Siouan uses seven of the eight principles, ignoring only the life or death of connecting relative. In Basque, the most ancient of languages spoken in Europe, kinship terms do indicate the life or death of connecting relatives.

An almost endless variety of kinship systems can be imagined by recognizing that they must differentiate themselves on the basis of (a) which of the 8 principles of kinship they use, and (b) which of these they emphasize, and (c) the specific logic they use for lumping terms. Literally thousands of kinship systems have been recorded; virtually every culture has its own brand. Most of them can be sorted into six organizational types. Anthropologists have named these after the societies for which some ethnographer first figured out how the natives arranged their kinfolk terminologically. Each of these types is found among many different peoples on several continents.

Bilateral Systems

If your culture reckons kinship ties through both male and female links (*bilateral descent*), then you are a member of both of the kinship groups from which your parents hailed—whatever your surname may be.

The advantage to having two families you belong to equally is that each set of grandparents and other relatives is a backup system for the other in case something goes wrong. Just how many people are immediately responsible for and with you depends on which particular kinship principles your culture's kinship system uses.

Hawaii

The absolute minimum number of kinship principles necessary to indicate differentiated relationships well enough to avoid incest and promote cooperation, is two. These, for obvious reasons, are always generation and sex of relative. Thus Hawaii equates the importance of differences between generations with the differences between sexes—which has interesting philosophical and organizational implications.

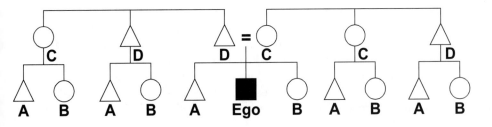

Figure 4.   Hawaii Terminology

This diagram is a schematic; in real terminology records you would encounter the actual terms that native speakers use for these relationships instead of A, B, C, etc. Note that as few as four terms can suffice to differentiate relatives, no matter how many generations are involved, because everyone can tell the difference between an old person and a child. In such a case, "A" would need to be translated as "male in my generation," and "C" as "female in other generation." But more commonly, Ego will use six or eight terms to identify three or four generations: own, parents' and children's. Grandparents, perhaps.

Among peoples who reckon bilateral descent, Hawaii is the most common type of cousin terminology. It reckons descent laterally; it assumes that your mother's people are no more and no less your relatives than your father's. Hawaii kinship systems make no terminological distinction between cross- and parallel-cousins, and calls both by the same reference terms as Ego's siblings of the same sex. It also calls Fa, FaBr and MoBr by a single term. Relating to so many people just as you relate to your parents makes life very secure for children and adolescents; such broad intimacy also makes it easy to choose the group you'll affiliate and live with: the gang you hang with. Perhaps with some of your father's people, perhaps with some of your mother's. (This method of reckoning descent is technically called *ambilineality*.)

Now for the most important hint in kinship analysis: *if two relatives are called by the same referential term, they will interact with the same expectations of their relationship.* What that means for romance is that if Ego is female, then all the males called A or D are sexually taboo to her because all As are equivalent to brothers, all Ds extend her relationship with her father, and the universal incest taboo prohibits mating or marriage with anyone carrying a nuclear family kinship term. Similarly, if Ego is male, then hands off all Bs and Cs.

So whom does Ego marry?

No one on this chart. That means that Hawaii types must marry beyond cousins. The incest taboo, if extended, is extended bilaterally. The incest taboo always means that your mate must come from beyond the class of all people that your culture defines as your relatives. For Hawaii kinship systems, that is not a great hardship because, since they lack lineality, they have no organizational need to extend the incest taboo very far upward generationally—meaning that blood relations not defined as kin are seldom far away.

Hawaii types always lack a recognition of nuclear families. Their households are extended and ambilocal, meaning that the new couple lives near or with either spouse's kinfolk, often joining a married brother or sister there. A typical household occupies a large building or compound with separate residential areas for each couple and their children. Any adult acts as a parent toward any child in the unit. Theoretically this is as tolerant as a kinship system can be. Both monogamy and polygyny can be practiced since neither will confuse descent lines. It does not matter to kinship reckoning whether a polygynous man marries sisters or unrelated women. Theoretically polyandry should be allowed too, but there are no examples of it: Hawaii is not found in environments that make survival of the next generation chancy.

Let me remind you that ideal categories of cultural phenomena, such as kinship nomenclature systems, are often—like colors or musical tones—only points on a continuum. Most actual genealogies show people using "creative accounting" to make kinship do what they want it to do, even when that is by definition impossible. For example, "my" Kwinti have what looks at first like a straight Hawaii system: their terminology uses only generation and sex of relative, and sibling = X-Co = //-Co. But the Kwinti are a clan with three lineages—which makes them unilineal and non-Hawaii by definition.

To sum up the Hawaii kinship type:

- *Principles:* generation and sex of relative
- *Descent:* bilateral, ambilineal
- *Corporate groupings:* no clans, lineages, or nuclear families
- *Cousin terminology:* sibling = FaBrCh = FaSiCh = MoBrCh = MoSiCh
- *Marriage type:* monogamy and limited general polygyny
- *Residence:* usually ambilocal
- *Household:* bilaterally extended family

Eskimo

The other way to be bilateral is Eskimo. All Eskimo-type kinship systems add the principle of lineality to generation and sex. Like Hawaii, Eskimo assumes equivalency between Ego's maternal and paternal relatives in descent and affiliation, but it insists that the people you grew up with are categorically different from all other relatives. So every Eskimo system uses a special vocabulary to distinguish Fa from FaBr and MoBr, and Mo from MoSi and FaSi; Br and Si from all //-Co and X-Co; So from FaBrSo, FaSiSo, MoBrSo, and MoSiSo; etc. Eskimo thus recognizes both lateral and lineal descent reckoning.

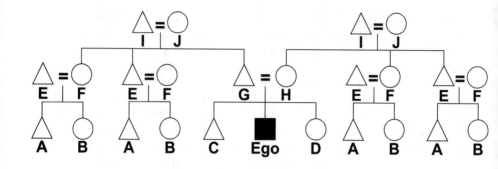

Figure 5. Eskimo Terminology

Ideally, Eskimo households contain only a husband, a wife, and their children living in a single domicile separate from both parents' relatives. Eskimo is always monogamous: you simply cannot have polygyny with neolocal nuclear families, not when that sort of family life demands both economic and psychological interdependence between the parents heading that reproductive and consumptive unit. Moreover, polygyny (even sororal) would hopelessly confuse lines of descent for the next generation, and threaten the nuclear family. (But note that a successful Eskimo hunter could assume responsibility through marriage for a second wife, usually a widow and her children. Inuit culture was very practical.)

So-called "serial polygamy" (marriage, divorce, marriage) is, of course, another story. Where allowed, that works for both sexes because it causes no confusion about who the two adults in charge of the household are.

Because this system reckons descent bilaterally, there are no unilineal organizations such as lineages or clans. Some Eskimo-type societies, especially in Madagascar and Southeast Asia (where ideas of endogamy, descent and territory can be inextricably intertwined) have developed bilateral kin groups called *demes* that perform many of the functions of unilineal descent organizations. But most preurban bilateral systems lack descent groups to fulfill society's necessary roles. About the best Hawaii or Eskimo can offer is *the kindred, an Ego-based bilateral network of relatives* (the clique of blood and in-law kin you work and play with) that shares members with other people's kindreds, and is therefore unsuitable for the formation of corporate groups. Although kindreds exist in many societies, they have no standard form or functions.

Eskimo is common among hunting-and-gathering peoples everywhere.

So whom do you marry?

As with Hawaiian, the incest taboo covers everyone on the diagram and may be extended bilaterally. Lineality and neolocality combine to make Eskimo types look for spouses among strangers, that is, people who are not related very closely in blood or territory. And all these factors, in turn, increase the incidence of mismatching and domestic violence.

If, by now, you have noticed how familiar this system sounds, you are right: Eskimo, the kinship system of the frozen north's Inuit, is essentially identical to that of the English-speaking United States. It is often referred to as Eskimo-Yankee.

To sum up the Eskimo-Yankee kinship type:

- *Principles:* generation, sex of relative, and lineality
- *Descent:* bilateral
- *Corporate groupings:* the nuclear family dominates. No clans or lineages
- *Cousin terminology:* sibling $\neq$ (FaBrCh = FaSiCh = MoBrCh = MoSiCh)
- *Marriage type:* monogamy
- *Residence:* neolocality preferred
- *Household:* nuclear

Unilineal Systems

There are far more societies with unilineal than bilateral kinship systems, for several reasons. Unilineal descent allows you to create organizations that can manage greater numbers of people than bilateral systems can. Their kinship rules can create a potentially immortal organization with a reach and power far beyond that of even the largest extended family, one whose officers control and manage the organization's resource bases—like any other corporation's.

Unilineality confers upon you at birth full membership in an ancient institution with its own customs and beliefs, a functional group larger than your birth family but smaller than your tribe or nation. That means you always know who you are and where you fit, because your kin are the people you grow up with, work with, fight with, party with. All your life. Unilineal people develop an almost ethnic "kin-patriotism" that is not typical of bilateral societies.

Patrilineality

In patrilineal societies, affiliation is handled in the same way that surnames are assigned to Western peoples: you inherit your father's membership. If you are a male, it's yours for life and your kids belong to the same lineage as you. If you are a female, you trade it for or add it to your husband's, and your kids belong to his lineage.

If your culture reckons descent only through male links (*patrilineal descent*), then you are a member of your father's kinship group *IF* he married your mother. If he did not, you are in trouble. How deep depends on local custom. In some cultures, if your father acknowledges that he sired you without marrying your mother, you still have certain rights in his kin group. In other societies his honesty makes no difference: the child of an unmarried woman is the responsibility of the mother and her people, and no one else. In either case, if you are female, your children will belong to your husband's family, as you did to your father's. If you have no husband, you can be pretty sure that you will be down-graded for having a child out of wedlock.

In most patrilineal societies, if you are a male, your wife's children belong to your family, and so will any kids you've caused outside the bond of matrimony, *if* you admit you fathered them. But you can be pretty sure that you'll be pressured by your own relatives *not* to acknowledge your bastard, because that could hurt the bottom line for your legitimate heirs, who are members of your own kinship group and therefore deserve your primary loyalty.

Patrilineal kinship is more prevalent than the other forms of descent—possibly because it is so well suited to polygyny and masculine hierarchies. The most populous nation-state, China, is patrilineal; so were most empires in the past. The custom of tracing surnames only through the male line is a vestige of patriliny—at least the ruling elites of Eurasia's most powerful societies were patrilineal.

Patrilineality can easily lead into patriarchy, which means rule by men, especially by the oldest male. And wherever it does, it diminishes the life chances of women. A man uses his success to arrange his womenfolk's marriages, because that brings him the alliances and prestige that will keep other men from toppling him. In other words: *with language and culture, and unlike any other male-dominance organization in nature, human males can perpetuate their elite position.* And once culture evolves into stratification, a man's power, property, and prestige can be made permanent through inheritance and the founding of a dynasty.

Matrilineality

If your culture reckons kinship only through female links in *matrilineal descent*, you are a member of your mother's family or lineage or clan without further ado. She legitimates your membership, and there can be no argument about it because she bore you. Illegitimacy is not the horror it is in patrilineality. If you are female, your own children will be members of your mother's family—which is yours. But if you are a male, your kids will belong to your wife's family, not to the one you and your mother belong to.

In matrilineal societies the most important male authority figure is not the father, but the mother's brother. That man, MoBr, is expected to pass on his property, knowledge, and inheritable offices to his sisters' children, not to his own. This splits his loyalties to the next generation, which may have important implications.

Matrilineality used to be widespread among the world's cultures. But no example of a matrilineal nation-state survives.

Corporate Descent Groups

In the days and places where family was the sole or major agency for doing what needed to be done in society, the principles of descent were used to create kinship structures that could organize many generations of people. The two major types of unilineal organizations are lineages and clans.

A lineage is an exogamous, corporate, unilineal descent group that traces its membership to a known human ancestor; a female for matrilineages, a male for patrilineages. "Corporate" means that the unit holds certain rights and properties in common and that its members are responsible for each other.

A lineage typically controls such basic goods as arable land and approval of marriage. It also has specific rights and obligations in the larger community: lineage A may bury the dead of lineage B and vice versa, for example, or the occupants for a certain ritual office can only be elected from lineage C. Lineages can grow only so large before they become too unwieldy for the face-to-face interactions that typify their management and conduct.

In some societies, related lineages are united into larger units called clans. *A clan is a corporate unilineal descent group that traces its membership to an assumed or mythical ancestor.* Clans are typically composed of lineages that cannot prove their shared origin. The Kwinti tribe, for example, constitutes a single matriclan made up of three lineages descended from three biologically unrelated women who separately escaped from different plantations on Suriname's coast. Each woman's descendants eventually joined up with those of the two others and wound up on the Coppename River. The mythic ancestor uniting these three Kwinti lineages into a single clan is these women's shared Mother: Africa.

All six Maroon tribes combine Hawaii-type kinship with matriclans. This is a successful syncretism (blending of elements derived from different traditions) because Hawaii is simple and crosscuts all the different ancestral tribal traditions out of which Suriname's Maroons had to fashion their unique cultures, and matrilineages and matriclans gave these male-dominated societies of runaways their egalitarian organization.

Sometimes clans can be united into still larger units that anthropologists call phratries. Even so, there is a limit to what a particular kind of organization can handle, and clans lack the organizational know-how to run a modern state, as Somalia and Afghanistan have recently demonstrated. These are societies in which the nation-state barely exists because the individual's patriotism is still focused on the clan.

Usually, clans are exogamous—otherwise the boundaries between paternal and maternal relatives would be lost and the clan would lose its unilineality. Individuals have specific obligations to, and special privileges with, their mother's relatives, and a different set of both with their father's people. If individuals could marry within their clan, these special relationships would become confused: some of the people who normally would be Ego's paternal relatives would now also be Ego's mother's kin, meaning that a person who would normally be Ego's moral sanctioner could also be Ego's privileged-joking relative, confusing everybody.

Like nonkinship corporations, clans often identify themselves through symbolic representations such as totems (your equivalent would be logos). These symbols acquire vast psychological power and may be defended against real or imagined injury with violence or its modern moral equivalent, legal action.

In societies organized by unilineal descent, everything that needs doing is done by relatives. That minimizes social differentiation and inequality because it lets social relationships remain face to face. But because only a limited number of people can be organized effectively, clans tend to be replaced by nonkinship associations. Wherever the nation-state has taken over, corporate kinship has been replaced with the impersonal offices of bureaucracy.

Until the invention of bureaucracies, clans were the most efficient and the largest organizers of human effort. Clans can grow massively as the generations pass: clans with a million members exist in West Africa. Some Chinese clans are much more numerous than that: the Lee clan claimed 72 million living members in 1998, making Lee the most common surname in the world. But clans of that size lack any meaningful organization.

There is a limit to how many people can be united effectively through kinship ties.

Sudan

Relationships are expressed in two-way expectations and obligations. In theory, kinship terms describe relationships, not people, but in fact, most nomenclature systems describe only the "important" ones. Sudan is different. It uses a purely descriptive kinship terminology in which every term denotes an exact relationship to Ego. Sudan does this by adding bifurcate collateral to generation, sex of relative, and lineality. Literally, "to bifurcate" means "to split in two," and "bifurcate collateral" means the splitting continues on both sides of Ego's descent line. Sudan thus covers all systems that indicate every type of cousin by a different term.

Remember the hint that *if two relatives are called by the same referential term, then Ego's ideal relationship with both of them will be the same?* Now for the second hint in kinship analysis: *If two of Ego's relationships are termed differently, then the connecting relatives must also be indicated by different terms.* In other words: *Ego's connectors to different relationships themselves carry different terminology.*

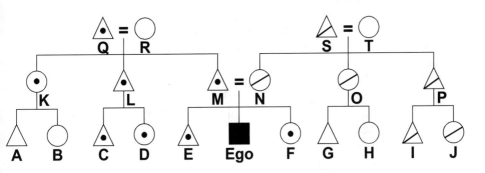

Figure 6.   Sudan Terminology

Ego's fellow clan members are indicated with a dot. **C** and **D** are members of the same clan as Ego and Ego's siblings, **E** and **F**. Mother's clan is indiated with a slash. **G** and **H** are not of Ego's MoClan, but of MoSiHu's clan. **I** and **J** are MoClan. **A** and **B,** as children of FaSiHu, belong neither to Ego's own or MoClan and are not parallel cousins. They are in a clan not necessarily related to Ego in any way.

So whom do you marry?

Obviously no one in your own clan: that would be incest. In many Sudan systems, including China's, a man's preferred marriage is with a FaSiDa. In all other unilineal systems, marriage into your own mother's clan is incest.

But just to show that value assumptions make a difference, the Sudanese and some other Arabs prefer marriage between a male Ego and his FaBrDa, "because that keeps wealth and power from leaving the lineage and the clan."

Sudan forbids sororal polygyny, but not nonsororal. Say a male Ego such as **M** (Ego's Fa) contemplates polygyny by marrying both **N** and **O**. Why can he not marry sisters?

Because that would make **G** and **H** Ego's half–siblings and members of his patriclan while they are already members of his mother's patriclan. Cousins would be siblings with different mothers. MoClan would lose the chance to make another alliance through marriage. A new set of terms would be needed to describe this anomaly, one which does not occur in polygynous marriage with unrelated women.

Say a male Ego such as **M** (Ego's Fa) contemplates polygyny by marrying both **N** and **O**. Why can he not marry sisters?

Because that would make **G** and **H** Ego's half-siblings and members of his patriclan. Cousins would be siblings with different mothers. MoClan would lose the chance to make another alliance through marriage. A new set of terms would be needed to describe this anomaly, one that does not occur in polygynous marriage with nonsisters.

In terms of the number of societies that use it, Sudan is the rarest of the six major types of kinship organization. But with the Chinese and the Arabs practicing Sudan, it is how perhaps one quarter of all human beings reckons kinship.

To sum up the Sudan kinship type:

- *Principles:* generation, sex of relative, lineality and bifurcate collateral
- *Descent:* patrilineal
- *Corporate groupings:* patriclans, lineages, patrilocally extended families or independent polygynous families
- *Cousin terminology:* sibling $\neq$ FaBrCh $\neq$ FaSiCh $\neq$ MoBrCh $\neq$ MoSiCh
- *Marriage type:* nonsororal polygyny
- *Residence:* patrilocal (couple moves into HuFa's household)
- *Household:* patrilineally extended

Societies using Sudan kinship are traditionally run by and for men. Women there have a subordinate and seldom enviable status. Fortunately, one of the side effects of modernization is that such traditions become impossible to maintain. In China today, for example, we see the addition of nuclear families to the Sudan model. This has great potential for improving the position of women but threatens the venerable role of the oldest male child as caregiver for his parents in their old age—especially where the one-child-per-family rule is rigidly enforced.

If you are wondering what it would take to make, say, Saudi Arabia or Afghanistan let their female citizens have the same rights and freedoms as males, there can be only one answer: a fundamental change in the way these societies reckon kinship. As the population of the Middle East grows denser, and individual family units are forced to compete for ever fewer natural resources, Eskimo-type bilateral kinship *might* replace Sudan there. But kinship systems are highly resistant to change: they are everywhere seen as expressions of society's most fundamental assumptions. Consider how often "the family" and "family values" are invoked in your own country to deny adaptive social change.

Unilineality can become so important in certain kinship systems that there are many societies in which the clan, not the family or the lineage, is the reference from which all kinship terms are reckoned. Such societies typically use three of the principles of relationship: generation, sex of relative, and bifurcate merging. Bifurcate merging recognizes some male and female links but ignores collaterality. In the kinship terminologies of the three most common clan-dominated kinship types (Iroquois, Omaha and Crow), Fa and FaBr are indicated by one term, Mo and MoSi are indicated by another single term, but MoBr and FaSi are given separate terms. Because (in terms of their matrilateral and patrilateral clan situations) Ego's siblings are so much like Ego's parallel cousins, they are all indicated by the same two, sex-specific, terms.

Iroquois

This matrilineal system uses generation, sex of relative, and bifurcate merging. What typifies it is its cousin terminology, which has a single set of terms for cross-cousins. Iroquois has matriclans and matrilineally-extended families. It has no true nuclear family orientation, yet practices monogamy or sororal polygyny.

Ego's fellow clan members are indicated with a dot, Ego's father's clan with a slash.

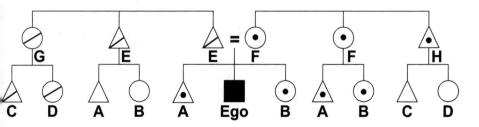

Figure 7. Iroquois Terminology

Iroquois is typically matrilocal: when a couple gets married, they move in with, or near to, the bride's mother. As do her sisters. The combination of matrilineality and matrilocality creates stable family units growing from an endless chain of MoDa links to which males from other clans are attached as husbands. Usually, the men born to the clan continue to make most of its policies on war and other important events, but that means they must meet at their (grand)mother's home, where the female core of the clan can be certain to have input, and often, final say.

So whom can Ego marry?

No parallel cousin, of course; they're the same thing as siblings, referentially. Not MoBrCh: that would be marrying a child of a fellow clan member and break the incest taboo which, as you would expect, is matrilaterally extended. That leaves FaSiCh. Your father is not in your clan; mating with his sister's offspring would not be incest. If male Ego did marry FaSiDa, he would live with, and his children would be members of, his own father's clan. Which is not his own, but nevertheless family of a sort, and therefore safe and easy to adjust to. Of course there are usually more than two clans to choose spouses from. Note that Ego can marry his/her cross-cousin on father's side but not on his/her mother's side, even though these are indicated by the same term.

So why wouldn't general or nonsororal polygyny work here?

Because these people are always matrilocal. If a man marries sisters, he moves to where they live, in their mother's extended household; it makes no difference to the clan whether he marries one sister or six. But if he married two unrelated women, he would have to live with two families in two localities, and that is physically impossible.

Why would sisters want to bring the same guy home to Mother to be their husband?

Because the fewer strange men there are around the core group of women, children, the elderly and the still unmarried brothers, the less chance there is for physical violence with or between the strangers and for domestic violence to occur. (Sisters can gang up on an errant husband, and their brothers will punish the outsider.) Sororal polygyny of this type can maximize the independence of sisters on their own home turf.

To sum up the Iroquois kinship type:

- *Principles:* generation, sex of relative, and bifurcate merging
- *Descent:* matrilineal
- *Corporate groupings:* matriclans, matrilocally extended monogamous and sororal polygynous families

- *Cousin terminology:* (sibling = FaBrCh = MoSiCh) ≠ (FaSiCh = MoBrCh)
- *Marriage type:* monogamy and sororal polygyny
- *Residence:* matrilocal
- *Household:* matrilineally extended

Crow

This kinship type is generally considered the ultimate matriclan system. It requires either matrilineal or double descent—here we will focus on the former. Crow uses generation, sex of relative, and bifurcate merging, but with asymmetrical cross-cousin terminologies—meaning that cross-cousins on father's and mother's side have different reference terms. Relatives who are members of your clan are distinguished terminologically from those who are not, and people who have the same relationship to Ego will be addressed by the same term regardless of generational distance.

Crow has clans and matrilineally extended families. Although it has no true nuclear family orientation, it is typically monogamous. Fellow clan members are indicated with a dot.

Note that Crow cousin terminology differs from Iroquois in that it distinguishes cross-cousins from each other, and does so in a very unusual manner: a male Ego calls FaSiDa by the same term as FaSi, and as FaSiDaDa! Here these are all indicated as **F**. Moreover, he uses the same terms for MoBrCh as for his own children and BrCh.

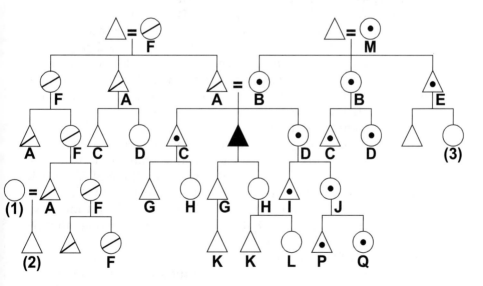

Figure 8. Crow Terminology

So how would you translate **F**? Certainly not as "cousin," that term is meaningless in this context. Father's sister or aunt? Ditto. No, the only way to make sense out of Crow (I promised that kinship reckoning could be a mind-bending exercise) is to think of **F** as "female in my father's matriclan." Ego thus has an eternal line of women in father's clan, who all have the same relationship to him as his father's sister.

Now let's look at the implications. Remember, if your brother and sister refer to the woman your father married as "Mother," then you do too. So why is Ego's FaSiDaSo an **A**, the same as Fa and FaBr?

The answer is in the chart: Because the brothers of females in Ego's father's matriclan are called **A**.

What does Ego call (1), FaSiDaSoWi?

The logic goes like this: FaSiDaSo is an **A**, like Ego's Fa. According to the terminology on the chart, the wife of an **A** (see FaWi) is a **B**. So FaSiDaSoWi is a **B** because FaSiDaSo is an **A**.

In other words, Ego has the equivalent of mother-child relationships with generations of women married to the men in father's matriclan. All that, as backup to Ego's relations in his own clan. Talk about redundant psychological security!

Try this one: what is (2), FaSiDaSoSo?

Well, he's the son of one of Ego's classificatory fathers, so he is indicated by the same term as any son of any **A**, which is **C**, the term for a classificatory brother, even though he is two generations removed.

Finally, what does Ego call (3), MoBrDa?

MoBr, like Ego himself, is a male in Ego's matriclan. MoBrCh thus belong to his wife's clan, just as Ego's Ch and Ego's brother's Ch belong to *their* wives' clans. Children of males in Ego's matriclan are referred to as G and H, terms which therefore translate as "son and daughter of a male in my clan." Since E, MoBr, is also a male in Ego's clan, his children are likely to also be called G and H. So (3), MoBrDa, is an H.

So whom does Ego marry?

Nobody in his clan, and no child of a male clan member. Certainly no female in his father's clan, because that would terminologically be incestuous also, since **F**s are the mothers of **A**'s and **A** is the term for one's own father. Typically, the incest taboo in Crow systems is extended matrilineally or bilaterally. If matrilineally, Ego might be able to marry FaBrDa, because she belongs to neither Ego's nor Ego's father's matriclan. If bilaterally, he will have to marry into a third clan.

This system institutionalizes redundant copies of every nuclear family relationship at every generation of Ego's father's clan and adds those to the securities already existing within Ego's own matriclan. Add monogamy and matrilocality, and you can see why Crow is the most child-friendly, woman-empowering kinship system ever devised.

To sum up the Crow kinship type:

Principles: generation, sex of relative, and bifurcate merging

Descent: matrilineal

Corporate groupings: clans and matrilineally extended families

Cousin terminology: sibling = //-Co ≠ (FaSiCh ≠ MoBrCh)

Marriage type: monogamy

Residence: matrilocal

Household: matrilineally extended

Omaha

This is the most highly developed of all patrilineal clan systems. In that Omaha uses generation, sex of relative, and bifurcate merging, it mirrors Crow. But because it is always patrilineal and patrilocal, it functions very differently.

Omaha kinship is characterized by patriclans, patrilocal residence, general and sororal polygyny, and independent nuclear or polygynous families. General polygyny can work here because descent is both patrilineal and patrilocal: the clan's core group is made up of males. Women from anywhere can be joined to the core through marriage regardless of what other clans they come from, or whether they come alone or as sisters or in unrelated groups.

Normally, the incest taboo is patrilaterally extended throughout the clan.

Again, it is necessary to overcome your Eskimo kinship habits if you are to make any sense of this terminology, for in Omaha, not even such concepts as father and mother are directly translatable.

Patrilateral cross-cousins are termed equivalent to SiCh, meaning that the terms translate as "child of woman in my clan." Since clan membership only goes through male links, this terminology implies that these children are not of Ego's clan.

Note next that matrilateral cross-cousins are termed identically to MoBr and Mo. So these terms must be translated in effect as "man and woman in my mother's clan."

That immediately makes the whole chart comprehensible:

MoSiHu = (same term as) Fa, because, like Fa, he is married to a "woman in my clan." So the husbands of all **B**s are **X**s: addressed the same as Ego's biological father. ("The husband of a mother is a father.")

When it comes to children, it makes a difference whether Ego

Figure 9. Omaha Terminology

is male or female. If male, his children belong to his (father's) clan like BrCh; if female, her children belong to her husband's clan like SiCh. Since clan dominates, these two categories of nieces and nephews would bear different classificatory terms.

Within the clan, Omaha terminologies distinguish clearly between the generations. But outside of the patriclan, relatives are indicated essentially as "male and female members of mother's patriclan." The terms for FaBr's descent line duplicate those for Fa, but FaSi's, whose offspring belong to FaSiHu, is categorically separate and distinct—even if FaBrSi married MoBr—which she could, since he is no clan relation to her or her mother. In any case, her children will be seen and termed as equivalent to Ego's SiCh, FaBrDaCh, and MoSiDaCh: that is, as relatives lost to both Ego's FaClan and Ego's MoClan.

Question: What is **(1)**, FaBrSoSo, called by Ego?

Answer: **(1)** is the son of a **C**. Sons of **C**s are **E**s (see BrSo).

Now test yourself on **(2)**, **(3)**, **(4)**, and **(5)**. That will prove to you that the logic of kinship terminology can be very alien indeed.

So whom does Ego marry?

Nobody in his own clan; nobody in mother's clan; no classificatory parent, sibling, or child. But everybody else is fair game. Note that if Ego had been female, the same answer would apply, but her children would have been **G** and **H**, like her sister's.

To sum up the Omaha kinship type:

- *Principles:* generation, sex of relative, and bifurcate merging
- *Descent:* patrilineal
- *Corporate groupings:* patriclans, patrilineally extended and polygynous families
- *Cousin terminology:* sibling = //-Co $\neq$ (FaSiCh $\neq$ MoBrCh)

- *Marriage type:* monogamy, sororal or general polygyny
- *Residence:* patrilocal
- *Household:* patrilineally extended or independent nuclear families

KINSHIP AS IDEAL CONSTRUCT

The six types of kinship outlined in this chapter are ideal types, and any specialist in kinship studies can list exceptions to some of their major characteristics: Hawaii doesn't have clans but Suriname's Maroons all have clans even though they use Hawaii nomenclature; Crow-type terminologies are not always associated with matrilineal descent; and so forth. This in no way denies the usefulness of the typology, especially in a general introduction, because it illustrates the ceaseless transforming of cultures, and it underlines an important consideration regarding the difficulty of collecting accurate kinship nomenclatures.

In all societies, the structure of kinship is seen as a reflection of how the universe is ordained to operate. The rules of kinship are therefore an ideological construction, and in real life no society can follow them exactly and still satisfy the needs of its individuals. Especially in some small societies with complicated rules governing marriage, some people must either cheat or not marry.

For example, consider an Australian aboriginal kinship such as the Murngin's. Over the last century, several ethnographers have recorded and analyzed its arcana, and published their findings with kinship nomenclatures that in at least one case (Lloyd Warner's 50-page publication in 1930) covered many fold-out pages illustrating five generations and seven levels of kinship from FaFaFaFaFaSiDaDa to MoMoMoBrSoSoSoSo. Yet no two experts agree on how the Murngin system works. Not because the anthropologists were incompetent, but because the people using it were often so frustrated by its rules for finding mates that they created theoretically indefensible exceptions to those rules. But these individuals would certainly not admit to outsiders that they were committing incest (by their culture's definition), so they explained the facts in torturous logic that the ethnographers copied down verbatim—and found to be different from what the previous outsider had been told to explain another inconsistency.

Ranon, a Six–Section System

To show you what Aborigines (and their ethnographers) are up against, here is an example of Ranon, a much simpler system than the Murngins', used by a Melanesian population in the New Hebrides and Pentecost Islands, some 1,200 miles east of Australia.

Ranon is a six-section system: it has three patrisibs (unilateral descent groups similar to clans, here indicated as A, B, and C), and two moieties (literally: halves; one of two groups into which a tribe may be organizationally divided, here labeled 1 and 2).

Ranon has three rules for locating Ego in social space:

- All patrisibs and moieties are exogamous.
- Children inherit sib membership from Fa, moiety from Mo.
- Males cannot marry into Mo patrisib, females can.

Consider the complexity of cousin nomenclature in this system.

- Parallel cousins are always in the same moiety as Ego.
- Cross-cousins are always in the other moiety.
- Patrilateral //-Co share Ego's sib and moiety.
- Matrilateral //-Co can be or may belong to FaMo sib.
- Patrilateral X-Co may be members of Mo sib, or of FaMo sib.
- Matrilateral X-Co are always members of Mo sib.

What all this means in terms of mate selection is that:

- Male Ego cannot marry matrilaterally; he can marry his patrilateral X-Co only if she is B1, thus not a member of his mother's clan. If she is C-1, he is out of luck.
- Female Ego can always marry matrilaterally, but cannot marry her patrilateral X-Co because he would then be marrying into his Mo sib. Thus she can only marry her matrilateral cross-cousin.
- Ego's MoBr must marry a B if his mother is an A, an A if she is a B.

Would polygyny work here?

It would, *if* there were two or more women in the same section

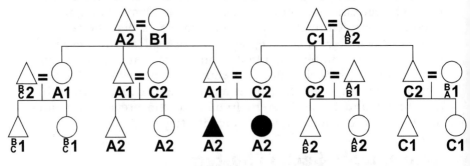

Figure 10. Ranon, a Six-Section System

cell (for sororal polygyny) or *if* the would-be husband could marry into two cells at once (nonsororal), and *if* these particular women had not already been spoken for by other men with very limited choices in a spouse—an unlikely event.

You can see why these people would cheat the system if no mates were available in their appointed sections. You can also understand that in such societies the politics of kinship are the most important thing in the world: it is everybody's business who has children, because everybody's own child will need a spouse.

SIGNIFICANCE

All kinship systems are not created equal, they have different survival implications. Marriage in patrilineal societies forces the females out of the nest to live among strangers and be dependent on their husbands. Men there gain the power that women lose, making their dominance unchallengeable.

There are other ramifications. Say that you and your spouse die in an accident. Who will take care of your children? In a matrilineal society like the Kwinti they must go to their mother's relatives. In a patrilineal society like the Bedouin they must be cared for by their father's people. In a bilateral society like the United States, they may be raised by whoever wants and can afford them on either side of the family.

In *any* system, if your parents were married you have relatives in two family lines even if you are a member of only one. If they were not married, you have relatives in only one family line, your mother's, which means you have no backup system if something goes wrong in your relationship with them. Illegitimacy basically cuts your support system in half, which means that your life chances are diminished that much. For all the millennia during which kinship was the only thing that stood between the individual and extinction, the fact that kids are better off with two sets of kinship ties than one set may have been sufficient to underwrite marriage and the incest taboo.

Sudan probably confers the greatest number of disadvantages to the individual, especially to women and their illegitimate children.

Crow is probably the most egalitarian: by maintaining the core group of women and adding husbands, the men, even though they are politically dominant, cannot become tyrannical.

Eskimo-Yankee seems slated to become the most common kinship type as, under the pressure of overpopulation, humanity grudgingly metamorphoses into a true societal species. But Eskimo is far from the ideal system for that purpose, because it isolates individuals, because its nuclear families are much more vulnerable to economic exploitation than extended families, and because illegitimacy here is as much of a problem as among patrilinealists.

Lineages and clans could still become important in complex urban societies. In the United States, several Asian immigrant populations contribute to lineage or clan coffers for the education or business opportunities of distant relatives, who are obligated to do as much when their ship comes in. This principle would serve people from other ethnic backgrounds just as well, if they could learn to accept the collective power of kinship in this sense.

Moreover, all those young women trapped in dependency by today's unwise tolerance of illegitimacy would benefit inestimably from a consciously introduced matrilineality, especially from matriclans. Clan-sisterhood would help them succeed in raising their children without gangs or day-care, and help them escape from poverty and abuse—domestic violence remains the number-one cause of injury for young women in the United States. But because such a switch would threaten the Eskimo-Yankee system to which your culture is addicted, matriclans won't be an easy trait to diffuse.

Thinking It Through

1. Suriname's Maroon tribes combine a Hawaii nomenclature with clans. Would it be possible to combine Eskimo with matriclans? How would that work, or why couldn't it? Diagram it for three generations, and include spouses, to prove your point.
2. On the Crow kinship chart, how would you translate the terms G and H? Where does Crow nomenclature differ when Ego is female?
3. Collect a four-generation nomenclature chart from an immigrant from an alien culture. Can you identify its kinship type, find if and where it deviates from its type in some detail, and connect that variance to a relevant datum about the society's marital or inheritance patterns?
4. Can you explain why a Western woman contemplating marriage to a man in a Sudan kinship society risks subservience and the loss of many rights and freedoms she grew up with? What other cultural factors determine her degree of risk?
5. The different aspects of a well-integrated culture all support each other. Even in rapidly changing cultures such as your own, certain basic traits seem impossible to change without wreaking chaos. List and explain what it would take to turn the bilateral descent of Western societies with Eskimo-style kinship into a unilineal descent system such as Crow or Iroquois. Consider, for example, inheritance laws, marriage, and religion. Can you think of any technological/economic adjustments that would be needed?

The Shaft, and How You Got It

Inequality

"All that any man has the right to expect, ask, give or receive in this world, is fair play."

—Frederick Douglass (1817–1895)

"We hold these Truths to be self-evident, that all Men are created equal, that they are endowed by their Creator with certain unalienable Rights, that among these are Life, Liberty and the Pursuit of Happiness—"

—Thomas Jefferson, (1743–1826)

Any division of labor implies cooperative effort, separation of tasks, coordinating functions and therefore, social differentiation. Some degree of inequality is necessary, but the extremes to which distinctions in human rights and rewards are being driven today are neither necessary nor advisable.

R-i-i-i-ght. Obviously the celebrated quote from Jefferson's Declaration of Independence was not a descriptive statement but an ideological one, because inequality was then—and is now—rife in everything from life expectancy to wealth and power. More than in any other modern nation, the death rows of America are crammed with prisoners who, having lost their liberty, await the taking of their lives—usually because they have taken someone else's. Meanwhile happiness for many is a transient state of brain chemistry amenable to drugs and medication.

On the other hand, Americans whose ancestors came from Africa are no longer on the open market; their vote now counts as much as that of women and Native Americans, which is as much as that of the white male property holders by whom and for whom the Constitution was written. The average American takes for granted luxuries and entertainments that kings and queens could not have even imagined a century ago. And all of us are living longer.

On the third hand, it now takes both parents working full-time to support households in which no one minds the kids; a majority of eligible voters no longer bothers to go to the polls because only corporations and the obscenely rich get to choose the candidates; we spend more money on buying and fighting drugs than on education; the United States stores a larger percentage of its surplus males in prisons than any other country; year for year, their incarceration costs more than sending them to college would have.

Inequality is alive and well.

Should it be?

I recognize that much of what you will read in this chapter may seem incendiary, but you really do need to know what is going on with the way your culture is organized. Everything I say on the subject of inequality has been said by others, but almost always in the service of some "ism" that promises to correct the injustice if you'll only follow its political or ideological program. The fact is, no ism so far has ever created an adequate social system. It is *not* my purpose, here or anywhere, to tell you how you should live and

137

what you should believe. It *is* my purpose to make you aware of your culture's assumptions and how they operate on you.

THE ATTRIBUTES OF INEQUALITY

At birth, you evidence only two characteristics of interest to *all* societies: your sex and your dependency. Because of the latter, women's work has always been different from men's. As you mature you will pass through a number of life stages, each with its own roles and rewards. Sex and infant dependency are the legitimating and operating considerations behind all the different ways that societies divide labor and its rewards and are therefore the wellsprings of inequality.

In every culture, no matter how simple or complex, there are certain jobs nobody wants and others that everybody covets. Somebody has to do the nasty work, take the risks, pay the price. Others get to make the decisions, interpret the supernatural will, and enforce the rules for the rest. To continue operating, any society requires allegiance, cooperation and performance from its individuals. Every society therefore rewards its members, though none has ever done so with perfect equability. Your backpacking ancestors, wherever they lived, spent their lives in their family, so they rewarded each other in personal ways. Today's city life is lived among strangers, meaning that most of your contacts are impersonal.

The four Ps

In our ancestral societies you were rewarded for what you were and what you did with one or more of these four universal compensations:

> **Power**—*control over something people know is necessary.* In hunting-and-gathering societies, role differentiation was almost exclusively a function of age and sex. There were no true specialists, no true leaders, no bosses. Power was held only situationally and temporarily, as in being leader of the hunt.

> **Property**—*exclusive rights of possession, use and disposal.* For backpackers this was limited to tools, weapons, clothes and decorations, and such intangibles as names, songs, magical rites, stories and other things now called "intellectual property." There were no rich people, there were no poor.

> **Prestige**—*status, respect, dignity.* Social evaluation was pragmatic and therefore different at successive life stages. Because favoritism and invidious comparisons would tear

small societies apart, there were no stars, there were no losers, but still, there was enough differentiation to reward the outstanding and indicate the less-than-competent.

Pleasure—any personal satisfaction in work and play beyond the previous three. Gratification resulted directly and ultimately from your adequacy in fulfilling obligations and the group's expectations. There were enough individualized rewards that almost everybody could realistically expect to lead a satisfying life.

You may find it tricky to differentiate pleasure from prestige or one of the other social rewards. Modern cultures differentiate work from play; no doubt you are convinced you know the difference as well as anyone else does. But in many other societies the distinction is not always clear and may even be denied in many circumstances. Here's an example many fieldworkers in the tropics have experienced:

Work or Play?

The Volkswagen Beetle lurches to the right as its front tire goes flat. The ethnographer brings it to a halt. The men on top jump off, everybody else gets out to inspect the damage. Someone reaches inside to release the hood latch. Someone else raises the hood and gets out the spare. A third grabs the jack and begins raising the car. A fourth takes off the wheel and breaks the bead on the tire so that a fifth can patch its inner tube and reassemble the wheel to be the new spare for the next time when a tire goes flat in a knife-edged pothole in the ore-surfaced path that serves as road in this region. The jungle steams like a sauna; everyone is dripping sweat. The pregnant woman moves heavily into the shadow of the trees. Those for whom there is no assigned job contribute too: they sing and beat on the fenders for rhythmic accompaniment. Everybody sings to encourage the workers: this is a party. Drinks are passed; warm water, sun-heated softdrinks and maybe a hot beer for the driver. When the task is completed and all the parts have been returned to their rightful places, the journey continues: four men and the woman inside, two men on the roof and a seventh on the rear bumper. It's another thirty miles to the government clinic, and the woman is in labor. The ethnographer drives as fast as he dares: 20 miles an hour. Bang! There goes the left rear. Laughter erupts. Everybody piles out and off and the impromptu pit crew gets busy. Someone comes up with the words for another stanza in the ballad of this trip. Everybody is happy because the woman is being helped by her kinsmen, and each of them can justify the space he takes up. This is an adventure; certainly there are hazards, but there is camaraderie and fun and gleeful anticipation of telling the tale of this odyssey. Is this work, or is this pleasure? Can work be as pleasurable when it is removed from a social context, when it is involuntary, or when its roles are rigidly prescribed? ∂

Expressing Inequality

From your perspective at the beginning of the Third Millennium, life in a band society may seem inconceivably remote. Yet for you, too, inequality between individuals and among groups is still expressed in "the Four Ps"—that is, in differences in power, property, prestige and pleasure. For your backpacker ancestors, it was enough to compensate performance with just one or two of these societal rewards. Brave men risked death not for property ("What, something else to carry?"), but for prestige—nonmaterial recognition of their courage, skill or acumen: that which made the young women want you and the adult males make room for you in their councils. Power, in those days, was diffuse and familial. Many—perhaps most—of life's tasks had immediate survival implications; performing them brought instant rewards in people's approval and appreciation.

But all that changed when societies became sedentary, when land and its resources could be privately owned or publicly confiscated. Today, we come in different sizes, shapes and colors, with varying lifestyles, expectations and demands on us. For you, unlike your ancient ancestors, wealth (property) largely determines how you fare on the other rewards: being wealthy means having power, prestige and the pleasure of luxuries. Poverty (lack of property) means being exploitably dependent, politically insignificant and preoccupied with necessities.

Historically, Americans profess more preoccupation with the unfairness of social differentiation than do people in other cultures, but in spite of that we'd all rather be rich, smart and good-looking than poor, dumb and ugly—and damn the social consequences. Nevertheless, when asked *how* you are unequal, you probably cannot answer the question.

THE CONSEQUENCES OF INEQUALITY

This may help: *Inequality between individuals or groups is always expressed in differences in life chances and lifestyles.*

Life chances indicate the probability that you, because of your membership in social categories, will encounter certain experiences that affect your viability. Say you finally succumb to the persistence of an insurance salesman and let him sell you $25,000 of term life. You may have to take a physical, but for so small an amount, a mere interview over the phone may suffice. So you tell him your age and sex, the health of your parents and siblings or the causes of their deaths at what ages. He checks the actuarial tables (industry-generated statistics on the employment histories, finances, accidents, causes of death and a few thousand other facts about people like you). Then he gives you a quote, you sign, and you have $25,000 of life insurance.

Say 15 years pass while you become a success, with responsibilities to a family and a profitable business of your own. You decide to upgrade your insurance. To $5 million. This time the company is not satisfied with a few answers over the phone: you are much older now and there is serious money at stake. A team of specialists will give you the most thorough physical examination of your life, and you'll be asked a thousand questions about your lifestyle: Do you skydive or race cars? Were you raised on the farm or in the city? How much booze do you drink? Have you ever had a homosexual encounter? Do you cheat on your spouse? The insurance company is making book on your life chances, and it is not in business to lose money. Its bid, when you finally get it, wagers that you will live long enough to provide the company with a healthy profit beyond the sum that your death will cost them. They are The House, and they know the odds.

Life chances include not just your relative longevity, but also the odds that you will go to college, become a successful professional, be elected, be arrested. They are your statistical chances of getting married and being divorced, becoming mentally ill, unemployed or murdered, contracting various fatal diseases, dying in a work- or sports-related accident, being drafted into the infantry, becoming morbidly obese, having more children than you can afford to raise, et cetera, et cetera. And all these odds are based on the fact that you, since your birth, have belonged to "categories."

Where you were born, and to whom, practically determines how you will speak and about what; the conditions of your upbringing affect who knows how many other important things. Your life chances were set in your family, but you can adjust them up or down—depending on whether you treat them as a self-fulfilling prophecy, as a curse or as a challenge. In America, "being successful" often means "having beaten the odds of one's life chances."

Lifestyle is a population's adaptation to its particular profile of life chances (in its technical sense "lifestyle" does not refer to the behavior of an individual). In complex societies, lifestyle implies both a maximization of the group's self-perceived life chances and its defense against those who would compete for them.

Let's say that I, a truck driver, visit you, a banker, to convince you to lend me money for a new truck. I park my old but well-maintained and therefore still valuable rig in the bank's lot; you look up from your spreadsheet analysis when I enter. I show you my profit-and-loss statements and my tax returns. You check my credit history and collateral. We find each other's vocabularies and pronunciations difficult: I talk of sixteen-geared twelve-wheelers until your eyes glaze over; you talk of compound interest and tax arcana until I am half asleep. After we finally agree and sign the papers, I take the wife out to celebrate: first a pizza, then bowling. You toast your bride at an exclusive restaurant and hit the golf course. Sunday the wife and I go to our storefront church to thank God in ecstatic tongues; you listen from your family pew as a specialist speaks to God for you. If you ever dropped into my neighborhood bar, you'd be challenged for slumming. I'd never make it past the guards at your country club. We may both be Americans, but we belong to different classes. Our lifestyles express that: we differ in technology, organization, values and language. *Lifestyle, in other words, is another term for the expression of culture.*

THE ORIGINS OF INEQUALITY

We humans are simultaneously creatures of biology and culture. We can therefore trace the roots of inequality to both our physical and social attributes.

Biological Sources

If you've ever visited the baby ward in a hospital, you may have noted that some newborns lie quietly, enduring whatever indignities life inflicts. Others, apparently mourning the loss of Paradise, weep softly, wearily, hopelessly. Still others scream a killer rage in red-faced, fist-clenched fury. Although it is nearly always an error to anthropomorphize infants, you won't find it difficult to believe that the basics of personality are inborn. Babies may all look like Winston Churchill, but they do differ from each other.

As time goes by, interaction with their social environments causes some of these distinctions in newborns' character traits to be exaggerated while others diminish. All peoples find it necessary to try to standardize the behavior of their uniquely hardwired little immigrants into something society needs or at least can get along with. And though all inevitably fall short of complete "standardization," behavior that is encouraged in one place or time might get suppressed in another.

As babies grow up, they demonstrate differences in natural immunities, irritability, intelligence, metabolic efficiency, height, weight, athletic potential and a variety of other attributes that the people around them may or may not find interesting. These help determine where they fit in their peer groups, how educable they are and (if they survive into adolescence and beyond) whether they will be lionized or ignored by the opposite sex. We are speaking here of physiological determinants of life chances.

Clearly, beautiful people have different life chances than plain people, even in areas in which looks should be irrelevant. That is grossly unfair, but no more so than the fact that genes can also determine which of us will live to a hundred, who will almost never be ill and who will be doomed to poor health, who will store fat in their breasts and who will pack it in their thighs, whose skin will burn in spite of SPF 500 sunblock and whose is impervious to the most brutal sunlight, who will gray late and who will go bald early, who will be squat and who will be linear. There must be a thousand ways in which we can differ biologically, and no doubt every one of us would like to exchange some part of our physiques. Still, when you and I decry inequality, we are usually less preoccupied with anatomical differences than with what they mean in the social context of our lives.

Cultural Sources

You act differently at work than at play, with relatives than with strangers, as a parent than as a spouse, on the job than off-duty. You have, in other words, many roles. In each of them you will be evaluated; each brings you a separate status.

Achievement versus Ascription

Your various roles and statuses are either achieved by you or ascribed to you. "Achieved" means you bring inequality on yourself (for example, by going to college so that you won't have to live and work the way your parents did or by lawbreaking your way into prison). "Ascribed" means that inequality is thrust upon you (for being born into a rich family or to a poor single mother). In our backpacker past, about the only ascribed status was gender: as soon as a baby was born, people knew whether it was male or female, and that determined at which pursuits it would spend its life. But from that point on, all its personal statuses were achieved, for all that the range of things a person could achieve was narrow. Today, modern life is rife with ascription at the same time that the range of achievement is broad.

Division of Labor

You are a societal organism, which means that a truly solitary existence is, if not impossible, at least highly improbable for you. You need society to survive, but society also needs you. To maintain itself as a distinct and self-perpetuating entity, every society has to satisfy at least these six functional prerequisites:

- *Communication*—the transfer of comprehensible information among its individuals and institutions;
- *Production*—the manufacture of goods and services for its people and institutions
- *Distribution*—the transfer of surpluses to those who need them for sustenance or raw materials
- *Member replacement*—the training of children and immigrants to fill the roles left by the dead
- *Social control*—the maintenance of order among its people and institutions and the control of intrasocietal violence
- *Defense*—the readiness to apply violence to outsiders to deter them from using its products or people as a resource

One way or another, you are or will be involved in most of these functions, because society itself cannot perform them without you. Therefore the primal reason for ascribing status to individuals is to ensure that society's essential roles will be staffed. But note that *the functional prerequisites for a society in no way demand or imply the need for invidious (unjustly discriminating) distinctions between society's members and certainly do not specify inheritable inequalities as a condition for survival.*

At their simplest, human societies lump all necessary tasks into two piles: one for males, the other for females. Although in theory that opens up the potential for such abuses as the exploitation of women by men, in fact people with primitive technologies too obviously need each other's willing cooperation for sexism to become much of a problem among food collectors. Neither sex is ever expected to "do it all." Society survives as long as men's work and women's work dovetail together well enough to satisfy the needs of both and of their children. However, cultures are never totally logical about their sexual divisions of labor, and surely the most venerable inequities are those imposed upon you because of your sex.

Any division of labor presupposes (1) differentiation of tasks and (2) a coordinating authority. It is this organization that can be elaborated virtually endlessly to create the structures of inequality that we in the modern world take for granted.

Whenever different individuals are expected to cooperate by completing different tasks, there has to be some mechanism—a person or agency—that can tell them to adjust their performances. Say, for example, that your club plans to assemble left-handed veeblefritzes from parts, to sell at the fair. One of you must sort the pieces and direct them to the assemblers. Then one of those must bolt the frame together, give it to the second who must screw in the whoopenlooper and hand it off to the third, who'll weld on the torqual stabilizer, and so forth until the whole veeblefritz has been completed and your last club member seals the package and tosses it onto the truck. Congratulations: you are differentiating tasks.

Like it or not, however, it is impossible to make all the separate tasks equally difficult or time consuming, so your assembly line will jerk along fitfully: some people will be working their tails off while others get bored waiting. The only way to keep people from walking off the job in disgust is to give one of you the authority to say, "You, go help her for a while because things are piling up there." But who?

Theoretically there are several ways to choose an administrator (and in the beginning that was all that chiefs and rulers were):

- randomly (spin the bottle)
- in rotation (Suzie's turn today)
- by acclaim (vote for John)
- by inheritance (Charlie always oversaw the assembly line, and Dale is Charlie's kid . . .)

In fact, as you have no doubt noticed, for most of history only the last of these four ways ever got practiced. You'll see why in a few pages.

Note that it doesn't really make that much difference who gets to stand on the box for a better view; as long as *somebody* does and *everybody* accepts that, the veeblefritzes will roll off the assembly line, or the hunt will be successful, or the ritual will be completed, or the bridge will be built.

Note further that, though it may become necessary to differentiate those who have gained great success and authority from those who haven't done as well, there is never any need to reward such individuals excessively in more than one of the Four Ps. In fact, until very recently *no* society considered doing so a good idea.

As cultures become more complex, the division of labor gets almost infinitely subdivided among specialists. And the occupants of the separate status of manager will strive mightily to convince everybody else that it matters very much indeed who gets to stand on the box, and that boxstanders are made categorically different, probably "more important and better" than those they tower over, and that they, and of course their children, too, should be rewarded far more opulently.

Any division of labor will also require some category of persons to pay more heavily into the cost of society than the others. In pre-literate societies, that is usually the young women because their specialized role, childbearing, is the most dangerous necessary act that humans at that level of culture routinely perform. However, once civilizations develop fairly competent gynecological special-ists, it becomes young men's turn (they have always been expend-able): they die in construction, exploration, war, industry and other dangerous pursuits "for the good of society," which far too often turns out to mean: for the private interests of the boxstanders.

Cultures of Inequality

When you look beyond the sexual division of labor in complex societies, you find a standard organizational model regardless of what political system is in place. Everywhere the bulk of the popu-lation works hard to raise enough children to replace itself in the necessary tasks. Everywhere some unfortunate category or group is targeted for scapegoating and performing the jobs that no one will do voluntarily. And everywhere some others lead lives of unchallengeable authority and deniable accountability.

This realization affects our sense of fairness much more than the (often devastating) biological inequities visited on some of us by God or Fate or Nature. Perhaps we feel so strongly about social discrimination (ascribed inequality) because we know it is not inevitable and suspect it isn't even necessary!

Egalitarian Societies

In your ancestors' bands, individuals had equal access to status and to goods and services—meaning that if you were good at something (whistling, cooking, running, hunting, setting broken bones, making peace, midwifery, dancing, whatever) the people around you would give you credit for that. Except for sex-assigned functions, all statuses were achieved. We now call such societies "egalitarian." That does not mean that everybody was equal but that access to the Four Ps was—and that typically individuals were rewarded on only one or two of those four attributes of ine-quality so that nobody could hog it all. Differences in status and role were essentially based on merit, but individuals were not ranked, because in their face-to-face familial organizations no one was able to lord it over the rest. The people who recognized that you were good at something also knew that you were bad at something else, and they never forgot you were one of them. Whoever you were and whatever your roles, you were family, one of Us, and you got the same shot at a meal or a place near the fire as any other relative.

Ranked Societies

When bands evolved into tribes, with ritual leaders and a few (semi) specialized roles, access to certain important statuses and roles became ascribed. For example, chiefs of a federation of bands or descent lines might be selected from only one lineage. But such individuals lived no more ostentatiously and ate no better than anyone else. Nowadays we call those "ranked" systems.

Ranked societies use nonhereditary individual differentiation to achieve their organizational goals: they may have Big Men to deal with political problems, ritual virgins to embody some religious concept or medicine singers to help the ill. But the children of such individuals do not gain any important advantage over others: a Big Man's son does not inherit his title or status. And the vast majority of work, especially subsistence labor, is still done by the domestic household: people grow their own food and make their own tools, weapons, clothing, houses—whatever they need.

Most societies use ranking for some roles, but true ranked societies typically do not reward people with all four attributes of inequality simultaneously; high status or wealth is not directly inherited, but individually achieved; and for all roles other than the few ranked ceremonial ones, competition is open—within the limits of sex and age. Moreover, the four societal rewards are not convertible: in ranked societies you cannot buy power with mere wealth or use power to achieve wealth—the system is not set up for that.

Stratified Societies

State societies are an outgrowth of the Agricultural Revolution. They extend the idea of limiting access to its logical extreme. Market-based cultures, like your own, control access not only to all statuses but also to all goods and services: almost everything has a price, and most of us cannot afford it all. In stratified societies most roles become specialized. Because specialists do not have time to grow their own food or build their own houses (unless doing so *is* their specialty), they have to interact with a great variety of other specialists in order to satisfy their needs. *Extreme specialization inevitably exaggerates the perceived importance of administrators.*

States (including all mass societies) organize populations hierarchically, that is, with a series of levels whose top enjoys the fruits of the good life that inequality can offer and controls the access to the Four Ps of all the other levels. Hierarchic societies resemble food chains or pecking orders. Authority is centralized at the top, and the tasks of providing for people are distributed among the different levels. This kind of society is labeled "stratified" because its clustered life chances and lifestyles are arranged, like the layers of a cake, in levels, or strata. The occupants of each ascending stratum are rewarded with more property, power, prestige and pleasure than those at the level below them, regardless of whether they perform any greater (or even any recognizable) service to the whole. The real indignity imposed on those born to the lower ranks is, of course, the limit placed on their expectations. That limit always means that their children, regardless of talent or drive, will inherit their lowly position.

In any large hierarchical organization—whether a state, a corporation, a religion, an army or some other cultural ecology—the people at each level share a specific set of traits that mark their difference from people in the other levels. In the lower strata, where life chances are least secure, lifestyles necessarily include a wary and jealous defense of "turf" (territory, resources, honors and privileges) against other groups scrambling for survival or advantage. Consequently, discrimination and prejudice of every sort are most visible and violent at the bottom of the heap; the well-to-do can more readily afford to be tolerant.

Hereditary inequality is a relatively recent invention. It feels perfectly normal to you because you were born to it and were never taught that there could be an alternative. But during most of our species' history it was not even imaginable and was always a condition devoutly to be avoided.

THE PREREQUISITES FOR STRATIFICATION

How did the human race and its cultures evolve from the broad egalitarianism of hunting-and-gathering economies to the invidious social distinctions of feudalism, caste and class? We know now that the very success of band societies' lifestyles ultimately doomed them: as cultures succeeded in keeping more people alive than some area could support (exceeding its "carrying capacity"), some people were forced to start producing food. Here and there, hard-pressed bands settled down to garden or took up herding, and sometimes these were so successful that they began to dominate their area. Civilizations grew from those humble beginnings. Today there are only a few food-collecting societies left, on the fringes of the modern world, on land no one else wants. Yet.

It took some huge leaps to move from egalitarian food collecting to hereditary inequality, and by far the majority of societies did not evolve into the latter. Most people live in places where stratification was forced on the local population.

Judging from those peoples and cultures that first made inequality inheritable, it now appears that a society must meet the following four necessary preconditions before it can stratify. These preconditions are discussed in the following sections.

A Storable Surplus

For specialization to occur, there must be time for some individuals to experiment and perfect their techniques while the rest produce enough to feed and house and clothe them as well as themselves. Not just any surplus will do: if an Eskimo paddling his kayak around a promontory finds a dozen beached whales, he will indeed have a surplus, but it will putrefy into uselessness long before his village can become dependent on it. "Storable surplus" implies staples like grains or legumes that can last through the winter; or techniques for drying, pickling, smoking or otherwise extending the shelf life of perishables; or meat on the hoof in the form of a breeding population of food animals. And it demands granaries, corrals or other storage facilities.

Of course, once a society has a stored surplus, it needs some agency to distribute it. That in turn requires the invention of standards for eligibility and of specialists for making the decisions—requirements that open all sorts of cans of worms.

A Permanent Power Base

Rulers can be effective and secure only as long as the governed accept their right to wield power. Without public acceptance of the idea that authority is a permanent attribute of office, there can be no stratification.

Power without Privilege

In band societies, all power is situational and temporary, and so is authority. No one is Best Hunter or Wisest Woman forever. In ranked systems too, authority is limited. Tribal Chief Afiti of Suriname's Kwinti, when in his seventies, succumbed to malnutrition in his well-fed village of Bitagron. He was the last surviving member of his lineage, so when he became too old and senile to hunt and fish and work his own garden, there was no one left who had a family obligation to feed the old man. Anybody would have, if he had only asked, but he was chief and he was proud: he couldn't—and people forgot too often. His authority remained unchallenged, however; until the day he died he could stop fights with a wave of his pakkawood cane, but that didn't give him the right to live off other people. ᴥ

In the evolution of societal complexity, it is primarily legal and transcendental precepts that make permanent inequities possible. Authority is the right to use power. *A power base becomes secure, meaning permanent, when the authority it confers can no longer be challenged.* That happens when it has the force of supernatural sanctions behind it. *If* you can be made to believe that the sun is a being responsible for creating all of this, and *if* you have been taught all your life that I am a legitimate heir or incarnation of the sun, then it follows that you will damn well do as I say. Or, *if* you can be made to believe that people dead two centuries ago knew what would be best for us today, and *if* you have been taught all your life that a line of authority descends from those founders, then we can get you to vote for one of only two candidates for political office even though each has greed and gall as his only qualifications. In both cases we will have succeeded in making office more important than occupant. It is what armies everywhere teach their recruits: "Salute the uniform, not the man!"

The Acceptance of Status Inheritance

Fans of beauty contests would be outraged if Miss America were selected exclusively from among daughters of previous winners of the Miss America title. Members of egalitarian societies would similarly choke on the idea that the son of the hunting chief is destined to replace him or that the daughter of the midwife must become the next midwife. Yet moderns have shown no trouble swallowing the idea that the idiot kid of the king should be their next ruler or that the boss's wastrel son is heir apparent to the company. In fact, ascribed status everywhere still outranks achievement—think of old money and *nouveaux riches*, of hereditary nobility and university faculties. So how did the practice of inheriting ascribed statuses get started?

Probably it spread from the idea that whoever stood on the box to organize the assembly of veeblefritzes (or whatever labor your forefathers divided) was too busy to also do all the subsistence maintenance that "regular" people were expected to do to survive. They all paid taxes so that he could eat and be housed while he did what they needed to have done for them so that society would work right. Once sedentarism is resorted to, once surpluses have been stored and are being doled out, *the management role in any division of labor can and will be aggrandized.*

We become dependent on the office and confuse that with dependency on the occupant because we can see him and not it. So when our grand poobah dies or becomes incapacitated, we could spin the bottle, or say it's X's turn to be grand poobah, or elect our favorite tap dancer. But more likely we will have learned to venerate the mind that ran things and the hand that disciplined us. Our very submission will have convinced us that the grand poobah has a god-given, ancestor-approved calling to be in charge—because (and therefore) he is somehow different from the rest of us. And his kids must be, too, because they live with him in the house we built for him, they eat the food we grew for him, they sometimes even climb on the box with him—they must have been born to his job. Clearly—we hear and believe—the grand poobah's son was divinely selected to inherit the grand poobah's status and role.

Population Surpluses

Every human society elaborates its roles beyond those that its ecology and culture necessitate, if for no other reason than that the occupants of those roles embellish them to increase their personal share of the Four Ps. The more roles a society supports, the more people it takes to act them out and to keep them organized.

Band societies can make do with few members because everybody is a generalist, their material culture is minimalist, and so a hundred or fewer of them can carry it on forever. But as soon as specialization occurs, with ranking, the number of roles and people they need increase dramatically. The Kwinti numbered only about 450 souls in the 1970s, and that was enough for them to carry on their slash-and-burn gardening, raise their families, build their houses, perform their family rituals and still have some of the men do wage labor outside tribal territory so that they could buy sewing machines, outboard motors and beer. But unlike the other five Maroon tribes in Suriname, the Kwinti had no musical instruments other than drums, they did no woodcarving, and most telling of all: their major shrines were managed by men born in other tribes. There simply weren't enough Kwinti to staff all the roles and to do all the things typical of the Maroon culture area. How many Kwinti it would have taken to do everything themselves no one knows, but judging from the next larger tribe—which *is* completely representative—perhaps a thousand people. As a society, the Kwinti will never be stratified: they are too few. But inevitably, they are losing their culture and becoming stratified into the bottom layers of the larger Creole society of coastal Suriname.

A society that fulfills only the first three prerequisites for stratification will not yet be able to organize itself into levels identified by distinct lifestyles. The final qualification for stratification requires an elite to succeed in keeping enough people so economically dependent upon itself that they will perform the tasks that the lifestyle of the dominant culture requires. That means that *stratification demands a surplus population competing for survival.* Once that has been achieved, the elite will be able to pursue a set of lifestyles conspicuously different from those raised in the managerial, professional, and laboring strata.

It takes a lot of personnel to operate all those different technologies, to play all the roles in all those organizations, to maintain all those identifying values and to express all that in characteristic jargons. Because local conditions can vary so much, no one can say how many people are required to operate a stratified society, but it seems safe to say that a large surplus population is necessary. A society as complex as yours, with highways and refrigerators, television and newspapers, defense contractors and supermarkets, universities and a welfare system, must require many millions of contributors, a surplus population large enough to be a permanent reminder to workers of how terrible life without jobs can be, and an almost inconceivably powerful and remote elite.

Types of Stratification

There are three basic organizational models of stratification: caste, feudalism and class. In each, a dominant elite strives, just like every lower stratum, to defend its lifestyle and to maximize its life chances—which has the effect of maintaining and embellishing systemic hereditary inequality. Stratification is a dominance game; it requires competition and violence for its establishment and maintenance. For reasons of security as much as to avoid contamination and empathy with those it needs to exploit to make its own lifestyle possible, a ruling elite typically distances itself from the lower strata through language and behavior, values and status display. But each of these three models is legitimated by a different assumption.

Feudalism or Estate Systems

The most common way to create a stratified society is through military conquest. Feudalism maintains social distance among its three strata (called "estates") through religious belief backed, as it was imposed, by lethal force. *An estate is a legally defined status group traditionally described in terms of its relationship to land.* Feudal societies are organized pyramidally: the nobility or aristocracy, a tiny landowning elite that is itself subdivided into many layers from king to knight, rules the peasantry or serfdom—a vast economic base of people who cannot leave the land and whose productivity is taxed to underwrite the lifestyle of the elite. Alongside these two there is always a third estate that legitimates the laws defining and perpetuating inequality: the priesthood or clergy that functions everywhere to convince the serfs that divine will ordains their submission to the nobles.

Feudalism today tends to be called military dictatorship. In just the last decades of the twentieth century, bullies with armies have subjugated populations in Africa and Southeast Asia, turning them into serfs and themselves into unquestionable rulers. In most other places the old forms continue: the essentially feudal organization of most Latin American nations may recently have been tempered somewhat by democratic formalities but has certainly not been replaced by them. Landowners still rule. Most of El Salvador, for example, is owned by 16 families. More than half of Brazil's arable land, much of it unused, is owned by 2 percent of its population—which is what drives the destruction of the Amazonian rain forest as landless peasants seek to carve out a living there.

In traditional feudalism, personal mobility was severely limited. Bullies could become mercenaries but, fairy tales notwithstanding, heroic serfs were more likely to be murdered by their liege lords than to be knighted: peasant heroes would have made very dangerous role models for their estate. Occasionally some bright serf lad might be given to a monastery by his master, and occasionally one of those might even enter the lower levels of the priesthood. But that was as far as mobility could go: the princes of the church were always of noble birth.

In many forms of modern feudalism, however, it is possible (although still unlikely) for talent and drive to offer a way out of the physical and intellectual poverty of serfdom. Today's established nobilities tolerate a fourth estate (no, not the press): a small but necessary "middle class" of technicians and experts who maximize the quality of life for the first and ruling estate.

In Europe's Dark Ages, a similar category of specialists was tolerated to perform a service that Christians could not then perform themselves: the lending of money. Feudalism is always and everywhere a system in which aristocrats compete for power and privilege through warfare, and wars are expensive: they take more money than can be squeezed from peasants. But the Bible's edict against usury (the lending of money at interest) was then still interpreted to mean that only non-Christians could lend money, and so a special caste of people (the Jews) was forced to remain separate from the traditional estates in order to pool its monies so that there would be bankers to underwrite the aristocracy's wars. In many places Jews were forbidden to own land, forcing them into trade, which was the source of their income. Their villages survived on the goodwill of some local lord—a goodwill that could be rescinded whenever he needed cash. And there you have the origin of anti-Semitism.

In general, feudal societies are the most unstable of the three forms of stratification. One reason is their predilection to settle disputes with warfare—which always costs more blood and suffering among the serfs than in the estate that caused it. Another reason is that feudal rulers' legitimacy is ultimately rooted in a willingness to use force on their own people. A third is purely cultural: their lifestyle marks the ruling elite as grossly different from those they rule, which makes them targets for resentment. Revolutions are a constant threat.

Feudalism operates through law, and can be changed by more law but never replaced through it. Internationally, those laws say that no government can be done away with legally, it takes illegal means to remove a corrupt government. The U.S. Constitution has its Second Amendment because The Founding Fathers didn't know how to create a government that could be disbanded at will by the governed, but they did know that the need to do so would arise, and that it would take force of arms to do satisfy it. That is why Americans have the right to own weapons, and why Thomas Jefferson wanted a revolution in every generation. We are way overdue, but it is too dangerous to have a revolution among the world's best-armed civilians.

It is popular to believe that the days of feudalism died out with the advent of modern democracies, that the remaining European kings and queens are mere symbols of days gone by. True, the trappings are hollow, but they hide a greater truth: that the basic elements of feudalism operate all around you and that you could not imagine your life without them.

Long ago and everywhere, laws were passed that said that all people and animals living on a nobleman's land belonged to that land and must remain there as resources for the nobleman's lifestyle and that of his entourage. Serfs cannot leave, no more than a slave can. The distinction between serf and slave is moot in many other areas, too, especially when compared with the debt-ridden worker at an intolerable job like some indentured servant.

The assumptions underlying modern life are almost all feudal. It has always been the mark of hereditary inequality that a few men control the rest and live off their labors in any way they like. When the exploitation is blatant and achieved with brute force, we speak of tyranny and despotism—that is, kennel-level feudalism. When it is done subtly, when the cattle are allowed to roam relatively freely, and only conditioning and obligations are used to keep them fenced in, exploitation is called business and government. But the combination of money and law corrupts every form of government and reduces life for the many to the kennel-level of feudalism. Hear the dogs barking?

Feudal law rules all stratified societies; even in the most tolerable it exists to ensure that its elites can safely transfer the coin of life chances from the non-elite to their own accounts.

Caste Systems

A caste is an endogamous hereditary status group traditionally associated with a particular occupation. As in feudalism, people in caste systems are taught that their stratum's hereditary role in the larger economy, as well as its relative status, are functions of divine will. Although castes are fairly common (you noted the Jews in Europe's Middle Ages; now think of the pre–World War II roles and statuses of black Americans when compared with whites), the organization of entire societies by caste is exceedingly rare. The main surviving example is Hindu India.

There, social distance is achieved and maintained not by law but through supernatural edict: people in the upper caste are holy by definition. Ideally every separate task in the societal economy is assigned to a different population. For example, there must be people to haul (sacred) dead cows out of populated areas, others to skin these animals, still others to tan the hides into leather, people to make sandals out of the leather, and some to sell sandals. The production of every other necessity can be similarly subdivided and the separate tasks assigned to hereditary groups. And so there are castes of food growers, of weavers, soldiers, thieves, carpenters, soothsayers, and so on. As culture changes, new castes are added or old ones slowly evolve new roles: there have long been taxi-driver castes in the major cities, and some castes are striving to gain exclusive rights over computer-related functions.

Originally, there were four ancestral occupation-status categories called *varna*: the highest contained the priests and intellectuals, the next the warriors and rulers, followed by the farmers and craftsmen, and finally the laborers and servants. Below this lowest varna was a category of people who did not belong to a caste for some ritual or historical reason. These outcastes or untouchables therefore could be expected to perform the most unpleasant tasks in society; they had the lowest standard of living imaginable, and no one owed them a thing.

Over time the varna became subdivided into literally thousands of *jati*, or castes, each local in its definition of membership, roles and relative status position. Much of that evolution resulted from the feudal aspects of life associated with the warrior varna and castes: conquest, rape and pillaging, dominance and submission.

If this were all there was to caste, it would simply be a way to ensure that all the tasks that need to be done to keep a society going will indeed be performed. But the organizational principles of caste are less important than their religious underpinning.

One of Hinduism's central tenets is that the spark that distinguishes the living from the dead is an immortal aspect of the Divine and that it progresses more or less fitfully through reincarnation from the simplest life-forms to the most enlightened. Humanity itself is but the final set of steps in an evolutionary ladder that the soul must climb before it can achieve reunification with the Divine from which it sprang. So your spark must have animated a flea before it could be born into a bird, a cat before it could vitalize a tiger, a beast before it could be the soul of a human in a lower caste, and that before it could be born into a member of a "twice-born" higher caste. In each incarnation (fleshed expression) the spark is expected to perform the lifestyle of that species or jati correctly. If it doesn't, it may be forced to repeat the course—or worse, it may be forced some or even all steps back to the beginning. When you are a cat you must act like a cat, a good cat, or you will be born a cat again until you get it right. If you go around chasing dogs and cars, you may find yourself reincarnated as a frog or a cockroach. Or, if you were born in, say, a servants' caste but you disobey your master or prevent him physically from beating you, then you are not a good servant and you may be reincarnated in some lower caste or even as an animal.

Consequently each caste not only has its own economic specialization but its own rituals, habits, dress, organization, social controls, even—literally—religious beliefs. Dogma dictates that no two castes are ranked exactly equal, which means that it is almost impossible for a devout Hindu to marry outside of his or her caste. Only a few jati have been linked into larger endogamous (in-marrying) groupings. The upper and the lower castes are culturally so different from each other that they require other castes to mediate their interaction.

Certain concepts deriving logically from this religious perspective have major social repercussions. The first is the idea of spiritual pollution. Physical pollution is only part of that: some necessary tasks, like dragging dead animals out of the village or emptying septic pools, are essentially dirtier than such others as selling shoes or designing bridges. But because each step on the ladder of life has its own cultural characteristics and behavioral requirements and because you are forbidden to act like a dog when you are a cat, or to behave like a person from another caste, contact with people in other jati can be spiritually dangerous to you. The rule holds that no one can pollute downward, but everybody pollutes upward. So if you are high-caste and you come (knowingly or not) into certain kinds of contact with a member of a low caste, you will be polluted, which means that a (suitably expensive) ritual has to be performed by some member of a sufficiently high priestly caste to repurify you.

Note here that the idea that no two things are exactly equal permeates all of Hindu life: in India almost everything is ranked "better than Y but not as good as X." But until a newly independent India outlawed the more pernicious aspects of caste—in effect returning its social structure to something approximating the original varna—the concept of spiritual pollution was crucially vital. And it still carries great weight—you can outlaw prejudice but you cannot keep people from feeling it.

The idea of spiritual pollution is nastily complicated by the fact that internal pollution is harder to remove than external pollution. Consider lunch. If you eat food touched by a person of a lower caste, that may so pollute you that your own family will disown you and declare you Untouchable. It follows that restaurants have to be run and staffed by people from higher castes, who cannot pollute their customers.

And then consider sex. If a woman has intercourse with a higher-caste male, even against her will, she cannot be ritually polluted. He can be, but for him it is external and his ablutions will probably take care of the whole thing unless she was really way below his caste, in which case he gets purified ritually. So prostitution is in. But when a higher-caste woman loves or is raped by a lower-caste male, her pollution is internal and probably dooms her and her children to life and death on the streets as an outcaste—regardless of how much her family may regret that. For they cannot retain their own caste purity if they tolerate pollution of even one member. Consequently, in warfare in this part of the world, the rape of women by lower-caste males has been institutionalized as a terror mechanism. It also means that women are much more dependent on the protection of men than in other stratification systems. The fact that jati are endogamous also handicaps women, because these relatively small groupings (most range from a handful to a few thousand members) offer only a limited choice in mates.

A second by-product of organizing occupations by heredity is that there is no reward for expertise. If you need a surgeon, then anyone from the surgeon caste can apply, for no one else will do such polluting work (blood is highly polluting, another strike against women). But *most people in any caste do not practice the occupation that defines the caste.* So traditionally, your surgeon might know less about medicine than about farming (which all castes are allowed to do for themselves) or fighting (ditto).

As a believer in the system and its theological basis, you cannot, of course, complain about having been stuck with incompetent medical care (or with any other kind of hereditary service) because that would imply that you question the divinely mandated. Besides, what would it matter if you died at some klutz's unhygienic hands? You'll earn another ride as a reincarnated individual, and as long as you died in the faith—here meaning "while putting up with whatever someone of your caste is expected to put up with"—your next incarnation may be a step up.

There is an uglier side effect. No matter how brilliant and talented you may be, if you were born in a shoe-shining caste in traditional India, you would never be allowed to express your abilities. You would shine shoes or risk being outcaste. Caste denies and prevents social mobility. To be sure, some jati have slowly—usually over many generations—altered their relative position on the status ladder by avoiding the sort of work that is polluting for their varna. And it's also true that a populous caste can organize itself by any feasible method: democratically, theocratically, feudally, even by individual merit. But again, most jati don't affiliate large numbers and must interact with other castes for life's necessities.

Caste is no doubt the most stable of all forms of organization because it integrates economics and theology—the four varnas were already mentioned in the Vedas, Hinduism's 3,500-year-old sacred texts. Its division of labor makes it almost impossible to create organizational alternatives. Because everyone recognizes that it is futile to defy the will of the gods and agrees that the reality of the ladder of life is as inescapable as death itself, there is not the constant threat of revolution against established authority as there is in feudalism. There is, however, a realistic fear that the system may be undermined by alien religious alternatives. Hence Hindu India's hatred for feudal Muslim Pakistan.

With urbanization and the advent of technology, especially since independence, India has found it necessary to blunt the effects of caste. The untouchables or outcastes who make up one-fifth of India's population now have rights and opportunities, including access to higher education. New technologies, which are based on principles not mentioned in the ancient Holy Writ, are therefore not polluting and are open to all castes. It should not surprise you, then, that India has a computer software industry second only to that of the United States. In the cities people do not want to know that they have been polluted by brushing against a member of a lower caste; who could afford all those purification rites? So caste markings are disappearing, and a true middle class has been born. But that means that in the conservative country-side, where most of the people still live, the cities are seen as cess-pools of sin and pollution.

Class Systems

Class structure, the form of stratification increasingly found in mass societies, emphasizes individual achievement and social mobility. *A class is a hereditary cultural grouping defined in terms of power and property, but characterized by fluid boundaries that allow individual mobility on the basis of accomplishment, luck, looks or anything else that can be converted into status and wealth.*

Because class societies evolved out of feudal systems, they continue the latter's dependence on legality instead of justice and similarly concentrate power and wealth in the same hands. How-ever, the elites in class societies, having learned from the decline of feudalism that their lifestyle and security are best assured through distance and invisibility, rule indirectly, through such managerial structures as legislatures and boards of directors. And they generally govern without bloodshed—if not without causing massive economic casualties.

Unlike castes or estates, classes are not easily identified by behavior, dress or language. What few class markers exist tend to be impermanent (like fashion) or largely unconscious (like speech). Individuals strive to differentiate themselves by age and taste crite-ria rather than by class markers, but any cultural indicator that becomes associated with membership in the upper class is imme-diately copied throughout the social system. In this way the bor-ders between classes are constantly being blurred, which means that you'll have difficulty not only in determining where one class ends and another begins, but also in discovering just how many classes there are in your society. Until the middle of the twentieth century, Americans stoutly denied that they even *had* a class sys-tem. Since then, most people who are neither homeless nor billion-aires have called themselves middle class in spite of the fact that workers and managers, farmers and urbanites, Mercedes drivers and hitchhikers vary tremendously in life chances and lifestyles.

Where the model for feudalism is a pyramid and that for caste systems a ladder, the model for class societies is an aquarium. One with a self-sustaining, sealed ecology: the resources for existence are produced by the life-forms within it. It must have soil with minerals and plants to produce food as well as oxygen for the various life-forms that crawl and swim in its space and whose interaction results in the life and death of individuals and the continuation of species.

Within the bounded, finite volume in which aquarium life takes place, some species tend to be bottom feeders, others skim the top, and most spend their lives at some ill-defined but nevertheless typical level between these extremes. Individuals of every species can dart up or down but generally tend to return to their typical level. Balance is maintained as long as the waste produced by the population's metabolizations can be utilized by the plants to grow the resources that the creatures need.

That, however, can be a tenuous balance. In the competition for resources, some fish grow larger than their comrades. When this happens, their bulk affects the freedom of movement of others. Moreover, they may supplement their diet with their smaller companions. And they produce more waste. When difference in size becomes extreme, the smaller fish have to compete with each other for whatever crumbs the big fish misses or disdains as it sucks up most of the resources, and they have to do so while swimming through the big fish's feces, which eventually can overwhelm the ecology's ability to regulate the waste-to-food cycle. Periodically the economy collapses, leading to die-offs.

This may seem an excessively unpleasant analogy for the system that has made your existence and mine possible for so long. But it does not distort reality. Again, before you start calling me a communist or an anarchist or whatever, let me remind you that I neither invented your class system nor do I offer you any political or ideological alternative to it. My intent is simply to make you sufficiently aware of how it works so that you will be able not only to survive but also to improve it. You have no viable alternative after all: you cannot return to some idealized primitive state to live without toilet paper or electricity, and you would certainly not want to live in a caste or feudal society—especially if you're female.

The overwhelming advantage of class over feudalism and caste is, of course, its dependence on individual effort and social mobility. You must recognize, however, that much of this vaunted mobility is illusory. In caste and feudal societies, the ascription of status and role meant not only that you couldn't rise much through personal effort, but also that you couldn't fall very far for lack of trying. Not so with class; as Alice was told by the Red Queen in *Through the Looking-Glass*: "Now *here* you see, it takes all the running *you* can do, just to keep in the same place." People in class systems probably work harder than anywhere else. Moreover, although there are all sorts of mobility, most of them are horizontal: you can expect to move from one career or job to another without dramatically improving your lot in life. Most people occupy roughly the same relative position in the social hierarchy at death as they did at birth—if that weren't so, class would not be a form of stratification.

A secondary characteristic of class, one that many hold to be its greatest advantage, is the fact that even its ruling elite is not hermetically sealed off. Although in fact no one ever moves into the upper class in one generation by the accumulation of wealth alone (cultural differences prevent it), the boundaries of the ruling class are permeable to the children of those who gain enough wealth and power to underwrite their offspring's entrance to the schools and clubs—thus the culture—of the hereditary elite. Unfortunately that also means that *the ruling elites in any class society are constantly reinforced by the most predatory and ruthless of the economic strivers from lower strata, which in turn means that inequality in class systems keeps growing.*

Nevertheless, the benefits of class clearly outweigh its costs. Its insatiable thirst for new products and ideas creates opportunities and lifestyles in which most people live better and longer than in any other culture type. For women especially, life in a modern class society is preferable over every alternative. For both sexes it simply offers more ways to live a satisfying life than any other form of stratification so far encountered.

Although class is replacing feudalism in more and more societies, it is most advanced—and advantageous—among those that have practiced it longest. (That's why millions of people have risked often horrendous dangers to come to or to break into the United States: here they can escape the limitations they face elsewhere.) Class systems nevertheless perpetuate some of the organizational problems of their antecedents. As in feudalism, relationships and most other aspects of life are legally defined, and lawyers occupy much the same role in the institutionalization of inequality and order as priests once did. The point of politics remains having control over the power to write laws for other people to live by. Also as in feudalism, class societies—including the one you live in—use elements of caste to benefit elites.

Americans with any African ancestry were long kept segregated, by force of law and violence, in an endogamous hereditary status group traditionally associated with a particular occupation—that of servant and laborer. In other words, blacks formed a distinct caste, one without access to adequate education or political representation. To a lesser extent this sort of differentiation has been applied to every other group whose culture or physiology was identifiably different from the local norm. However, none of those, not even the Native Americans your culture displaced, ever constituted a true caste the way Americans classified as "Africa-derived" did.

But class systems, especially those based on the American model, tend to be preoccupied with self-purification. The feudal legalisms that prevented some segments of the population from participating fully in the culture have been canceled. As a result, African, Asian and Native Americans now have considerable representation in the higher-income middle class of educated professionals.

Still, the feudal origin of class remains its Achilles heel. The enshrinement of competition still encourages centralization of power and wealth. This is especially dangerous when modern media are enlisted to convince you that class equals property—or worse, that capitalism equals democracy. The CEOs of major banks and corporations routinely tell you that the reason for their merger is, "We are at war [with other banks and corporations], and we damn well intend to win." Such statements demonstrate that the feudal "urge to be dominant" has replaced business's societal function of "distributing goods and services for the welfare of society's members." Economic competition has become the latest "moral equivalent of warfare." To appreciate the implications of that, you need to remember that in modern warfare there are no noncombatants and that everyone is a target. Mergers and monopolies do *not* mean lower prices or better service or more varied choices, but only increased power over you in the hands of people with their own agendas.

The oldest continuous form of stratification is India's caste system. The most widespread and violently unstable is feudalism. It remains to be seen whether class is a viable alternative to both, or whether its inherent design flaws make class but a transient stage in the evolution of feudalism, that class is an organizational experiment that must collapse when the world runs out of resources.

But even before that happens, the logic of class-based inequality will have been defeated.

Modern culture melds all of the four Ps (the original rewards for contributing to society) into a single one: Money = Power + Property + Prestige + Pleasure. It thereby nullifies the checks and balances in our ancestral societies.

Nowhere is this more true than in the United States, a country of immigrants and therefore of exploitable strangers. The Enron, Anderson, Xerox, WorldCom and other political-financial scandals of our age prove that the unification of the Four Ps in money will corrupt any form of democracy. The combination of multinationals and for-profit law corrupts every level of government and either nullifies it or converts it to authoritarianism or worse: the kennel- level feudalism of brutish men with guns. The United States, at one-quarter billion people, contains about one-twenty-fifth of the world's population, which is distributed among some 193 separate nations, each with its own laws, courts, judges and lawyers. But one of every three lawyers on Earth practices in the United States, and each decade the census details how inequality is growing.

Sexual and Racial Inequality

There were no surplus human males until civilization arose. But stratification could not exist without them because surplus males are not merely a problem; they are a vital resource for elites who figure out how to employ them for their own purposes.

In tribal societies as among bands, sexual differentiation of tasks does not usually carry with it any stigma of inferiority or superiority. True, there are jobs only men may do, but so are there tasks that only women are permitted to handle, and both are rec- ognized as equally necessary to the community's well-being. The face-to-face kinship principles by which prestratified societies operate tend to mitigate whatever individual dominance or prefer- ence patterns men and women may have evolved in their families.

Small-scale societies often look like permanent battlegrounds in a war between the sexes, but mutual dependence usually guar- antees that the two sides remain well matched and respectful of each other, and the battles are political rather than physical. Most societies could not survive otherwise.

Dispatches from the Front

In Suriname's Maroon tribes, for example, the sexes are forever jockey- ing for short-term advantage—or at least long-term equity. Typically they do so through religious ritual. In 1973 some men in Bitagron became pos- sessed by the Kromanti, an African warrior spirit whose shrine was a small, low hut. Kromanti made them drink a lot of beer, act boisterous and gener- ally raise hell. There were other shrines in Bitagron. Perhaps the least impressive, a structure the size of a doghouse, belonged to the village's Mamagron, the guardian spirit of the soil on which Bitagron stands. One day the Mamagron took possession of a woman to announce that it now required a hut larger than the Kromanti's, one large enough for the devotee and her daughter to live in while the Mamagron straightened out the moral mess in Bitagron. And Mamagron wanted it now, or sickness would come to the village. Soon thereafter, everybody caught the sniffles. The new domicile for Mamagron was completed with unprecedented alacrity. Next its interpreter made all sorts of demands from there, organizing events for which, more often than not, the men wound up paying. I was told by men as well as by women that the reason for the uproar was that the Mamagron had felt slighted by all the attention given to the Kromanti: "the woman's side of life needed to be brought up even." A couple of months later, the men regained lost ground when someone died, and the *olomans*, the (all-male) gravedigger association, made *its* demands by interrogating the corpse. But soon thereafter a *kunu*, a hereditary curse that strikes matrilineages to correct past wrongs, trumped the men again. And so it went and probably still goes: sexual differentiation exists, but sexual inequality is tempered by acknowledged mutual dependence. ✑

In stratified societies, however, people are rewarded not on their total contribution to the whole, but according to their specialized usefulness to the ruling elite and its managers. Feudalism, the oldest form of stratification, exists through and for warfare—a condition that emphasizes the importance of men at the cost of women. Your own society, whose structure was derived from feudalism, still carries that taint in its legal and employment spheres: as of this writing, women still make less money than men in many jobs.

Although the first factory workers were women, they were soon displaced by men as the Industrial Revolution transferred legions of surplus males from subsistence farms to factories, there to be attendant to indefatigable machines. The demands of factory labor converted men into organic *robots* (in its original language the word means "worker") who were denied their volition in satisfying such natural necessities as time for rest and bodily functions: "Hold it till your shift is over. The machine can't wait." Working men were impressed with the fact that, to their employers at least, they had less value than machinery.

Men's distance from their families and the dehumanizing conditions of labor destroyed the traditional interdependence of the sexes. Left alone with their children, robbed of men's familiar aid in return for a meager stipend with which to buy what in an earlier age people had grown themselves, women became pauperized and turned into dependents. Men, brutalized into being a commodity for their employers and driven as much as ever by their need for sex, converted women into a commodity for their own use and comfort. That often required forced subjugation, and it always meant a lowering of life chances and lifestyle for women and children.

Industrialization thus reduced the life chances of the lower class into a condition resembling slavery: men were inescapably enslaved by their jobs; women to their husbands and fathers. The term "slavery" was always carefully avoided in this context, however. Slaves were black, and endured what everyone "knew" was a still-worse fate than industrial bondage—by whatever name.

The case can be made that black slavery served—and was maintained—as much as a terror device to keep the white working class "in its place" as to ensure that dangerous and unpopular tasks were performed by other segments of the population. History shows, for example, that slaves were seldom used for really dangerous jobs in the American South: they represented a capital investment that was worth protecting; Irish immigrants did not. Not surprisingly, in the areas where slavery was actually practiced, its repeal was resented most strongly by the whites who were at the bottom of the social pyramid: free black men constituted not only potential competition for survival-level jobs, but a reminder that there was now nobody for poor whites to look down on ("At least I'm not a black slave."). No wonder that the elimination of this ego defense caused destitute whites to incorporate hatred and dehumanization of blacks into their class culture. And no wonder no ruling elite ever saw fit to counteract what was basically a safety valve for the effects of its exploitive excesses.

Racism and sexism have always been intertwined. Even the most die-hard and embittered racists will gladly "use" black women sexually, but the very idea of a black man reversing the compliment will send white men into literally homicidal rage. In the context of race relations—as in rape—masculine sexuality demonstrates dominance.

Since the beginning of civilization, even in racially homogeneous societies, these transformations in the egalitarian interdependence of the sexes have occurred everywhere that nation-states acquired new territory and populations. True sexual and racial inequality are thus a by-product of stratification.

The removal of men from women's daily realm also meant that individual young women had a far more restricted pool of males from which to choose their life partners. Driven by poverty, many women were forced to accept *any* offer of marriage—no matter how brutish and unattractive the suitor. Other destitute women were driven into prostitution to serve the sexual needs of the great masses of men living around the factories. Prostitution of the streetwalker type is unique to stratified societies.

Ruling elites meanwhile maintained their own women in the most luxurious lifestyles possible. In part this was an aspect of stratum defense; in part it expressed competitive conspicuous consumption. But elite women were also categorically different from their culturally disadvantaged sisters in the attitudes and sophistication that come with a life in which the Four Ps are taken for granted. It would never do for the upper class (or caste or estate) to treat its women the way working men treated theirs. The next social stratum, the professional and managerial categories, everywhere emulated their employers in this as in all things. Except that they minimized their own women's potential for independence from men by denying them meaningful educations and any roles other than those of wife, mother and hostess.

There has been considerable organizational evolution since the Industrial Revolution changed life for all time. Unions of determined wage earners have limited the power of employers; women are getting more college degrees than men; both the armed forces and the workplace are becoming sexually integrated. The problems attendant upon these changes are being addressed in law and sensitivity training to recognize and avoid sexual harassment.

But it is not at all clear that this signals a victory for either womanhood or humanity. Crimes against women have increased. Most men no longer dare smile at female children, let alone touch them affectionately. Half a century ago, a man could support a woman and their offspring, expect to lead a better (that is, longer, more comfortable, more varied) life than his parents had and watch his kids do better yet. But since the 1980s, economic inequality has returned with a vengeance: it now takes both father and mother working outside the home to supply the children with basic necessities as these are now defined. That means that children spend much of their lives warehoused under the supervision of strangers—which is no way to produce responsible, caring and competent adults. Society at large pays a high price for the cancellation of parental control: juvenile crime is at an all-time high and is more vicious and destructive than that of adults.

The Purposes of Inequality

We hold these things to be self-evident, that all men are created equal. . . ." So why is there all this institutionalized unfairness? Here? Today?

Because we are not interchangeable in our interests and skills; because we have children even though we lack the wherewithal to raise them adequately; because parents want their children to have advantages even though that must necessarily disadvantage other children; because we can get away with it; because we don't know any better.

There is nothing wrong with social differentiation if it is based on achievement: why *shouldn't* an authority have more say than an ignoramus? Why should a doctor not make more money than a truck driver? But why should either make less than a guy hitting a ball with a stick? There is nothing wrong with the idea of differences in lifestyles—as long as they are not ascribed and inherited, and as long as some are not parasitic on the others. Without social differentiation, no division of labor can grow very complex. We need specialists and farmers, judges and construction workers, inventors and teachers, coordinators and baby-sitters. But roles should go to those who want and prepare for them; they should not be assigned on the basis of irrelevant considerations like sex or gender, race or parents' income. For when they are, misfitting occurs, disaster and red tape follow, the purposes of organization become frustrated, and social life declines into mutual cannibalism. There is nothing natural or inevitable about a culture that allows a CEO to lay off a thousand workers, forcing the rest of his employees to fill in the gaps, all so that he can add the "savings" to his own salary or retirement.

Inequality exists because it is unavoidable. Some forms of it, like the power difference between parent and child, are necessary for society to function and for people to survive.

But *hereditary* inequality is neither unavoidable nor necessary. No form of stratification now practiced is inevitable. Or defensible.

Thinking It Through

1. Can you define and distinguish class, estate, and caste?
2. What are the origins, manifestations and personal consequences of inequality? How can you tell if you are unequal?
3. In a class system like the one in the United States, how do ruling elites maintain their power when so many strivers from the middle class are aching to replace them?
4. What is wrong with inheritable inequality if it has brought America its quality of life?
5. Try to imagine a world or a modern society without inheritable inequality. How would the necessary functions of inequality be fulfilled?

If It Works, It's Obsolete

Technology and Culture Change

"Printing, gunpowder, and the mariner's compass—
these three have changed the whole face and state of
things throughout the world."

—Francis Bacon (1561–1626)

"We were born, our generation, to save the Earth.
And Creation."

—Helen Caldicott (1938–)

*Technology concerns the materials,
knowledge and habits through which
people secure food and manufacture
tools, weapons, clothing, shelter,
containers and everything else they use
or need. As such, technology involves
not only artifacts but also the knowledge
and skills needed to make them and
the techniques for using them.*

*T*he energy that all life-forms need to operate can only come from outside themselves. Plants can live directly off the sun's power, but animals must get their energy second- or third-hand: by eating plants or by eating the animals that eat plants. So you see where that puts you.

You need a lot more than food, of course. The trick has always been how to get it. For your size and weight as a mammal, you are slow and weak and clumsy. You have no fangs or claws, no wings or poisons. Any nonhuman primate at half your body weight can steal your candy. Nevertheless, thousands of generations of your kind survived to raise viable offspring before your mother tried to. So how did your ancestors survive without guns or medicines, electricity or automobiles, so long ago that the horse was still good only for eating?

Well, their environment demanded extreme fitness and a willingness to engage frequently in violent exercise: life was exciting and short. But even back then they could do something no other species has managed to do to this day: with language they could *teach* what they had learned to each other and to their offspring. Language and memory let them keep adding to their cultural store—and as they did, they increased their adaptability.

FROM FIRE TO THE STARS

Half a million years ago or so, some creatures virtually indistinguishable from you from the neck down managed to make fire work for them. Immediately and fundamentally, that differentiated them from all other life-forms: to this day only humans use fire. And what a difference it has made! Not only did fire provide heat, light, and safety from dangerous animals, but also it made more plants and animals—and more parts of them—edible, thus vastly improving those ancestors' diet and greatly reducing their need to risk their lives in getting food.

Their new security allowed them to change physically: it made certain mutations (variations on the basic genetic model) viable; even babies with thinner bones and bigger brains survived. Evolution speeded up: 100,000 years ago your ancestors were already fully modern biologically.

Culture evolved as well. By a quarter million years B.P. (before the present), your progenitors had acquired a basic tool kit: the knife, lever, projectiles, tailored clothing, shelter, and perhaps boats all date back at least that far. Weapons made human males as formidable as any animal, and men gradually succeeded in doing what other primates never had: driving out or killing off the large predators that ate people.

The human population grew. Fire and weapons let people pioneer new lands with new climates and new resources, including new animals to fear and exploit. That response to population pressure worked until about 10,000 years ago, when people first ran out of space.

Until that time, all human economies had been based on the standard model for ground-dwelling primates. Today we call it *food collecting* or *hunting and gathering*. By 10,000 B.P., food collectors had entered the last major frontiers: the Americas and Australia. After that, wherever there got to be too many mouths to feed with a food-collecting economy, people were forced into *food producing*: the raising of food plants and animals.

Probably because it is difficult to imagine what life must have been like before agriculture, it is now popular to believe that once your ancestors "finally" figured out how to plant and harvest and raise livestock, they leaped at the opportunity. That turns out not to have been very likely.

Food-Collecting Societies

Hunter-gatherers attempted no control over their resource bases; they didn't dig ditches or plant fields, and although many had long enjoyed the companionship (and emergency protein) of dogs, they domesticated no other animals. Such people often used their environment very efficiently but did little to change it. Their cultures were poor in artifacts—not least because they had to backpack every possession from one known resource area to another as the seasons changed. Judging from those who survived into the twentieth century, their societies (bands) were small (usually between 20 and 200 souls) and spread sparsely across the landscape. Adapted to local conditions, their cultures varied. Throughout history they ranged from the technological sophistication of the Eskimo and the social complexity of the Northwest Coast Indians to the absolute minimalism of the Tasmanians.

But everywhere, food-collecting lifeways offered good reasons why people had to be *forced* into food production. Hunter-gatherer bands were egalitarian, face-to-face groups. You knew everyone in your own and neighboring bands; everyone knew your roles; you were needed and respected. Life was essentially secure: sure, there was danger—enough to keep it interesting, but seldom enough to threaten the community's survival. From long experience of wandering across its territory, every band knew alternatives when fire, drought or flood devastated a favorite spot. Work, the actual business of making a living, demanded far less time than it does now—and none of today's regimentation. Strangers were perhaps not to be totally trusted, but they were welcomed for their novelty and information; wars were rare and limited. Young men undoubtedly fought over young women, but social stresses were easily alleviated: when two people didn't get along, one moved out to join another band. All in all it was a good life; people whose traditions recall those days view them as their Eden.

Long before necessity forced them to risk agriculture, human beings understood the relationship between seed and fruit. They avoided basing their economies on that knowledge because of the horrendous insecurities in being sedentary. Food production has always been a hazardous undertaking: after you prepare the soil by removing unwanted plants (a major operation before there were iron gardening tools), you must invest seed that you could have eaten and then wait many hungry months before some of that buried seed turns into edible plants. To bring that about, rains must come at the right times, insects and animals must be kept at bay, and the crop must be defended against all who might steal or destroy it. Giving up primordial hunting and gathering meant trading an interesting and secure lifeway for backbreaking labor and constant worry. The evidence is clear in the skeletons of populations that actually made that change: those of the transitional generations are stunted in height, with spinal and bone deformations from the ceaseless labor. Their very bones attest a rise in disease.

This is not meant to imply that your ancestors one day traded their hunting weapons for gardening tools and never looked back. In most places and times, people continued to supplement their vegetable diet with game. But sedentarism means that a village's hunters always cover the same area, and eventually they eradicate the animals around them. Then the population's dependence on plants—or on domesticated animals—notches up again, and the need for back-breaking labor increases.

So your ancestors had to be forced out of food collecting. But on the other hand, food production opened up a whole range of new alternatives.

Gardening Societies

Timeless nomadism ends when a family or society wagers its future on a piece of land. Gardening societies use human-powered technology (the hoe) to produce food. Their settlements are necessarily sedentary. Staying in one place, living off seasonal surpluses, people could not get out of each other's way as they did before; that in turn made it necessary to create new forms of social control—and the roles and statuses to implement them. Sedentary lifestyles made it far easier for young women to accumulate the surplus body fat needed before pregnancy can occur. Birth rates skyrocketed—and so did deaths in childbirth.

Surpluses also meant that not everybody needed to do the same things to survive: there could be more than just men's work and women's work, and almost immediately there was part-time specialization. A woman experienced in birthing might become a recognized midwife; a man good at settling disputes could become a specialist at arbitration; the insecurities of life were addressed by persons believed to have a pipeline to the supernatural world via dreams or drugs or magic. So settlement, in creating insecurities and new threats, furthered social differentiation. As population densities increased vastly more than they could in the old nomadic days, every sector of culture evolved.

Herding Societies

One alternative to domesticating plants was to continue living off large animals, but to tame them so that you didn't have to chase them down. People who elected this option led lives very different from those who took up horticulture; for one thing, they could continue to be nomadic. Animals are dangerous, which means that the division of labor in herding societies is always far more sex-specific than among gardeners. Herds need fodder and water, and in good years, when there is plenty of both, the size of herds explodes. But in bad years—and those come around everywhere— there is never enough grass or water for all the beasts, and then herders are forced to compete for the few good places. War is therefore endemic in herding societies, and their military preparedness and organization are more complex than those of horticulturalists and vastly more important than those of food collectors. Because fighting and tending the beasts are men's work, men are deemed more important than women among herders, and sexual inequality is rife.

Where resource scarcity brought them into conflict with horticulturalists, herders tended to win. In fact, until the nineteenth century there had never been empires more extensive than those founded by conquering mounted nomads such as the Mongols. But efficient or not, the herding lifeway produces less energy than raising grains or other plant staples.

True Agricultural Societies

Once domesticated animals were enlisted to help till the soil, true agricultural societies evolved. Beast-powered plows made more territory tillable than the hoe could, produced greater surpluses, and therefore freed more individuals to invent new techniques, tools and ideas. With the plow, human populations and cultures once again exploded. By the time Egypt and China arose, we had the wheel, the pulley and the bow, full-time priests, soldiers, administrators and specialists in a variety of occupations. Writing made knowledge permanent, enabling the accumulation of alternatives far beyond the memories of the elderly. It made records and therefore bureaucracy possible and encouraged cultural diffusion and further role specialization.

Civilizations

Societies in China, India, Egypt, Mesopotamia, Central America, the Andes, Zimbabwe and other areas independently learned how to produce and store surpluses, to keep records, and to divide the tasks of cooperative living into differently rewarded specialties. Many developed metallurgy. Most important: all had cities—that defining characteristic of civilization that has replaced almost all other forms of society.

Today, because your own culture is so heavily dependent on developments in science and technology, you naturally assume that technology has always and everywhere been the driving force behind the evolution of civilization, but that is not true. At one time or another, each of the major aspects of culture (technology, organization and ideology) has somewhere been in the forefront of change. Often a future has been determined by greater *organizational* efficiency, as when soldiers—who are disciplined to fight as teams—defeated warriors who, though equally armed and brave and strong, fought as individuals for personal glory. Other times an innovative *idea* has triggered massive culture change, as when Muhammad's legions converted the people of North Africa and the Middle East to Islam. Or when the scientific method, borne on the printed word, brought forth the Modern Age.

The archeological evidence of human evolution also makes it absurd to single out technology as the reason for early humanity's ascendancy over the animal kingdom. Compared with dire wolves, saber-toothed tigers, mastodons and cave bears, even the brawniest of our ancestors were puny, slow and vulnerable to the predators and prey they had to contend with. What saved them, and us, was not their ability to fling stones and sharp sticks, or even that they built fires, but the facts that they learned from every encounter that didn't kill them, that language enabled them to cooperate far better than any beasts, and that they could stand together where any mere animal would have fled. Ideas, communication, and organization were always as important as tools and weapons—and they still are.

THE REVOLUTIONARY INVENTIONS

Nevertheless, you owe your material culture and your customary lifeway to some revolutionary changes in the way human beings dealt with the world around them.

Fire brought heat, light, and safety from wild animals, as well as making more (of) foods edible.

Basic technology—knives and needles, spears and projectiles, the pulley, clothing, tents, boats—greatly increased the energy efficiency and effectiveness of human activity. They made your ancestors the equal of any beast and enabled them to spread into new environments.

Domestication of plants and animals widened humanity's ecological niche to include all areas where food plants and animals can survive.

Writing made possible the accumulation of knowledge of alternatives—a store of information—beyond single minds and single generations. Vicarious learning is vastly safer and faster than personal experience.

The scientific method made it possible to separate factual data from superstition and other irrelevancies and offered a cornucopia of new alternatives.

Electricity has proven as seminal as fire itself: you cannot imagine modern life without its power.

Industrial mass production, coupled to all the foregoing, has standardized products, work, and language. It has enabled the societies that utilize it to supplant the cultures of societies that don't; it has raised the material possessions and welfare of their consumers to levels not dreamed of in centuries gone by.

Public health measures such as sewage treatment and pure drinking water have reduced or eliminated such scourges of civilization as cholera and diarrhea (still the number one killer of children in the Third World) wherever they are practiced.

Effective birth control has made it possible for the first time to separate sexual intercourse from reproduction and is rapidly altering the moral and legal attitudes of people everywhere. Largely because of the other inventions, however, especially those in public health, our species' numbers quintupled during the twentieth century in spite of the Pill, endangering your own and your children's future.

Computers, software, and the Internet are everywhere forcing the rate of culture change to explode exponentially. In every area of science and technology, cybernetic-derived alternatives are being realized almost as fast as they can be imagined. Already, human beings can do things that just a generation ago only deities were thought capable of, and no one knows where or when this trend will end. But there is also a growing generation gap in the ability to use the new technologies; older ones—and their practitioners—are made obsolete at horrendous social and psychological cost; inevitably, the technology is being turned against you by economic and political predators; and your very ability to make plans for a predictable future is being obliterated.

There are many other inventions—the automobile, for example—that have caused tremendous changes in the way humans think and behave, but they are essentially evolutionary, not revolutionary, in origin. However, that's quibbling. More interesting is the question of how new ideas and new materials enter a culture.

Change and Evolution

Not every new idea or technique becomes accepted. Electric cars never gained popularity even though their promise was at least as great as the gas-guzzlers' and even though their long-term costs would have been infinitely easier on the environment and your health. Another good idea, "Government of the people, by the people and for the people," is honored only as a slogan, without demonstrable application to elections. One reason so few people vote nowadays may be that they see elections as no more than cosmetic procedures in the process of empowering a "government of the corporations, by the corporations, for the corporations."

Moreover, culture change is never a freebie. Because change in any one aspect or area of culture requires compensatory changes elsewhere, individuals and societies are likely to experience unanticipated consequences that may be very dangerous. (What *are* we going to do with all that nuclear waste?) Every new laborsaving gadget or software program throws people out of work and, too often, out of a marginally bearable lifeway onto the mean and hopeless streets. Every attempt to introduce the Gospel or wage-labor to economically primitive people has added to the population of slums in big cities. The acceptance of any new idea requires some old perspective and its practitioners to become devalued. In every revolution people die, and it is never only those who profited most from the previous status quo. Even in relatively noncompetitive, cooperation-based societies, the introduction of any culture trait that benefits some can do so only at the cost of raising discontent in others. Because whether your culture acknowledges the fact or not, *resources are finite but human wants are not, so whatever benefits some must do so at a cost to others.*

Whenever change beckons, it will be opposed by those who recognize in it some threat to their life chances and lifestyles. Therefore, societies and social groups with the fewest alternatives and the greatest vulnerabilities—and hence, you may say, the greatest need!—are the very ones most likely to object to new ideas, new technologies and new ways of doing things. After all, about all the poor own is their beliefs and their customs, and they will defend those (regardless of the fact that their poverty indicates they have not been well-served by them) *because* these are all they have. Perhaps this helps explain why it is so often the oppressed themselves who perpetuate the habits and ideologies of oppression. Change is necessarily most threatening to people who live on the edge of survival. They know what has worked for them (however uncertainly); they dare not trade the devil they know for one they don't.

Still, culture change and therefore cultural evolution are inevitable: the image of a society that has not changed for generations is simply fantasy. This may seem self-evident to anyone raised in a world where a two-year-old computer is obsolete and a twenty-year-old one is "collectible," but the inevitability of change was assuredly not so obvious to your or to anyone else's ancestors: this self-evidence is itself an expression of change!

A half-century ago, appalled Americans read about homeless people living and dying on the streets of teeming cities in Asia. But today, because our culture has changed, you can step across homeless street people right here. At some point you really need to ask yourself whether today's tolerance for (if not addiction to) culture change is a healthy long-term adaptation for your society, your species, and yourself.

Predicting Culture Change

A few general rules can help predict whether a particular innovation or diffused trait is likely to become part of this or that culture.

Change is most likely to be accepted when it is introduced or supported by individuals with high status—which explains "celebrity" advertising, but not the phenomenon of celebrity.

It helps if the new can be shown to have aspects or components with which people are already familiar. Universal identification cards, such a divisive issue in the United States at present, would be fairly easily accepted if they instantly replaced drivers licenses, Medicare and Social Security cards, especially if they also speeded up boarding at airports.

Proposed changes must not conflict with traditional beliefs and values, unless those no longer satisfy. Among Suriname's Maroons, two centuries of Christian proselytizing have had little effect on people's religious behavior, because native belief systems do a better job of illuminating tribal life with its unique inequities and tragedies than either the Moravian mission schools or the Catholic priests. On the other hand, certain items of modern technology, like outboard motors and chainsaws, were accepted immediately, because they did the job faster and easier than canoe paddles and axes.

Change originates inevitably from within the culture but can come from contact between cultures or be imposed by force from outside. In either case, evolution means adaptation to changes in the environment, which, for any society, includes those other cultures with which it deals.

External Sources of Culture Change

Cultures have always grown by adapting ideas, techniques and artifacts from people in other societies. Never has this process of diffusion been more important than it is today: culture traits now diffuse so rapidly that a single world culture is taking shape before our eyes (although it will probably never replace family cultures or regional cultures).

When peoples of different cultural backgrounds first meet, fighting and trading are the most likely outcomes. In either case, if contact is maintained, both parties will be changed by it. This is true even when their relative power is vastly unequal, as it was when the West met indigenous peoples in the Old and New Worlds—though the effect of Western power on the aboriginal Americans, Africans and Australians has been immeasurably more devastating than the reverse. Conquest, missionizing, and relocation all forced local societies to adapt to the needs of the dominant culture, whose ever it was. As a result, native belief and control systems were shattered; traditional statuses and roles were abandoned, and often-marginal members of the native society were empowered to intermediate between the new rulers and the local population.

Peaceful diffusion—trade demands at least a minimal peace— usually results in less cataclysmic changes within borrowing cultures. Nevertheless, the introduction of certain items and ideas can upset the balance between belief and behavior or between status and power. For example: many of New Guinea's forest-gardening societies traditionally maintained territorial separation through ritual warfare in which only a very few people got hurt or killed, and even then only sporadically. The introduction of modern weapons upset this perennial balance: guns make massacres and genocide possible, and you know how people are: if something is possible, then someone will try it.

When the trait-receiving or -borrowing society is not destroyed by contact, it adjusts to the new ideas and technology by blending them into its existing culture to produce a uniquely new trait complex. This is most easily seen in syncretic religions, those in which native and borrowed elements are mixed and reinterpreted into a new tradition. Probably the most famous example of that is voodoo. But Christianity itself is a syncretic religion, perhaps the most successful one on record.

Syncretism is not restricted to religion, however; as exemplified by the modern North American diet, it is a general feature of all cultures over time. Suriname's Maroon cultures incorporate alien ideas and artifacts with an aplomb that outsiders can only admire. But individuals pay for it through stresses in the social fabric as well as in their individual lives. Just as North Americans do.

Internal Sources of Culture Change

Internal change always originates in individual deviance or innovation. Every society does its best to socialize its newborns to its prevailing standards: you were taught to speak and believe and act like your parents—at least until adolescence. But no society succeeds totally in replicating its adult members; there are too many genetic and social variables to make enculturation (imparting your first culture) a sure thing. Deviance (divergence from social norms) is thus an unavoidable phenomenon in all human societies. For cultures as well as individuals, it is also a source of creativity and innovation.

A deviant individual may be absolutely or relatively divergent. Absolute deviance means being unable to deal with the stresses of everyday existence; if you suffer this pathological condition, you cannot function in the outside world and are therefore unable to initiate culture change. Relative deviance means you are able to function in society but exhibit nonstandard attitudes, values or behaviors. There are three sources for relative deviance.

Incongruent Socialization

If you were adequately raised in another society to speak its language, to believe in its values and to perform its roles, then you will not only have an accent (if you learned this language after age 12 or so), but you will also have some habits and attitudes different enough to raise comment. If you were raised to be egalitarian, your attitudes in a strongly sexist society will get you into trouble; if you were raised to be a successful urban predator, your existence in a cooperative, face-to-face social environment will be difficult.

Incongruent socialization need not, however, threaten either society or yourself. On the contrary: It may be the source of a sufficiently oblique perspective to enable you to see things the locals cannot and thereby afford you an opportunity to innovate, to come up with new answers to old problems or with old answers (your original culture's) to new problems. It may even show you problems no one else has noticed. In a nutshell, this is why the United States has for so long been the fountainhead for inventions and technological innovations: it is a nation of immigrants, of incongruently socialized people.

Inadequate Socialization

In every society some individuals do not receive adequate enculturation (acquisition of first culture), meaning that they perform below the minimum level expected of people at their stage of maturation. The reasons for this vary on the personal level, from mental subnormality to refusal to submit to schooling, and on the social level, from low subcultural expectations to public policy: whole segments of populations—women, minorities—have at one time or another been denied educations.

In modern society, you have been inadequately socialized if as an adult you cannot read a newspaper, make change, follow instructions, or, today, if you do not have at least a high school education. If you've been handicapped that way, for whatever reason, you'd be unlikely to know enough about the way your culture works to be able to participate in it fully, and you'd certainly be unlikely to innovate or to imagine alternatives that will change it. Instead, you'd probably do scut work and live in a slum or an institution. America's prisons are filled with semiliterates.

Excessive Socialization

Every society also produces a few individuals who are abnormally preoccupied with some generally espoused value or goal. These include the miser who turns thrift into a social disease, the anorexic who starves herself into a skeleton because "thin is beautiful," and the Korean War's posthumous Medal of Honor winner who, when ordered to retreat with his battalion, "was last seen engaging the enemy with his entrenching tool."

But excessive socialization is not always a negative concept. It brings forth champions, saints and martyrs for every cause; it accounts for at least some of the dogged persistence that led Thomas Edison to the light bulb and for the strength of conviction that helped Mahatma Gandhi and Nelson Mandela survive the unendurable and change the mind-set of the normally socialized.

EVOLUTION: ADAPTATION TO ONGOING CHANGE

Cultural phenomena are interdependent: you cannot expect a hunting-and-gathering culture to build a seven-story, air-conditioned cathedral in which to crown its kings, because each of these technological and organizational traits presupposes others that simply do not fit with a food-collecting lifestyle. Before such a culture *can* embody those traits, it must fulfill the prerequisites for stratification and industrialization. (Its people, of course, need only desert their ancestral culture in favor of one that already has the traits they seek.)

The interdependence of cultural phenomena also means that there is, along with the already-indicated sources for change, an ongoing process within every culture through which it adapts to the new traits it has already accepted. *Change in any aspect of culture must be balanced by compensatory changes in all the other aspects, or the culture will be unstable.*

Consider, for example, the automobile.

A century ago, before the first horseless carriages, there were 20 miles of paved road in the United States. They had been built to accommodate bicycles. Ninety-five percent of the nation's inhabitants lived on farms or in towns of fewer than 10,000 people. The nation held six distinct regions, each with its own dialect, political orientation, and basic lifestyle:

1. In the Northeast flourished the closest thing to participatory democracy that the country has ever known: New

England, home of small farmers and shopkeepers, with its town meetings.

2. South of New England, the immigrant-powered Industrial North produced most of the material culture, causing "made in America" to become such a successful slogan—at the cost of child labor, sweatshops and unbridled political corruption.

3. Below the Mason-Dixon Line, the agrarian South, still smarting from its losses in the Civil War, remained essentially a feudal state in which the serfs were all black and the aristocrats all white.

4. The Midwest espoused self-reliance as the nation's breadbasket, its cities geared to process and export the bounty of farm and ranch.

5. In the Intermountain West, Mormonism's centrifugal theocracy pulled in converts from Europe but generally kept itself separate from life in the other regions.

6. The West Coast was the last frontier, a thinly populated region known only for gold and forests.

Life, law, and custom in each of these six regions were often quite at variance with those in the others. Into this cultural diorama rode The Car.

A famous editorial in *Scientific American* predicted that the automobile would finally end the pollution that had plagued every city since Ur. And by the standards of that day, it did. The dust from roads and horse manure no longer rots city dwellers' lungs, and the mud of horse urine no longer stains the hems of women's skirts. In part that is so because our city streets have been paved (to accommodate the automobile) and because hemlines have risen, but in the main it's true because we no longer use horses to transport all the goods and foods cities need.

So much land has now been paved over that virtually every inhabited place is accessible by car. That's cut the territories of many large animals into uselessly small pieces, contributing greatly to their rate of extinction. The construction and maintenance of roads has become one of government's primary functions and a major source of pork-barrel graft. And as the once ubiquitous water troughs for horses were replaced with filling stations for cars as the largest organizations ever attempted by human beings, the oil companies, became a reality and a major political force.

Changes in technology result in changes in organization. In fact, the car has made the modern city possible. Before, the biological parameters of the horse placed an absolute upper limit on how many people could live in one place. Now cities of 20 million exist, and tomorrow they'll be larger still.

The first use of automobiles in warfare was as ambulances during World War I, taking casualties from the front to the hospitals in the rear. The second was to drive replacements from the rear to the slaughter. Out of the idea of the car grew the tank and the fighter plane. Modern warfare is an entirely mechanized activity whose logistics and technologists keep the military the most complexly organized profession in the world.

Changes in technology result in changes in ideation. As the car moved Americans from every region to every other in search of The Good Life (or at least A Better One), they settled among others whose political, legal and moral assumptions differed from their own. In the process of mutual adaptation, the rough edges of regional distinctiveness were worn away to the point that now not only does every place look and taste like every other, but its laws and morality are much the same.

Elsewhere, the goods and products being shipped across the world affect the people who buy them. The car itself has led to international standards for traffic signs, highway construction, and so on, even among nations at war with each other. As the (so far) ultimate symbol of personal freedom, the automobile everywhere affects the perceptions of those who dream of independence.

The safety aspect of cars was instrumental in the rethinking of corporate responsibilities in producing consumer items. That very idea has grown to involve changes that are still not worked out in the culture at large.

Changes in technology result in changes in language. In randomizing people across the landscape, the automobile has caused speakers of every regional dialect to interact. Although local dialects survive, they are also affected by radio and television broadcasts in the Standard American English of the Midwest.

The major reason that English has become the world's lingua franca is that it is the language of the United States, the country that has dominated science and technology in the twentieth century. And the automobile is a quintessential American product: cultures that adopt the car usually also adopt the vocabulary that describes its parts and functions.

What's the Word for . . . ?

When the village chief of Bitagron came back from town on a motorcycle, he proudly described his new possession to the excited young men who had never seen such a machine: "The gas goes into this iron belly here. You turn this end of the horns [handlebars] to make it go. This little handle makes its eye [headlight] shine; this little thing makes it cry." But most of his impromptu labels were soon replaced with the English-derived terminology used by mechanics in the city. ≪

Meanwhile, as the other aspects of culture adjusted to the automobile, the device's side effects grew more threatening. Horse manure pollution may be gone, but exhaust pollution is a lot more sinister. Solitude is now an endangered concept. Alienation has exploded as more and more of us live anonymous lives—do *you* know the names of all your contiguous neighbors?—and so has crime, now that criminals can flee into instantaneous anonymity.

In the century since the automobile entered our culture we have improved it and made it safer to use, but we have neither mastered its side effects nor worked through all its implications. Unaddressed problems still face us: what will happen to the greenhouse effect when all the world uses cars the way Americans and Europeans now do? How can we stop building these mechanical monsters without imploding our economies? How will we feed ourselves after every acre is covered with roads? Where will we park?

The shock attending the introduction of the automobile still reverberates throughout the world's cultures. Legal systems continue to spit out laws in futile attempts to legislate standardization for a machine whose intent is essentially anarchic. Probably nothing else is so responsible for the anomie and alienation that typify modern society as the car. In short, we are nowhere *near* completing its integration into American culture—or into anyone else's.

Meanwhile there has been a spate of other innovations to promise heaven and bring us hell. Atomic power: you still don't know how to get rid of its immortal, poisonous wastes. The computer: you can't begin to imagine all the ways it'll affect you, but it has already changed everything you know and do. Medical breakthroughs: they offer you longevity and replacement parts and have already brought you the population explosion that threatens the entire web of life on Earth.

YOU AND CULTURE CHANGE

Stepping out of the Box

My most unforgettable Kwinti was a man called Awani, which means "he wants, he is greedy." Awani was one of the four *basia* (subchiefs) for

Bitagron village. He was the de facto chief of the tribe, even though he ranked below the village chief (whose appointment he had controlled) and the tribal chief, Afiti, who was old and senile. Like several other men, Awani ran a *winki,* a combination bar and store that sold beer, candy and a few other things. At first Awani distrusted me, but then he discovered ways in which I could be useful. I wrote letters for him to the government, and he became my best informant.

On my second fieldwork visit in 1975, I fell ill and required medical aid in the capital city of Paramaribo. During my recovery, I was reading beside the pool of the hotel Krasnapolski, the nearest thing to a modern guest facility in the whole country. The pool was on the top floor, as is common in the tropics. The waiter, a young Creole, advised me that "a person" was in the lobby asking to see me. Curious, and realizing that the put-down "a person" had to refer to a black tribesman (on whom Creoles normally look down), I gave permission for the intrusion. The waiter raised his eyebrows disapprovingly, but soon the door to the stairwell opened, and Awani came out, blinking in the blinding sunlight. He was an old man, dressed in dark trousers and a khaki uniform jacket that dripped with sweat from climbing stairs in the humid heat, and wearing too-large wingtip shoes without socks. I'd never seen him dressed other than in a loincloth.

We went through the greeting ritual, and I ordered us each a Parbo beer from the anxiously hovering waiter. We talked of Bitagron, my mysterious fever, and had another beer. Eventually the snooty waiter came over to ask if I would settle up the bill because he was going off duty. I gave him my credit card, he put it through the machine, and I signed the slip.

Awani watched silently. When the waiter was gone, he asked what that was all about. So I explained the idea of credit cards as well as I could: "It is a way that I can pay without having to carry a lot of money. Once a month I pay money to a bank in America, for using this card that only I can use. When I have a debt, I give this card, the machine checks with the bank in America, and the bank sends money to the business I owe money to."

His intelligent eyes narrowed speculatively. "I could do that," he finally said. "I've been planning to sell tires to the people whose cars break down on the road to Bitagron. I could get my own card and use it to buy the tires. In the month before I have to pay, I can sell them, and pay the bank with the people's money. And if they pay me with such a card, I wouldn't have to touch the money, and nobody could lose it or steal it.

I need one of those little machines. . . ."

I was blown away. Here this illiterate had grasped the basic principle of a concept and a technology that at the time was so new that most people in the United States had not even used it yet. We talked of banking, of interest rates, of long-range financial obligations. We drank more beer.

Finally Awani decided it was time to go. It was a long walk to his lodgings in town. I walked him to the elevator. "No, Bakra," he said turning towards the stairs, "I am leaving." I assured him I would see him out. He shrugged, giving up. The elevator arrived and I stepped inside. Awani looked at the little room I was standing in and shook his head. "I go now," he insisted, and turned around. "Yes," I said, "but let's take the elevator, it beats walking down all those stairs in the heat," and I pulled him inside. He stood there, patiently facing the crazy bakra who wouldn't let him go, and I pushed the button. It was a very smooth, slow elevator; you couldn't feel it move. When it stopped at the lobby, the doors behind him slid silently open.

"Okay," I said.

"Now can we go?" he asked.

"Turn around!" I said. He did, and his eyes grew enormous.

"How—How did you do that?" he asked. His expression shouted: White man's magic! This foolish bakra is more dangerous than I thought!

That broke me up. Here this genius, able to intuit a whole economic system of which he had never been a part, didn't know about elevators but thought I was a magician. He looked affronted, of course, and I wanted to say "Awani, you are a brilliant man limited by your culture, as we all are. If you'd been born in the States, you could be a billionaire, a Senator, anything!" But I didn't know how to say that in Kwinti, and besides, I knew I shouldn't. So we rode up and down with a couple more bottles of Parbo, while he pushed buttons for every floor until he understood the principle. ᭒

The river of culture flows like time itself. Wherever you were tossed into it at birth, its ever-changing current began permeating your being. Had you entered it at another point, you would have become and known something different. You are therefore the unique but ephemeral embodiment of a process: you identify a specific intersection between culture, genetics, and history.

The same is true for every other human being, of course, even as their cultures and experiences differ more from yours than their genes do. One effect of rapid culture change, which is now a fact of life for the whole world, is that there is more difference between generations than ever before. Rapid culture change will make your own children more alien to you than even you and your parents appear to each other.

Looking back at your nineteenth-century ancestors, you may get the feeling that you descend from some pretty ignorant people: they knew nothing about science, had never seen MTV or a computer, never heard stereo, didn't drive and wouldn't know enough to turn on the lights when it gets dark. No wonder politicians assure you that yours is the smartest, best-educated generation that ever drew breath. Don't believe them, though; they always say that when they plan to cut funding for schools. Certainly you know things your ancestors never imagined. But look at all they knew and could do that you cannot. Culture accumulates, but does that mean that your skull contains more culture than your forebears'?

Let's say that 20 percent of the things you talk about today did not even exist in people's vocabularies 25 years ago. Would that mean that you know 20 percent more than they did?

In a word, no. You've got only so much "RAM space," and the odds are that you've dumped 20 percent of the stuff everybody knew then, in order to make room for that 20 percent that is New and Improved. Culture accumulates in libraries, but *some* culture is continually lost from everyday access. Consider the early PCs—Osborne, Kaypro—and their operating arcana; who can still code CP/M? Early in 1998, President Clinton suggested that a special corps of computer programmers be set up to deal with the Millennium Bug, the programming error expected to drive most of the world's computers berserk on January 1, 2000. "Too late!" cried the industry. "There isn't anyone left who can program in the old computer languages!"

Which neatly points out the major problem with the rate of culture change that you must expect to endure. That rate is higher than any the world has ever seen, too high for all but some very (statistically) abnormal personalities to keep up with. We're all gonna die, that's old news. The new wrinkle is that, equally inescapably, *long before you're dead of old age you'll be functionally obsolete*. That's a challenge your culture has not yet prepared you for.

Thinking It Through

1. So what all did using fire do for your ancestors and for the evolution of culture?
2. The archeological evidence of human evolution makes it absurd to single out technology as the reason for early humanity's ascendancy over the animal kingdom. So what did do the trick?
3. Can you distinguish revolutionary from evolutionary inventions? How has the computer made a difference in the last quarter century?
4. Where does culture change come from, and how does it affect you?
5. Do you know more about the world and society than your ancestors did? Would you be able to live in their world more successfully than they would in yours? So are you really smarter than they?

The
Unquenchable Thirst

Knowing

"Truth supposes mankind: for whom and by whom alone the word is formed, and to whom only it is applicable. If no man, no truth. There is therefore no such thing as eternal, immutable, everlasting truth; unless, mankind, such as they are at present, be also eternal, immutable, and everlasting. Two persons may contradict each other, and yet both speak truth: for the truth of one person may be opposite to the truth of another."

—John Horne Tooke (1736–1812)

"Science must begin with myths, and with the criticism of myths."

—Sir Karl Poper (1902–1994)

*Ideation refers to the production
and systematization of sacred and
secular assumptions and definitions
about self, society, humanity, and the
universe. It determines the perceptions,
goals, and means of a human population
and therefore includes values, morals,
law, religion, science, ethics, and any other
intellectual device for promoting social
and personal survival.*

*O*ne common way to conceive of culture is as the Ultimate Encyclopedia, as the compilation of everything humanity has done and made and learned and believed Since We Began. If you do, that's certainly not wrong—as long as you realize that this particular encyclopedia contains a lot of inaccuracies and blank pages. However, you'd probably find it more useful to think of culture as a road map with a tool kit and a manual for standard operating procedures (SOP).

When your forerunners were still backpacking through life, they got their SOP from the mouths of the elderly, who had lived through similar situations. But whenever human beings spread into new ecosystems with new dangers and opportunities, they were forced to go beyond SOP: the Old Ways were not always applicable. Faced with the need to act and the necessity to decide, people had to innovate—and take new and unexpected risks.

From one valid point of view, the whole purpose of culture is to make it unnecessary for individuals to make decisions. If your culture is adequate to the tasks it sets you, SOP will carry you through. Or the flip side: as long as you deal only with the situations for which your culture was designed, you will have appropriate responses to every stimulus you encounter.

Unfortunately your existence isn't that predictable. Sooner or later you'll range beyond the scope of your culture's manual and get into situations for which nothing has prepared you.

HOW KNOWLEDGE IS GAINED

All cultural evolution, all deviation from norms, begins in the behavior of individuals. Some of it originates in deliberate analysis and experimentation, some in imprecision when following tradition and routine, and some comes from spontaneously innovative responses to situations novel to the culture or at least new to the individual.

Only a few genetic mutations ever make it into the gene pool; the rest are not reproduced. Similarly, most behavior variations and attempted innovations never enter any culture's trait inventory; they are simply errors, failures or incompetencies without effect on the direction in which culture flows. Nevertheless, in distinction with other animals, any novel experience that *you* survive need not necessarily be lost to those of us who did not share it.

Novel Encounters and New Adaptations

Say you suddenly come upon a bandersnatch coobeling arkedul. You haven't a clue what it is you are seeing, but your muscles tense for your response: flee, fight, feed, or fornicate? Watching you intently, the bandersnatch extends a crequou and squeezes an arkedul's ferantra. Beffaron spurts . . .

As does your adrenaline. "Have I run into a massacre?" you ask yourself, feeling the hair rise on the back of your neck. "Or is that creature only sort of . . . milking its cow?" No time for analysis—is there ever?—you're there! A second crequou waves . . . in warning? Threateningly? A greeting?

Heart hammering double-time, you scoop up the nearest arkedul and toss it at the creature, avoiding its fell eye as you leap across its squeezing crequou. Beffaron splashes your leg. You run. Replete with arkedul, the bandersnatch snides succulessly.

You live! To tell the tale. But you wonder out loud: Did I assume correctly, or was I just lucky?

Moving deeper into bandersnatch territory, every member of your band carries an arkedul along—just in case. Soon proof is abundant: the one time humans need not fear the bandersnatch is when it coobels arkedul. Arkey-raising becomes a part-time specialty, arkey luggers are traded far and wide, arkey-tossing teams compete for first choice in mates. Long after your death your feat remains the maxim in the legend at the core of the bandersnatch ritual. ✎

Cultural Conservatism

If you survive a novel challenge, your successful response may become a part of your culture. If you were not lucky, if you focused on some inappropriate characteristic of the singularity facing you and acted accordingly, you failed and may be dead.

From that perspective it is easy to see why traditional cultures are usually conservative: people stick with what works, rather than risking something new with who knows what results. And yet, for all their conservatism, they often evolve astonishing capacities that must have required persistent and deliberate analysis and experimentation.

Consider, for example, bitter cassava or manioc, a staple of South American lowland Indians, which now grows in many parts of Africa and other tropical regions. It is a tuber resembling a sweet potato. What makes it bitter is the prussic acid it contains, enough to kill a human being. Long before Old Worlders came to the New World, Native Americans (to whom you owe half of all the entrées in your diet) had learned how to turn this well-defended plant into food. The Kwinti practice the process to this day.

The tuber is peeled, grated, and packed wet into a seven-foot-long tube of flexible basketry shaped like a fire hose. This *metape* is squeezed by stretching it, which presses the cyanide-bearing sap from the mash, usually into a large bowl. The metape and its contents are then allowed to dry, after which the metape is collapsed from its ends so that the dry cassava cake falls out of the tube in cylindrical pieces. These are pounded into a powder that is baked into wheel-sized pancakes. These may be broken into pieces to be used like thick potato or tortilla chips, mixed in soups, and so forth. The "juice" in the bowl is used to poison fish in the river—and provides the traditional means for suicide. Left standing for a few days, the cyanide evaporates, and the remains can be used as a piquant but harmless spice.

Why would people go to all that trouble to make a poisonous plant edible? Probably because it can be grown easily: stick any leaf or twig or root of the cassava plant into the ground, and you soon have more tubers, year around. But the whole process makes you wonder just how many dogs and enemies the Indians tried that recipe on before it was perfected. It gives you a hint as to how expensive *all* knowledge must once have been.

Thousands of other examples show that your backpacking ancestors experimented quite purposefully long before they understood the protocols of science. For example, when Spanish Conquistadors met the Aztecs they were offered a drink unlike anything they had ever tasted before. English explorers in the Guyanas encountered the same taste in a more solid substance. The natives there collected a species of bitter-tasting nuts in the region's forests, fermented them twice, dried them, roasted them and ground them into powder to release the flavors that the nuts' 300-plus chemical compounds produce. The wild forests are long gone, but their heritage lives on in plantations, for "food of the gods" (as chocolate's scientific name translates) has become the most sought-after edible substance on Earth.

THE PERVASIVENESS OF MAGIC

One thing you can be sure of is that the modern production of cocoa and chocolate is more efficient and direct than the Indians' ever was. Nowadays the process is rigidly scientific; originally it was a combination of pragmatic treatments inextricably combined with irrelevancies, redundancies, and behaviors that had psychological but no effective functions. The reason for that is that you cannot always be sure why something suddenly works when you've been messing with it for a while.

If you randomly reward a hungry animal with food, its activity will begin to focus on whatever series of steps preceded its "success." Of course the same thing will work on human beings, which is why there is so much superstition in the world: *Magical thinking results from an inability to extract the operating factor out of a successful behavior sequence.*

The behavioral psychologist B. F. Skinner developed this idea into a technique to train animals to do virtually anything he wanted. When I was still a grad student in psychology, I once trained a hungry pigeon in less than two weeks to tap out the first line and a half of "The Star-Spangled Banner" on a toy xylophone. It's not that the poor bird had a musical ear, but that it discovered that when it pecked at three keys in a particular order ("O-oh say"), a desirable thing happened: a kernel of grain fell into its cage. After a while, however, that didn't work anymore. Then, "knowing" from experience that there was a connection between tapping and food, it kept madly tapping the three keys for a while before adding a fourth. When it hit the right one ("can"), food appeared again, soon ensuring that it played all four notes in the right order from then on. "You," "see" and "by" came easily, probably because they were next on the scale and the keyboard. "The" took longer, I suspect because we were reversing directions, and the bird had acquired a tendency to try pecking to the right of its last success. The experiment ended before I succeeded in teaching it "early."

Having watched myself and others working on modern devices, especially computers, I realize that though culture has come an incredibly long way, you and I are not much different from that pigeon when it comes to messing with stuff we don't understand but have to deal with. Try this, try that, try those: It worked! Okay, now let's do this that those again. Great! Again! Okay, okay, okay—uh-oh. This that those? Again? Hmm . . . Well, let's sacrifice a virgin and see if that helps.

Imagine that the two-seater airplane carrying you to your winter vacation crashes onto a nameless pond somewhere in Canada.

You wake up to freezing cold. Your guide, the pilot, is dead. When you move, you discover that your left leg is badly broken. The plane is slowly sinking; you *have* to get out of there. You carefully lower yourself onto the ice, painfully dragging your sleeping bag behind you, and make for the snow-laden trees crowding the shore. You crawl behind a fallen log to get out of the wind and manage to get the sleeping bag around you before you pass out.

You wake up once in darkness, your teeth chattering. When you wake again, it is light, but you cannot move; your whole body aches too much and your leg is on fire. You don't remember anything after that except, vaguely, a dark face speaking to you in a language you never heard before—and a pain you never imagined possible as someone moved your leg.

The next time you open your eyes, it is hot and close and noisy. Something smells of smoke and putrefaction. Women's voices wail atonally nearby, four half-naked men wearing grotesque masks dance to a monotonous drum; shadows leap wildly around the low-ceilinged hut while somebody tries to spoon broth into your mouth. Someone else has unpacked the mess tied around your leg and is putting a new poultice on the place where the bone had broken through the skin.

In short, you heal. You learn to speak a few words in your saviors' language and to understand many more. You learn to walk with a crutch and a limp. Eventually your rescuers take you to the nearest road, and you hitchhike home.

There, after celebrating your unexpected survival with your loved ones, you check into a hospital. Its orthopedic surgeon inspects your leg. You tell your story, enumerating every detail of the treatment that got you back on your feet. The doctor is fascinated but aghast: his training hasn't prepared him for a curing ritual involving prayer, warriors dancing, constant wailing by six widows to keep the evil spirits away or singing a healing chant at every dawn and dusk. "Magic," he mutters disapprovingly. He does allow that your native friends did a good job setting the compound fracture and is intrigued to learn that they packed the wound in a potion of cobwebs and breadcrumbs in some sort of salve after cleaning it with whiskey. "You're lucky to be alive!" he concludes.

Fact is, you *are* alive, and you wouldn't have been except for the people who found you and did the best they knew how for you. Once you had healed enough to be bored with bed rest, you asked the medicine man exactly what he had done to save you, and he told it to you so you could write it down. He explained that he knew from experience that when he treated a broken leg this way, the person usually got better and walked again. Of course you were not one of his people, so he had to make adjustments. He'd burned your wallet in a sacrifice to the Healing Spirits to make them aware of your alienness. But otherwise he'd been very careful that everything be done exactly and in the order that worked in the past.

Magic? Of course it was magic. The medicine man had followed a ritual involving many parts or steps without understanding or caring how any of these added to the desired result. That's how magic is done: success and safety depend on exact duplication of whatever worked in the past. Any deviation may not only bring failure, but something unexpected and possibly malevolent. The Supernaturals are not pleased when someone messes with their stuff, and they can get nasty.

SCIENTIFIC THINKING

Your doctor, having set many a broken leg himself, does not see the prayer as indispensable, the singing as obligatory or the dancing as prerequisite to healing. Physicians are scientists, trained to eliminate the extraneous from the necessary, and in their experience broken bones heal without all that jazz.

It may be that scientific thought begins whenever someone questions whether all the steps in a process are necessary. But it is fruitless to worry about whether science grew out of magic or whether its birth awaited a whole new way of looking at the universe: one doesn't deny the other.

In any case, it cannot be denied that magic and science begin at the same place: with the awareness and *observation* of some phenomenon. *Categorization* follows in both approaches: the observed data are classified according to some schema in the mind of the observer: color, shape, weight, size, texture, substance, effect, moral implication, peril, profit, whatever. (Individuals and societies differ in their ability to recognize and create new classificatory schemas.)

After this point, magic and science diverge. For the magician, classification determines what ritual process will be employed to acquire mastery over the phenomenon, and failure to achieve the goal means adding or replacing elements of the process until control is achieved.

For the scientist, after acknowledgment of the event or phenomenon, understanding it usually requires these next steps:

1. formulate a hypothesis to explain it;

2. then empirically test the hypothesis;

3. conclude whether the results confirm or reject it;

4. if necessary, reformulate the original hypothesis so that it explains both the results and the original event; and

5. integrate the validated hypothesis into existing theory.

For our purposes, let's agree that *Science refers to the systematic, objective study of empirical phenomena and to the bodies of knowledge resulting therefrom.*

Systematization of data means the scientific investigator now attempts to fit the observations into an order that shows how the various parts or aspects are linked. This requires the formulation of *hypotheses*, testable statements on the relationship among the observed phenomena and between them and the rest of the universe. Not every statement is testable (How would you prove that your deceased great-grandfather loved your deceased great-grandmother?); therefore much of the art in science lies in the ability to formulate meaningful hypotheses.

Once a hypothesis has been derived, *experimentation* or comparison will either confirm or deny it or, if the results are ambiguous, lead to further observation and analysis and a reformulation of the hypothesis. Experimentation is considered a hallmark of the natural sciences but is generally impossible for astronomers and anthropologists—you cannot drag a galaxy into the laboratory and we do not allow experiments on human beings. Although experimental cultures may well be humanity's most pressing unrecognized need, no one has figured out how to square them with our notions of liberty and self-determination. For these and other disciplines therefore, *comparison* is the critical factor.

Methodical comparison involves measurement against known parameters and logic. Ethnocentrism is the tendency to judge all alien ideas, artifacts, and behaviors against the standards of your own culture. Cross-cultural *comparison* has made it possible to separate ethnocentric opinion from objective data in the assessment of human behavior and capacities. *Fieldwork* is a specific variant of experimentation in that the fieldworker, unlike the laboratory scientist, doesn't attempt to eliminate all variables around the phenomenon to be studied, but sees them as context and therefore as part of the data to be recovered.

Once a hypothesis has been "proven" or supported, it must be integrated into a more general, overarching explanation of life and the universe. This is *theory*, the constantly adjusted and perfected body of general statements about the ways the universe actually works, which can predict and explain empirical (objectively demonstrated) phenomena. *Model* is another term for theory, one that focuses on its illustrative powers. Theories are constructions that integrate supported hypotheses into more powerful explanatory and predictive ideations. They are always—and this bothers the uninitiated the most—*statements of probability*. Unquestionable certainty is not science's province.

MAGICAL THINKING

But how can you be sure? you ask.

Face it, in science you can't be. But you can be certain enough to wager your life and wealth and good name: some odds are overwhelming. Nevertheless, the universe is a quirky place, and when you get into your car, you never really know for sure you'll arrive where you're going, do you? Probability statements are the only sane way to deal with the unforeseeable: you seldom see a meteorologist so foolish as to announce that there is an absolute certainty that it will (not) rain tomorrow.

You live in a scientific society, meaning that your environment, the entire modern world with the technology and medicine you take for granted, is based on theories and their realized implications. But the case can be made—*needs* to be made—that neither you nor anyone else is totally free of magical thinking. Odds are that your doctor has only the vaguest and most unscientific comprehension of most other disciplines that are not directly relevant to his or her interests; there's not much time in medical school for intellectual broadening. Odds are also that you, personally, are as magic ridden as any Stone Age warrior with a bone through his nose when it comes to technologies alien to your training. And I myself have memorized and repeat, as dumbly as any pigeon in a Skinner box, the ritual steps on which the demon in my software program seems to insist before it will let me type on this computer that I comprehend no better than my cat makes sense of my stereo.

Whenever any of us uses technology that is beyond our understanding we are, for all practical purposes, operating magically. Do you really know how and why those ubiquitous microchips work? Can you actually explain how an antibiotic cures you, in terms that are more sophisticated than "the good bugs shot into my butt find the bad bugs in my throat and kill them"?

HOW DO YOU KNOW?

In any case, magic-tainted or scientifically pure, all cultures survive by knowledge. And however it is packaged, it is worth a great deal not only to the individual but also to society. The Chinese sage K'ung Fu-tse (ca. 551–479 B.C.), whom we in the West know as Confucius, wrote, "To know that we know what we know, and that we don't know what we do not know, that is true knowledge." True! But even Confucius knew a great number of things that we now know were not true, and that brings up two questions: how *do* you know what you know, and how *do* you know that what you know is actually so?

There are only two possible answers for the first question. Either you possess the knowledge because you took somebody's word for it, or you trusted the evidence of your senses. You'll concede that the first category transcends the second by magnitudes. You're a cultured being after all, meaning that you have internalized the distilled experience of thousands of people who lived and died before you. Most of your knowledge is vicarious; that is, you read it or heard it or watched pictures of it. But your authorities (the somebodies whose word you took) may be honestly mistaken, trying to protect you from the truth, guessing, lying or even right on. But how do you know which? (Remember believing in Santa Claus? In politicians?)

That leaves the evidence of your senses, and right away there's a problem. You've been taught that you have five senses, but that's just one example of how culture can misinform. In fact, your body has separate sensory organs (meaning distinct anatomical structures) for hearing, seeing, tasting, smelling, touch, pain, temperature and balance, plus various others that gather less obvious but physiologically vital information such as the level of sugar in your blood.

Sensation

This is the operation of these organic receptors, your data-gathering organs. Everything you know has come to your brain via your senses. The two you count on most are hearing and seeing. Before rock concerts, young people with normal hearing could receive sound vibrations ranging from a low of about 15 to a high above 20,000 cycles per second. Normal human vision reacts to light waves ranging from .000040 to .000072 centimeters. Fortunately you don't react to every image and sound in your environment; you focus on what's important and ignore the rest.

Perception

The process whereby you screen information out of raw data or "noise," the mountain of sensory input your body sends to your brain every second of your existence, is called perception. Another word for that process is "focusing," paying attention to some aspect of what you see or hear by selectively ignoring everything else. You *learned* how to do that; no baby is born knowing what any sound or sight means. When you were born, the barrage of stimuli assaulting your senses was simply over-whelming. Over time, with the help of the people who raised you, your brain learned to make sense out of the chaos: pay attention to this, ignore that. So perception determines whether some-thing has significance, or meaning.

Perspective

The systematic and coherent bias you have in observing and manipulating information is called perspective. You got your basic perspectives very early as part of your *family culture*, along with language and perception itself. They include your basic values and assumptions about right and wrong, hierarchies of importance, justice, honesty, gender, and so on. These were later augmented by your *societal culture*: what friends, schooling, higher education, and professional standards taught you.

Meaning

This is therefore always a cultural artifact, and in different cul-tural contexts the same stimulus may have different meanings.

Take a symbol such as the swastika. This hooked cross has been used for millennia in societies ranging from bands to civiliza-tions. Some Native Americans used the swastika in sun worship; others saw it as a symbol for good luck if it turned to the right, of bad luck if it turned to the left. In India, the worshipers of Vishnu paint swastikas on their foreheads. In Nazi Germany, it turned to the right and symbolized the state and Adolph Hitler's ideology, which wasn't lucky for anybody. In North America today, the swastika is a mere visual obscenity, its major purpose to desecrate and irritate.

So what does it mean, you ask? It means what people believe it means! But what it means to *you* makes the difference. For exam-ple, it lets me predict categorically how you'll react to a swastika: You are more likely to come unglued at the sight of one if you are over sixty than if you are under thirty, if you are a Jew rather than a gentile, if you were born in Europe rather than in the Americas. In other words, what the thing means depends on you, not on it. *Meaning exists in the mind of the observer; meaning is not intrinsic in the observed.*

That may run counter to everything you believe, but it is nevertheless a fact of life that you have experienced every time you take an introductory course in any academic discipline. Such classes are mainly vocabulary builders: they redefine the world for you, teach you to see it in a new way and label its features accordingly. Until you take a course in geology, the shapes of rocks and mountains are just that. Afterwards, however, you will be able to say something more informative than "Ooh!" and "Ahh!" about any new countryside you drive through: terrain will have acquired *meaning* for you. It'll be a different sort of meaning than the same terrain achieves from your doing a stint in the infantry or a few years of farming. But in either case it is not the terrain that has changed, so its meaning is not in it, but in you, you see?

Human beings *impose* meaning on the universe; the universe apparently doesn't care whether you do so or not. Individually and collectively, people have a powerful need to make sense out of the surroundings they are born to and grow up in. All humans see patterns: it's what we do. You recognize faces and figures in clouds and blackboard erasures, you discover predetermination in random events, you find trends in the way the numbers come up in the lottery, you classify strangers by arbitrary standards. Why? Because you *have* to; you *need* to categorize your experiences in order to remember them, to make them useful. In the Bible and the Qur'an, that tendency is enshrined in the first task God assigned to Adam: to classify and label everything under the sun. That universal reflex of wanting to impose meaning is a distinguishing human attribute: The most frequent utterance of two-year-olds—after "No!"—is "What's that?" Infants at play often sort things almost compulsively. As an adult you still see patterns—whether or not they actually exist.

Here's an experiment to prove the point. Take a large piece of cardboard, spray it with flat-black paint. Toss a handful of fine glistening stuff, like foil confetti or small stars, toward the ceiling. Catch some on the wet paint as it comes down. You will then have a random distribution of sparkles against a black background. Frame the cardboard, hang it over the foot of your first-born's bed. Leave it there. When the kid is ten, he or she will show you that this was not a *random* distribution of sparkles, but a complexly *patterned* one: "See, Mommy? When you draw a line from here to there to there, it is a [whatever]." If you are still mentally flexible then, you too will be able to see the pattern your offspring imposed on randomness; in fact, you may never be able to find the randomness again! But wait, it gets better. Number-one kid will teach number-two kid what the patterns are. Number two will see even more of them. And, if your "Star Map of Another Galaxy" should become a family heirloom, so will *their* children.

If you cannot wait that long, just go outside, look at the stars and contemplate astrology.

How Do You Know That What You Know Is Actually So?

Any contemplation of the relativity of meaning soon forces you to face a potentially disturbing fact: that all perceptions and perspectives, all disciplines and ideologies—be they political, legal, religious, moral, mathematic or scientific—ultimately rest on unproven and usually untestable suppositions. You may find it difficult to accept that the bulk of what you know and believe is rooted in assumptions, in statements you take for granted without proof, in principles you have accepted on faith. Yet once you can bend your mind around that concept, it may be the most liberating mental tool you'll ever wield.

You'll probably have no trouble entertaining the idea as long as it is restricted to something supposedly as dispassionately objective as mathematics. Math is one of those things that people believe to be free of the "taint" of culture, but in this they are wrong: culture affects *every* aspect of human existence.

Around 300 B.C., Euclid, a Greek mathematician, wrote thirteen books called his *Elements*. Euclid's greatest contribution was his use of deduction to present his insights into geometry and numbers. He defined such concepts as point and line, postulating (that is, "assuming") certain unprovable attributes or axioms (unchallengeable or self-evident propositions) for these concepts, and then logically deduced a series of statements from them, including the famous fifth postulate: "One and only one line parallel to a given line can be drawn through a point external to that line," one of whose implications is that "parallel lines cannot meet."

Euclid's system dominated Western culture for over 2,000 years because it has worked well enough to measure territories, design complex structures and machinery and get ships to where they wanted to be. But in the early 1800s this "perennial" aspect of culture changed when it was discovered that Euclid's fifth postulate could not be proven from the others. That made room for alternatives. Soon there were non-Euclidian mathematics, based on different axioms, in some of which parallel lines *could* cross. One, Boolean algebra, became basic to the development of computers, and without its specific axioms we would not be able to program a landing on another planet.

There are several points to be made here.

1. Whether Euclidian or not, all mathematics are based on certain assumptions.

2. The issue is not whether these axioms are false or true in some unknowable sense, but whether they "work."

3. If an axiom is changed, the result of the logic deduced from it must also change, meaning that it may not work anymore or that it will have implications that cannot be totally predicted.

4. Therefore, society is unlikely to accept an alternative as long as it already has an axiom that works.

5. As long as it does work, you will not think of it as an assumption but as an established fact.

Now, don't all five of these points apply equally well to your concepts of law and religion, science and morality? Before you answer, remember that stating that something is an assumption is not the same as saying it is not true—or that it is.

Assumptions

Consider who and what you are, what you believe you stand for, what you consider important. Can you *prove* the truth or value of these things, or are they justified by the fact that you very much want to *believe* them because otherwise a lot of things wouldn't make sense?

Your very identity and personality are based as much on your assumptions as on nature or nurture. You derived most of the basic values you live by from your family culture. Therefore your personality (your being and behavior) must change if your culture and its basic assumptions change. But though that follows logically, it is difficult to prove, because basic assumptions are more resistant to change than any other aspect of culture or character. Just as it took millennia to change a single axiom in mathematics, so too the axioms and postulates underlying your culture and your personality are virtually immune to questioning.

Say your community is overrun with vandals who spray paint every surface of private and public property. Arresting them does no good: law enforcement is unable to catch most of them, and therefore their lawyers have argued successfully in court that punishing the occasional arrestee is cruel and unusual. Tired of the mindless degradation of its living space, your community passes a law that gives anyone who catches a tagger the right to remove his thumbs. Soon thereafter you actually get the drop on one who's desecrating your church or your home, and you chop off his thumbs.

Naturally he complains; the police arrest you, and your lawyer defends your act as legal because there is that new law you guys passed. But the court calls that law unconstitutional—meaning that it is in contradiction with the implications of a set of assumptions made centuries ago by people who couldn't even imagine spray paint.

You may point out the irrationality of this, insist that any assumptions made then do not cover the realities of today. But no one will listen: people are too terrified of the chaos they expect to follow any successful challenge to such seminal assumptions. Even those who privately agree that your argument is valid, and that nothing less will keep vandals from spraying, would much rather live with the old law's unfairness and inadequacies than change the rules of the game.

The basic assumptions underlying legal systems everywhere have the status of unquestionable referents. The most your culture can allow is their occasional reinterpretation. Nations have special agencies for that purpose, like the United States' Supreme Court, whose pronouncements are as unchallengeable as a pope's when he speaks ex cathedra. These agencies, again like the pope, reserve for themselves the right and power to retract or change decisions made in previous ideological pronouncements.

So *why* do people and societies make assumptions—besides the fact that you couldn't do math without them? Because you don't have all the information you need to make the decisions necessitated by your lack of instincts. Human beings do not tolerate ambiguity well.

Individually and collectively, you make assumptions whenever you have inadequate information yet must plan or choose. First you'll attempt to fit any unknown situation to a familiar precedent. Then, if the actuality is beyond your perceptual scope, you create models that let you envision what you are dealing with. These representations and the actions that flow from them necessarily assume values and priorities. Those in turn determine your behavior as an individual and as a member of such social structures. In this sense, *all of culture is the working out of profiles or combinations of assumptions.*

"There is common sense, the conventional wisdom!" I hear someone protest.

Perhaps, but what good is that? Individuals disagree on what it is because what is CS/CW to one society or group is often nonsense in another. CS/CW always suffers from preconceptions; it is usually moralistic, nonobjective and therefore useless for comparisons. Normally it offers only a prejudiced, post-facto explanation. No, it is fair to say that common sense is typically neither common nor sensible.

"But what about reality?"

Good question. You can assume to your heart's content, but in the final analysis there is a line between fiction and fact, and you have to know where it lies. If you get drunk and climb to the seventh story and the booze lets you assume you can fly, it matters less what the origin of your conviction was than that the result of your leaping into space will be "splat!" And since the same gravity will kill you no matter what your culture, there must be something in or about the universe that goes beyond assumption. But if that's what everybody calls "reality," what is it?

Reality

The short, flippant answer is that reality is a crutch. Although that's undeniable, on the cultural and psychological levels, it doesn't advance understanding a great deal.

The long, complicated answer is that *objective reality is a synthetic construct, predicated on a hypothetical universalization of subjective realities.* In other words, reality is whatever dominant thought in a society says it is.

When the Second Millennium was aborning in Europe, reality held that the Earth was flat, that the sun, moon, and stars orbited it, that men had one rib less than women, and that the right of rulers to rule was ordained by God. Now, at the dawn of the Third Millennium, reality holds that the Earth is a globe, that it and its moon orbit the sun, which is but one star among billions in a galaxy that is but one among billions of galaxies, that men and women are essentially identical except for the causes and effects of reproduction, and that the right of rulers to rule originates in the consent of the ruled. Any bets on what reality will look like when the Fourth Millennium rolls around? (Any bets that there will *be* a Fourth Millennium?)

Reality is a fluid concept. When culture change was still glacially slow and deliberate, reality (however it was locally defined) served as a perfectly adequate reference guide. Reality kept our ancestors from barging into the affairs of gods and other supernaturals; reality made them choose certain alternatives over others. Reality still keeps most of us out of jail and bankruptcy court. As such, reality may be "only" a crutch, but why is that a pejorative if you cannot move around without one?

Science "objectifies" reality by removing it from its provincial, culture-specific setting. A statement is objective reality, that is, considered representative of the way the universe actually is and operates, if it remains true regardless of who tests it. Pure water boils at 100°C (212°F) at sea level, regardless of whether you heat it in Florida, Holland, or Bangladesh.

Unfortunately, even objective reality nowadays has a short shelf life. I still own my college biology textbook, which taught me that human beings have 24 sets of chromosomes. If you stated that on a test today, you would be wrong. Now we have 23 sets.

That isn't meant to imply that biology is bunk or that the author of that text was incompetent. Until the twentieth century no one had even imagined chromosomes; when they were finally postulated, it took the invention of the electron microscope before their dim outline could be recognized. Further technological refinements, long after the text was published, finally made an accurate count possible. In the world of science, the latest word is valid only until still more refined knowledge is procured—but during that wait, it *is* the best, the most objective, information available. And that's what the author gave my generation of students.

Here's another example. In the 1930s, physicists knew enough about the way the atom worked to realize that they didn't know enough, and they hypothesized that there had to be another subatomic particle, which they named the neutrino. In the 1950s they were able to verify its existence. The neutrino turned out to be, as they'd expected, "a ghostly little thing" without electric charge or mass, good really only for balancing the equations that describe nuclear reactions. For four decades now, physicists and their college students have known and worked with this objective reality. Then, in 1998, it was convincingly demonstrated that at least one of the three known kinds of neutrinos does have some mass—not much, but enough to account for much of the "missing mass" in the universe and therefore enough to cause a reexamination and adjustment of cosmological theory. Is this the final statement? Is it ever, with science?

So the fact remains that the world is globular whether we acknowledge it or not, that male and female humans have always had the same number of ribs, and that the sun doesn't alter its course through our quadrant of the Milky Way simply to suit some mortal's beliefs.

Reality is a cultural artifact. Every society defines its own reality because it needs one and because it can. There are consequently at least as many objective realities as there are different cultures. And every reality we know about works well enough—as long as nothing challenges its assumptions. But as peoples from different climes and cultures meet in war, in trade and in bed, more and more alternative realities fall by the wayside and are replaced.

Does that mean that one reality is as good as another?

No, it does *not!* If by reality we mean some culture's ideational structure of the universe and your role in it, it makes a lot of difference whether you're told you are inferior or that you are equal, whether you're expected to live to labor or to worship, to obey, to conquer, to excel or to cooperate. It matters whether you are taught there are germs, that smoking kills, that doctors should wash their hands before surgery. We can argue forever on what "good" meant in the question, but let's face it, some cultures' realities are not worth living in, and others are worth dying for.

But how can you tell which is which?

When it comes to judging alternatives, you need a less pliant yardstick than reality, objective or otherwise.

Veridicality

"The belief in an external world independent of the perceiving subject is the basis of all natural science," Albert Einstein wrote in 1934. All we need add is that there's no reason to restrict that insight to the natural sciences. But we do require a single term to indicate this "external world independent of the perceiving subject," this ultimate referent.

I suggest *veridicality,* and define it for our purposes as *the actual conditions in the universe regardless of whether anyone knows them.*

That definition is, I admit, less than perfect. Especially because it includes humans and their cultures. The universe is not a stable place, so veridicality is probably neither immutable nor constant. But it does operate by rules that have a longer half-life than beliefs and theories and objective realities, and that, moreover, have remained in effect wherever and whenever human beings live. The value of veridicality lies in the fact that it is not contingent on our assumptions—it exists independent of them.

Veridicality cannot replace reality. For one thing, veridicality must remain unknowable, like the nature of God or the size of the infinite. Veridicality is in several important ways an intellectual equivalent to the concept of God. *If* it exists, veridicality has to be more than the sum total of all realities, because they are only cultural constructs. *That* it exists is evidenced in the fact that when a culture's assumptions run contrary to veridicality, thus to the way the universe actually works, that fact will eventually become obvious. And then its people will suffer unless and until they restructure their reality.

Nevertheless, we cannot prove the existence of veridicality because we cannot perceive it directly—that's why Einstein talked about a *belief* in an external world independent of the perceiving subject. Veridicality is an inescapable inference, but that doesn't *prove* it is Out There.

So cultured beings can continue to believe whatever they want and are likely to do just that until *what* they believe conflicts decisively with veridicality. They can assume and deduce to their heart's content, derive great ethical systems and codes of conduct, teach their children that they were brought by the stork, and their elderly that winged canoes will carry them off at death to unendurable pleasure indefinitely prolonged—or anything else that'll smooth the path. Various native prophets have promised aboriginal armies that the white man's bullets would not touch them. Various societies have fervently sacrificed so that their gods or ancestors would protect them from the Unthinkable. But the warriors died anyway, and all that remains of those societies is an archeological record.

You cannot escape the fact of your enculturation and the arbitrary meanings it taught you to place on the culture-filtered evidence of your senses. Certainly you can be aware of them in the behavior of others, and you may even come to recognize some of your own biases. But as a general rule, *human beings act according to their perceptions, not according to veridicality*. From that insight it follows that it is not veridicality that kills individuals and cultural traditions, but the conditioned inaccuracy of their perceptions of it.

"Let's see if I got it," you may interrupt. "All reality is based on assumptions, but all assumptions aren't equal because if I bet on the wrong one, veridicality can kill me. However, I can't know veridicality. So what good is it?"

Well, yes, that's about it. Except that we can roughly measure the odds that a particular datum or assumption is veridical, and our measurements are getting better all the time. Scientific statements are probability statements, and the probability in question always concerns how certain you can be that the conclusion arrived at does indeed reflect the actual conditions in the universe.

Face it: a lot of your life has never been tested for probability. For example, according to your own culture's reality, an ever-expanding economy will employ everybody, and happy consumers will raise happy children under the benevolent leadership of people so rich that they cannot even imagine the struggles of the poor. This sort of wishful thinking has occurred often before, even in preliterate societies. During the Great Depression many people sincerely believed that if we all just played enough miniature golf on each other's courses, the economy would right itself.

An earlier version of today's brand of lunacy occurred in seventeenth-century Holland; we now remember that as the Tulip Mania. It began in the 1630s when a virus genetically altered some bulbs that the flower-loving Dutch had imported from Turkey. These mutated tulips had a vastly greater range of colors and patterns than the original stock, and therefore became expensive. Bulbs increase in number when planted, so they were a good investment—up to a point. At the height of the folly, in 1637, prices increased twenty-fold in February alone, and a single celebrated bulb, the Semper Augustus, sold for an all-time record of $60,000 in today's money. Then, in the next three months, the tulip market lost 95 percent of its value. A century later, Semper Augustus bulbs went for 50 cents apiece. (Does this tell you something about the stock market?)

By all indications the capitalist happy talk of the year 2000 was no more veridical than the communist promise of the triumph of the working class, but it did serve to give the rich a far larger share of the communal American pie at the cost of the rest of us.

The question you should therefore ask is not "Will the American economy be able to dodge veridicality until I get mine?" but "Will America still be possible if we ignore veridicality any longer?"

But that gets us into another topic.

Thinking It Through

1. Why are preindustrial cultures and old people so conservative?
2. Can you contrast magic and the scientific method concerning medicine and disease?
3. Why does the introduction of any new trait designed to benefit only the few cause resentment and jealousy in the rest? Is this something that advertising agencies have to consider? Or does it only apply to things that give one an advantage?
4. In societies that brutalize women or that limit their opportunities far more than men's, it is nevertheless women who raise the children to accept these conditions as "natural." Why is it so often the oppressed themselves who perpetuate the habits and ideologies of oppression?
5. Can you distinguish between ideology, ideation, religion, magic, science, perception, reality and veridicality?

A Reason to Live Worth Dying For

Believing

"There are only two ways to live your life. One is as though nothing is a miracle. The other is as though everything is a miracle."

—Albert Einstein (1879–1955)

"The idea that there is one people in possession of the truth, one answer to the world's ills or one solution to humanity's needs, has done untold harm throughout history."

—Kofi Annan (1938–)

*The assumptions and values that
underlie knowledge and belief and
thereby determine human behavior
belong to an aspect of culture that until
recently only philosophers dared tackle.
The sciences concentrate on the objective,
material universe and shun the inherent
ambiguities and willful subjectivities of
religions and ideologies. The investigation
and analysis of the thousands of belief and
value systems in the world thus awaited
the founding of cultural anthropology.*

*a*ll of culture is based on the human capacity for communication, but the most nearly seamless connection is that between language and ideas. Beyond its most basic level of monkey-see-monkey-do imitation, technology requires symboling to understand, teach and learn, and for imagining improvements and alternatives. The same is true for organization: the structure of every society and its institutions is based on assumptions and decisions about roles and relationships, none of which is self-evident, all of which must be taught or inferred. But nothing in culture is more a matter of words than the shimmering patterns of conjecture and idealism that societies have constructed to explain the inexplicable, to validate the inexcusable and to reassure the inconsolable.

Knowledge itself is stored in words and other symbols.

Human beings grow up asking questions, and many of those (check the nearest kid) turn out to be unanswerable. You too have already had all sorts of questions for which your culture supplied no rational replies. Some of those you would have asked no matter what age or place you were born to, like the questions of being and becoming *(Who and what am I? Why am I here? What can I, what should I become?)*, the questions of sexual awakening *(Whom shall I sleep with, live with, commit to?)*, and the questions of mortality and survival *(What are the odds against me? How much do I have to put up with? When should I fold? Why me?)*. Others you asked specifically because you live in a mass society. Those were likely to be questions of politics, business and religion *(Whom or what can I believe in when everyone is lying?)* or questions of inequality, injustice and misfortune *(Why all this unfairness? Why do bad things happen to good people?)*.

No culture can satisfy such questions in the same way that it tells you how to do things or what things are named, because there is no "knowledge" about them. For tens of thousands of generations no one ever came back from the dead to tell us what lay beyond the Final Sleep; no one knew what caused disease and other misfortunes. Even today (*especially* today, some would insist), when we understand about germs and have all seen in a hundred TV shows how electric paddles applied to the chest shock people back to life, we still ask the universal questions for which knowledge has no answers.

STORIES

The human mind doesn't stop working just because it lacks veridical information. We are a storytelling species. Language makes it possible for us to juggle facts and fictions, and whatever is possible, we do that. As soon as children learn to talk, they learn to imagine, making up imaginary situations ("scenarios" we'd call those if children were adults) with imaginary beings doing imaginary things, and they'll happily share these stories if you let them. At the same time that children learn to fantasize, they learn to lie. It takes some doing on the part of adults to teach them the difference between truth and lies and that Mommy and Daddy respond better to one than the other. Lies, too, are stories.

Your mind is designed so that it can make up stories to fit any veridicality it encounters. Whenever a question was important enough, someone—hence the culture—has made up answers if no "knowledge" answer was available. When those satisfy your need to know, you'll accept them as if they were knowledge answers, but they are not; they are "belief" answers. They delineate your reality.

All answers begin as potential belief answers. Any hypothesis, any statement of possible relationships among phenomena, any sudden insight first has to be a statement of possibility, not probability: "Maybe what that bandersnatch is doing with that arkedul is like me milking a cow." If things would make sense if it were so, then there is your possible belief answer.

It is in the process of changing your evaluation from possibility to probability that knowledge or belief is created—and it is here that the scientific method has become so important in furthering culture. If you have compelling supportive evidence that can be tested by others, you have knowledge—right or wrong. If you lack objective and verifiable evidence, yet feel your faith in the likelihood of your insight grow stronger, you're experiencing belief.

To explain either result, you tell a story.

In that sense, theories are knowledge stories, stories tested for their veridical content, stories with a verifiably high probability content, but stories nevertheless. In that same sense, religious scriptures are belief stories, stories that are untestable for veridicality and therefore for probability, but stories that nevertheless satisfy the human need for a coherent reality. There are other kinds of stories, from polite little lies to novels to political ideologies, each with their own purposes and validations, but we won't bother with those here.

No defensible boundary separates knowledge from belief because, although you can know some things, that very knowledge is based on supposition, on things you take on faith but cannot know with absolute certainty. Even natural science is based on assumptions, including at least the following:

- The cosmos operates by rules that are not arbitrary and do not change capriciously.
- The entire universe operates according to the rules observed in our corner of it.
- We can learn the rules if we ask the right questions in the right ways.
- It is better to know than to be ignorant.

Plausibility

There is no way to ascertain whether any of these postulates are veridical, but scientists firmly *believe* in them, and so far they seem to work better than anything else available—well enough to have brought six billion of us to the Third Millennium. Veridicality remains forever unknowable; the best we can do is make theory approximate it ever more closely. In that sense, it is necessary to admit that all stories are based on assumptions. *But that does not mean that therefore any story is as good as any other.*

True theory is a story that explains how phenomena are interrelated and how some aspect of the universe therefore actually operates. For a theory to be sound, each step in the process of compiling and analyzing its information has been checked and verified, from the original observation through confirmation of the interactive processes to the story's predictive powers and its fit with other theories. In other words, *for a story to become accepted theory, the probability must be very high that it closely approximates veridicality, and it must not be contradicted by equally valid evidence and reasoning elsewhere.*

We humans are probably the only creatures who can satisfy our curiosity without actual data, because language lets us imagine scenarios and believe (in) them just as fervently as if they were factual. Wherever we need to know but cannot, that storytelling capacity comes into play to create imaginary answers, guidelines, and explanations: belief stories.

The most dangerous area for individuals in all of thought is the frontier between knowing and believing. Often knowledge is claimed where only belief operates; equally often, baseless beliefs are perpetuated long after the facts are in and understood. On the one hand, you don't *need* to understand something in order to use it; hasn't sexuality proven that? On the other hand, factual evidence is *usually* enough to change assumptions about how the physical universe operates.

But remember Galileo.

Astronomy is a topic that doesn't make people foam at the mouth anymore, but it certainly used to, until the competition between belief and knowledge in that terrain was settled. In the span of time that humans have thought about the stars, however, that was only a brief interlude.

When Oma and Opa Backpacker stared at the sky, they saw the same stars Einstein did. If they wanted to believe that stars are the distant campfires of the dead or that the moon is the eye of the First Mother, those were harmless but untestable propositions, and as stories they answered their questions well enough. I suspect that when clever animals like monkeys look up at night, they may also dimly wonder about all the little lights above them but, lacking language, they probably create no explanations. Oma and Opa Backpacker were no more knowledgeable about astronomy than a chimpanzee, but they could tell stories. Later, when Einstein looked at the sky, he saw it from a vastly more complex cultural base than theirs. The majority of things that Oma and Opa had only belief stories for, Einstein's culture had covered with knowledge stories.

Einstein's genius lay in his ability to integrate what was actually known and to reason from there into a breathtakingly comprehensive story about the birth, workings and death of the universe. What rates his particular story "genius caliber" is that he was able to tell it in testable hypotheses of such clarity that even today, long after his death, scientists still seek and find confirmation of the implications of his insight. The universe evolves, we now know; evolution is as undeniable as the existence of the sun or of Opa Backpacker's death.

There are people who refuse to sort through the conflicting stories of science and faith to see which serve best where. They would rather believe than understand. They insist on their right to deny knowledge stories—like evolution—without a shred of contrary evidence. When they say they do not believe in evolution, they refute it on the basis of unconquerable ignorance. They will not accept mere scientific evidence if it contradicts their beliefs, for to do so would collapse the explanatory support structure of the world as they understand it.

That is certainly a valid argument: as a general rule, the more you know, the less you will believe. Moreover, as the Bible says,

"In much wisdom is much grief, and he who acquires great knowledge acquires great sorrow" (Ecclesiastes 1:18). Anyone has the right to accept the story that the moon is made of green cheese or that the world was spontaneously created in 4004 B.C. But beliefs are systematized, and any belief system that makes its adherents deny fundamental scientific findings will also keep them from functioning as equals in the modern world.

Plausibility is in the mind of the beholder, but it is also measurable. In light of possibilities and probabilities and the ultimate iffy-ness of assumptions, you have the right to believe whatever you want, and I have successfully defended that right. But if in your mind the green cheese story is as valid as modern astronomy's view of our satellite, you may have a problem that reading books is not going to solve.

There is no easy solution to the problem of how to decide which sort of story to buy into—or why you should decide. You know how you know. But *why* do you *believe*?

The Burden of Mortality

Parents die. Children disappoint. Lovers leave. Leaders betray. Bodies fail. The grave yawns, waiting.

Knowledge is simply not enough.

One cost of being human is having to anticipate death. Most animals apparently don't. Until the moment their lives are actually being snuffed, they fully expect to outrun their destiny today as they did yesterday. But *you* have knowledge and foresight, words and memories. *You* can remember lying awake in a cold sweat from the paralyzing realization that sometime—maybe not this night, but some inexorable *some*time—you must die.

That recollection, which you share with almost everyone who ever lived past childhood, makes you characteristically human.

When you get past the terror of not-being, what probably galls you most about being mortal is the further realization that when you pack it in, everything will go on as if you had never been, as if you never counted, as if your existence meant no more to the universe than your shadow's. At some time, surely, you must have wondered: if life is meaningless (because death snatches the good as well as the evil) and also hard (as *subjectively* it may be for any of us, no matter how fortunate our supply of the Four Ps), why bother? Why not live only for pleasure until even that palls? Why not end it now and end the insecurity?

Must your only honest answer be: "Because I fear death?"

No, of course not. You are a member of a societal species: you have commitments to others, to relatives and friends, to comrade and partner, spouse and child, mentor and disciple—you cannot allow yourself to be the sort of person who would just quit and desert them all! You only need some reason, some good and sound reason why you should go on.

And culture eagerly supplies you with just what you need to refute meaninglessness: Goals. Values. Faith. Ideology.

Stories.

Does that mean that belief is *only* a hypothetical construct, like the "aether" that less than a century ago "explained" how radio works, or like the equally imaginary "phlogiston," which was invoked to define why fire burns? Is faith merely a necessary but arbitrary intellectual fudge factor, enabling society to explain and operate aspects of the universe it cannot understand yet?

Not necessarily. Your backpacking ancestors weren't expected to drudge their lives away in hollow, monotonous tasks for uncaring employers—and yet they, too, believed. Probably not in the same things you do, but they did believe in *some*thing. So what do you have in common with those people that can explain this shared penchant for believing unverifiable stories?

You, like them, were born cultureless, innocent, ignorant—but I repeat myself. Even before you understood that you cannot know it all, cannot do it all, and cannot have it all, you were obligated to commit yourself to socially approved roles. As a child you longed to be Big, because adulthood (so it then seemed) confers Freedom, which you conceived of as the right to do things children aren't allowed to do (Privilege), as not having to obey but making your own decisions (Power), as being able to keep others from messing with your stuff (Property), and as having fun your own way (Pleasure). But long before you reached your full growth, society hijacked Freedom from you by drafting you into schools or armies or dead-end jobs, by holding you responsible for the results of your actions (including your babies), blocking your access to the goodies of life, and in general making you long for the infantile security of being taken care of again.

So here you are, enmeshed in the expectations of others, working like some draft animal in the traces of society's cart, wondering if that's all there is. Freedom turns out to be only a carrot dangled in front of your nose: right there, always just out of reach. Survival demands that you keep lurching after the carrot, for when you tire of straining after it, you soon learn about the stick. Everything works smoother if you believe that you will eventually get to munch Freedom, if not in this life then surely in the next one that you hope—no, you must *believe!*—will follow. Because if it doesn't, pulling the damned cart wouldn't make any sense at all.

But you are more than a draft animal, you're a human being; your natural curiosity transcends that of donkeys. Every animal mentally maps its environment to the best of its abilities; it is obvious why. But you want more than simply knowing where things are. You want things to make sense and to have meaning.

Why do you have this need to impose order on nature and on yourself? Because you wonder if you aren't somebody's patsy for pulling the cart? Because you cannot stand the insecurity of not knowing when the ax will fall? Because you want to be assured that when it does, there is a good and sufficient reason for it? Because you want to be able to hope that you'll survive the ax?

That brings up the flip side of belief. You are needed not only for society to exist; it needs your willingness to assure its continuation—at the cost of your own life, if necessary. In the concise phrase of Martin Luther King Jr.: "A man who won't die for something is not fit to live." Every society teaches you stories about good deaths, noble deaths, deaths to be imitated: "If I am to die, let me die well." Mostly those are stories about men, but remember why: males have always been expendable. Until very recently everywhere, the most common cause of death was that of women in childbirth.

We have always needed reasons to live; we have always needed reasons to die. Culture supplies you with both in abundance.

Meaning

Meaning is that aspect of a phenomenon or thing that establishes its significance, its purpose, reason, or intent. Meaning is the answer to your "Why?" and "What's it for?" questions.

Meaning is as necessary to you as food and rest and respect.

The people who raised you knew that. That's why the culture they gave you came complete with a lot of knowledge that was specific only to your people at that time: ancient wisdom—much of it no doubt accumulated at great expense in human suffering—expressed in legend and aphorism, in myth and allegory. Stories so thrilling that they have not been forgotten as tastes changed over the generations; stories so universal that they retained meaning no matter how culture evolved.

For most of humanity's existence, all knowledge was magico-religious in the sense that, although much of it was necessarily practical, the cause-and-effect explanations for it were untested and often arbitrary. Even today, certain kinds of problems cannot be addressed scientifically because they are not "meaningful" in the scientific sense; that is, they cannot be formulated into testable hypotheses, they are not "falsifiable."

Ironically, inquiries about meaning are themselves not meaningful in the scientific sense. Unfortunately, that covers some of the most important questions you may have about the cosmos and your place in it. So *the fact that a statement is not scientifically meaningful certainly does not mean that it is meaningless.* One sad bit of evidence: In the twentieth century many more millions were butchered for scientifically nonmeaningful reasons (for belief stories) than over incontrovertible facts.

Still, the mind will work on questions that have no answers.

Comes culture to the rescue. Every society uses belief stories to define and defend its organization and the inequalities and injustices that flow from it. If words can create culture, words can destroy it. So society must have answers for all the questions and challenges posed by those whom Chance has permanently handicapped in accessing the Four Ps. Where society *lacks* answers, it invents rationales for silencing the challengers.

Values

People create (and cultures perpetuate) all sorts of guidelines for assessing the relative importance of things. These include stock answers for important questions, answers that are impossible to check (which doesn't make them wrong, of course, but certainly doesn't prove them right); answers to questions of precedence, of origin, of meaning, of purpose; answers about inequality and injustice, cruelty and greed; about accountability and responsibility, honor and dignity and anything else that might interest them, or you.

Values are locally unquestioned standards about relative importance or desirability, and how people should therefore act. Common values include such cultural attitudes as the sanctity of life (is killing and/or suicide permitted?); honesty and fairness in dealing with others (how to deal with kinfolk, with nonkin Us, with servants, superiors, strangers?); industriousness (is work a duty, a curse, or an opportunity?); courage (is it to be demonstrated only in battle or in any risk situation? Is cowardice ever acceptable?); competitiveness, greed, and so forth.

Values tell you what to submit to and what to resist, how to treat your friends and fight your enemies, how to live right, how to die well. They teach you about wealth and power, about honesty, love and trust, about building and destroying. Cross-culturally, any value exhibits a range of characteristics: the reaction to strangers, for example, may vary from paranoid to welcoming. But whichever preference is locally demonstrated, it ties in with that culture's expression of other assumptions: values tend to be part of a coherent idea system, both in society and in your personality.

Well-functioning value systems are always hierarchical, meaning that some values take precedence. Everything simply cannot be of equal importance. Some things must be more basic or pressing or momentous than others, and every culture instills those into its carriers as its referents. These are the postulates that determine its *goals—what individuals and groups will work toward*, and its *means—the acceptable roads to goals*.

Naturally, cultures disagree about which assumptions should constitute a decent person's values. What characteristics define the Good Man, the Good Woman, the Good Life? There appear to be few culture traits that no one has hung a value on—consider the collector craze, which seems to imply that "if anyone has ever noticed it, it has value."

Cultured life is therefore a life based on value *judgments*, and individual and group efforts are value driven. Although at one level shared values serve to integrate culture, at another level even *shared* values may be internally contradictory and thereby offer competing groups an opportunity to interpret or prioritize them differently so as to distinguish themselves from each other. Think of all the ways the Bible and the Qur'an have been interpreted, and how these variations have led to all the separate denominations within in Christianity and Islam—and to all the bloodbaths of the past, the present and, inevitably, your future.

Culture manipulates you by biasing your perception of your alternatives with values and backing those values with *sanctions— punishments and rewards*. Any normally socialized individual knows the difference between allowed and forbidden means and knows that if he or she is caught using the wrong ones to get a desired result, there will be unpleasant consequences. You are also expected to share (read "believe") the basic hierarchy of values of your society, so that when you have a value conflict, you will know which one trumps. Because value assumptions bias every decision you make, you cannot actually be free, but it is nice for you to think you are.

Values beget other values, which beget still more until everything you touch and think is permeated with implications that at heart are purely arbitrary, even when and if they are logically consistent. Cultural cautioning about how to live begets statements about how to be a good person, which beget admonitions about how to behave in public, which beget detailed regulations about how to walk and talk and sit and dress.

Modesty has an immense range of expressions that in most places involves keeping the genitals covered in public. But did you ever see a penis sheath? In some remote sectors of the New Guinea Highlands it is still customary for men to ensconce their penis and scrotum in a dried gourd. Some of these caricatures of permanent erections are so long that their tips need support from a string that goes around the proud wearer's neck. European men in the Middle Ages wore so-called codpieces, brightly decorated bags or flaps sown where trousers now have flies, which similarly called attention to the male's primary sexual characteristic. But for the ultimate expression of the relativity of modesty you cannot beat today's beach attire for women: may I refer you to the thong? Compare that to the Islamic chador, a shapeless garment that covers a woman from crown to foot, leaving only her eyes visible.

Across time and space, human beings have valued an infinitude of objects and ideas. The one thing all these beliefs have in common is that they were designed to make it possible for people to play the game of life as its rules were locally defined. From that perspective, nothing has changed.

From another, everything has. People believe because they *have* to, if their world is to be inhabitable in the ways they've been raised to aspire to live. As long as enough of them can continue to believe the stories their culture teaches, its reality will remain functional and life will be meaningful and satisfying because their universe operates as they think it does.

IDEOLOGY

It is obvious that individuals always have used and will continue to use things and ideas that they are incapable of explaining in any rational, scientific sense: I refer you to the fact that most people drive cars without ever looking under the hood because what they find there would mean nothing to them, and that they operate electronic devices without a clue as to what processes make them go—or refuse to. Nevertheless, there are occasions when even the ignorant are forced to attempt explanations, as when a child demands to know "Why?" and won't accept "I don't know" as a response, or when a specialist must defend an assumption in order for her proposal to be considered for funding.

Cultures, too, are posed questions for which they have no answers. The most dangerous ones are those that challenge the local definition of reality. Unlike people, cultures cannot say "I don't know." When a problem is raised for which no response exists, a culture must either reexamine its premises, come up with a new story that doesn't invalidate every other story in its repertory, or risk losing its carriers, its people. Small-scale societies cannot afford the third alternative. Every society avoids the first one at all cost, for once that can of worms is opened, it may never be closed again: to challenge an axiom (a basic assumption) is to nullify its conclusions, that is, the status quo.

That leaves the second. Every culture incorporates a general system of values and beliefs to explain the universe and guide its members through life. "Without a vision, the people perish" (Proverbs 29:18). Any systematic effort to define, explain, and (re)interpret "Reality" so as to define goals and means and to demand action is an ideological exercise. *Ideology is the "apologetic" branch of culture,* that area of thought that actively concerns itself with the establishment and defense of patterns of value and belief. *Ideology is what legitimates and integrates society's institutions.* We may thus define ideology as "the system of perceptions and assumptions (about self, society and the universe) that determines the goals and means of a society and therefore includes all its considerations of value, morality, law, science and belief.

You've already read that one prerequisite for society is a division of labor into performers and managers and that no particular advantage *need* accrue to the latter. But usually it does, or the insufferable unfairness of hereditary inequality could not have evolved. Since the people who run societies cannot survive unless they understand this, they always need to make the performers, the workers-peasants-taxpayers, accept the status quo as a given. The most efficient and least costly way to achieve that goal is to convince you, the performers, that the way the world is organized is due to divine design, immutable and unarguable, and that Divine Will has ordained that you pull the cart and they hold the reins. Of course this approach works best if you never learn enough about alternatives to be able to question the assumptions. (Which should give you some insight into the reasons for the state of education in your area.)

Ideologies can be either sacred (supernaturally based) or secular (law and logic based). Before the advent of science, ideology and religion were interchangeable concepts, because then *every* explanation and interpretation of the universe was based on supernatural assumptions. For billions of people, that remains true.

One universal characteristic of ideologies is that their ultimate justification is always a referent or authority who cannot be questioned, usually because he is dead. In preliterate societies the unquestionable sources are usually the deceased and the supernaturals. Although certain individuals manage to contact such entities through spiritual means such as divination and possession, they would not normally question basic assumptions. In literate societies, the will of the supernaturals is manifested in Holy

Writ: the Jews' Torah, the Christians' Bible, the Muhammadans' Qur'an, the Hindus' Veda.

Secular ideologies, because they evolved more recently and always in civilizations, use written records to legitimate themselves. Humanists and atheists are generally not organized into nations, and although they have their literatures, they profess no unchallengeable sources—perhaps because doing so would invalidate their most basic tenet. But the twentieth century's secular totalitarian regimes very much did insist that their intellectual founders were above question. In Communist Russia, the writings of Karl Marx, Friedrich Engels and V. I. Lenin functionally became Holy Writ. China made Mao Tse-tung's writings superior even to those. In Germany, the excesses of Nazism were legitimated by Hitler's *Mein Kampf.* The principle holds for all the other totalitarianisms that have plagued the twentieth century, from Albania's Enver Hoxha's to Cambodia's Pol Pot's.

Modern nations are all based on legal ideologies called constitutions, not all of which are written down (Great Britain's, for example, is not). The Constitution of the United States is one of the most elegant and moving political documents, designed to lift the human spirit and instill hope and dignity. In spite of its unparalleled status as the ultimate, unchallengeable authority in the United States, it is nevertheless an artifact of a particular time and place. As such it remains the main defense for rationales legitimating human exploitation and inequality. Most of the social advances in the United States grew from changes (amendments) to and reinterpretations of the Constitution. No one really knows what would happen if this document were ever to be successfully challenged. That is why there is so much opposition to the idea of holding a constitutional convention, even though knowledgeable citizens generally realize that some assumptions underlying the present Constitution are making life increasingly difficult for everyone except lawyers.

RELIGION

Writing about religion is a touchy problem, just as talking about it with strangers is. People get offended, often justifiably. The reason it's so easy to offend should be pretty obvious: if you don't know what my assumptions are and I don't know yours, we are in a sense speaking in different codes. But people usually don't realize this, because they've been conditioned to believe that as long as they are speaking the same language, what they mean with their words has the same meaning for everybody else. In fact, that isn't even true for stuff you can touch. Surely the intellectual imagery in which nonmaterial culture is expressed is more easily misinterpreted than nuts and bolts!

Religion expresses the distilled wisdom of a people, explaining how life and humanity originated, how the ancestors came to this place, and why life should be lived by certain standards. Once a basic discovery or insight has been made (once a Great Truth has been revealed), it needs to be expressed in terms and a context that will be meaningful to all those who hear of it; otherwise it will not be incorporated into the culture. This is why religion's stories, its myths and allegories, are woven so carefully, why their exact words are memorized and revered.

Any traditional religion has proven by its endurance that it can satisfy all the psychological needs people develop—as long as it remains within its original cultural context. That amending caution is there to let you know how every established religion manages to be simultaneously self-evident and wildly implausible. When seen from the outside by people who did not grow up with the fundamental assumptions upon which your religion is based, it is necessarily incomprehensible and may look absurd, like mine or anyone else's.

Say that as a college student you room with three others of your sex and that each of you belongs to a different religion. The four of you inevitably get into a discussion in which each of you—the Catholic, the Hindu, the Mormon, and the Muslim—explains some sacred assumptions underlying his respective worldviews. Since you are all tolerant and intelligent individuals, each of you can follow the logic and the implications of the others' theologies—but only up to a point. Beyond that, each of you may suddenly feel that you don't really know the other people, that the assumptions they take for granted are crazy—and you know how dangerous crazy people can be.

Believers handle such dissonances in various ways, ranging from viewing every alternative to their own beliefs as sinful error, to recognizing that there may be an infinite number of facets to Truth and that each religion presents a particular culture's contributing perspective.

Nonbelievers usually explain their particular psychological posture as the inevitable outgrowth of their recognition that the religious assumptions of other societies can be hilarious or dangerous or both, but never believable. From there is it but a small step to looking objectively at their own people's sacred precepts and to recognizing those as no more defensible than any others.

Again, there is no way to prove or disprove either position. Let it suffice here to note that since denial of supernaturalism is usually the result of intense but private thought, there are probably as many ways to be an atheist as to be religious.

But let's say that you and your roommates stay together for many years, that you eventually drag your spouses into the group, that you all keep talking and comparing and thinking things through, that you become a microcosm of America. You can see how over time your kids would believe in a mixture of the things that you four originals thought it important to keep apart. In just that way, continuous contact leads to religious evolution.

And therefore to religious differentiation. All those religions, all those beliefs, all those denials.

So which one of them is right?

That *is* the question, isn't it? Where should you place your bet in the roulette game called Life? All those cultures, all those perspectives, all those intelligent, sincere people without a shred of awareness of most of the forces that operate on and through them, all of them desperately trying to make sense out of things: Why death? Why inequality, cruelty, injustice, exploitation, misery, illness, misfortune?

Are faith and science necessarily incompatible? Will exposure to rational thought shrivel your religious convictions with all the eternal punishments thereunto appertaining?

You need not worry, unless you are convinced that you are not capable of translating alternative perspectives on What Is into the language of your own belief system without rupturing it. Knowledge and understanding are no threat to any adaptive value system, be it sacred or secular, private or communal. And if you weren't adaptation-oriented, you wouldn't be reading this. Go outside the box of your culture and its confinements of language and imagination. There, past your beliefs and your fears, beyond the realm of theories and facts, lies veridicality, the actual IS of everything in its infinities of alternatives—heedless of what you know and what you believe.

Judaism, Christianity and Islam, Hinduism and Buddhism, Communism and Capitalism, Animism and Zoroastrianism and myriad other belief systems past and present with their innumerable sects and subdivisions have each proven to be totally convincing to babies, and each would be so to you if only you had been raised to accept the premises it reasons from. But they are not veridical, neither individually nor collectively. Veridicality contains all of their perspectives the way a beach contains grains of sand: no two identical, not one sufficient to explain the history of the beach, let alone the action of the tides or the complexity of the world beyond the beach in any direction. Veridicality simply IS, regardless of points of view, and it is not static, because the universe evolves.

"Is veridicality then only another word for God?"

If you like, for then God would be, as most religions profess, both simple and complex beyond humanity's crude imagining.

But unlike the God or gods you are familiar with, veridicality does not require worship or ritual—unless you feel the need to think of science as a search for veridicality, and research protocols as its ritual.

"So what should I make of veridicality?"

As has been suggested under different circumstances by a sitting president of the United States: It all depends on what IS is—to *you*.

A Definition

All sacred ideologies are usually called religions, which in no way illuminates the concept because there are aspects to belief that not all religions share. For example, the idea of an afterlife is not universal, and neither are those of a single creator-god or of salvation. Anthropologists have found themselves unable to agree on a definition of religion, perhaps because, like culture itself, religion shows different attributes depending on which of its facets is being examined. (Remember the "liquid-filled bag with two air bubbles"? Definitions can only be judged by their usefulness.)

Sir Edward Burnett Tylor in 1871 defined religion as "belief in supernatural beings," but there are atheistic forms of Buddhism, and it is impossible to distinguish in any substantive sense between belief in supernaturals and belief in natural phenomena that are beyond your culture's understanding. Later anthropological thinkers attempted to redefine religion by focusing on its functions in ameliorating suffering and stress, on its personal role in defining reality, or its societal role in constantly working and reworking the basic contradictions evident in everyday life. All of these are intrinsically illuminating, but none by itself adequately describes and defines the topic.

For our purposes here, *religion is a systematic explanation of the relationship among the individual, society and the environment, which legitimates itself by reference to unchallengeable supernatural authority.*

Origins

Similar problems exist in establishing religion's antiquity. It is impossible to determine when religiosity began because evidence for belief doesn't outlast the believers.

The Neanderthals, an extinct branch of humanity that lived over much of the Old World from roughly 100,000 to 40,000 years ago, painted their dead before burying them—indicating belief in some sort of afterlife and therefore of religiosity. They were replaced during the last Ice Age by people we call the Cro-Magnon, who were anatomically identical to ourselves. Debate continues on whether there was any gene sharing between the two populations. Between 25,000 and 12,000 years ago, these Paleolithic people painted elegant pictures of horses, bison, and other animals in the deep limestone caves of northern Spain, south-central France, and elsewhere. They also left numerous engraved bits of bone and small carvings of stylized fat female figures that are usually interpreted as having ritual significance, whatever that means.

Religion, in short, seems to have been with us "always."

However, there are (and may always have been) individuals who do not accept their culture's supernatural claims, who do not and perhaps *cannot* believe—no matter how many different religious systems they examine. There may even be some irreducible personality factor at work here: I've heard thoughtful, educated people exclaim that they "lack the gene for religion." Perhaps nonbelievers can (or are willing to) understand only in the knowledge-story sense; perhaps they simply find it impossible to accept unquestionable sources. Whatever the explanation, either these individuals are not adequately enculturated, or the need for supernatural legitimation is not universal. What we *can* agree on is that the vast majority of human beings have always accepted the idea of invisible, transcendental entities that manipulate or at least influence human welfare.

The Evolution of Religion

In hunting-and-gathering lifeways, religion is usually a personal affair between you and whatever manifestations of the supernatural your culture recognizes. Any insight or status you gain from your supernatural connection is not usually binding on others.

In tribal situations also, there are usually no full-time religious specialists to intervene between you and the divine. But because the economics of settled populations are so much more perilous than those of food collectors, there is much more social effort and consequence in religion, and your private religious experiences, such as spirit possession, take place in a societal context. To explain all the incomprehensibilities in nature, simple animism is replaced with polytheism, the worship of many gods.

As soon as the state evolves, however, religion falls into support of the hereditary inequality on which all stratification rests. It is not an accident that there are knights and bishops in the ancient game of chess: in European feudalism and all its descendants, the aristocracy and the Church were always in league. The firstborn son of an aristocrat inherits the title and the property, which doesn't leave the second son much unless (a) he goes into the Church (bishops are princes of the Church), (b) he wrests an estate and its title from the neighbors, or (c) he goes overseas to conquer strangers and set up shop.

This "Problem of the Second Son" has brought the world (among others) the Vikings, the Conquistadors, the Colonists and the Church. It has been that way everywhere that feudalism flowered: in African, American, and Asian civilizations as much as those of Europe. Adjusted for local differences in religion and organization, it is as true of traditional Japan and China as of the Aztec, Inca, Egyptian and West African empires.

Conversion from polytheism to monotheism requires people to accept the idea that a single explanation accounts for all the effects of nature and culture. Unless one is taught this notion from birth, it is not easy to accept, which explains why there are only four surviving monotheistic traditions: Judaism, Christianity, Islam and Sikhism.

Christianity and Islam each believes itself to be the only true faith. Both proselytize; both have been forcibly imposed on populations with different beliefs; both have routinely practiced ethnocide and sometimes genocide. There have been bloody wars between them in the past, and there may be further conflict in the future.

FUNCTIONS OF RELIGION

Science and religion serve distinct social and psychological functions. Both seek answers, but in different ways and for different purposes. Religion claims its answers are eternally valid; it changes them only when they are no longer believed. Science claims its answers are only provisional approximations of veridicality, to be refined as soon as its next question of the universe provides more pertinent data.

Precedents and Antecedents

One example of the conservatism of cultures is that, in their jurisprudences and theologies, the validity of a judgment or conclusion normally depends on its continuity with tradition, that is, on its logical progression from what was already known and done. If there is no precedence for some finding, then it cannot be accepted without overturning the status quo, that cart we're (supposedly) all pulling. In other words, societies everywhere (and probably everywhen) agree that it would be dangerously disruptive, and therefore "wrong," to go against precedent.

This observation grows naturally out of the human need to agree on basic perceptions so that people can share goals and means and get on with life. But the urge to dig deeper, to ask questions, outlasts our individual childhoods, and there can be few if any societies in which the nature of reality is taken for granted by everyone. In ministering to humanity's universal search for comprehension and predictability, cultures create the explanatory stories we call cosmologies.

For our purposes, *a cosmology is any systematized set of sacred or secular propositions concerning the nature of the universe or cosmos.* Cosmologies usually postulate the structure and function of the supernatural, natural and cultural world. Cosmologies always include beliefs about death. The range of cosmologies encountered in the anthropological record—from detailed, complex and internally consistent ideological compositions on one end, to incoherent, incomplete and often self-contradicting explanations at the other—apparently depends on differences in societies' and individuals' need for this type of explanation. The Russian physicist Lev Landau may have said it best: "Cosmologists are often wrong, but never in doubt."

Antecedents are important in cosmologies, too. We are this way now, but how and what were we before? How did it all start? Not just us, but people, the land, the world, the universe? And where will it all end? If I must anticipate my own death, and yours, will the world die, too? Cosmologies usually include a *cosmogony: any explanation of the origin of the world or universe.* As creation myths or theories, cosmogonies make up a crucial part of all sacred and most secular ideologies. In different times and places, peoples differ in their need for detail and evidence, and a few cultures integrate the lives of their individuals so deeply into the natural environment that people do not ask the eternal questions. But such circumstances are vanishingly rare, and for the rest of us, ideologies contain cosmogonies because any that do not are soon replaced by others that do. Many civilized cosmologies, like those of the Aztec and the Maya, taught that the world is destroyed periodically, and that only the extreme effort and sacrifice of human beings can keep the gods from thrashing it once again. That idea persists in Christian cosmogony, which teaches that the world was once destroyed with water and still faces its demise in fire—which may be a self-fulfilling prophecy.

Explanations, like definitions and theories, can be useful without being accurate—or even germane. Modern science, with its continuously updated version of veridicality, did not spring full-blown into existence just before you were born. It evolved from primitive tools and clumsy approximations into the instrumentality that now allows humans to do what a single lifetime ago were miracles only the gods could effect. Explanations need only be good enough for their purposes and audiences. The natural conservatism of cultures keeps them holding on to whatever is proven to work, and no aspect of culture is more conservative in that sense than its ideology. Belief is often your only protection against the chilling winds of veridicality.

One of the most provocative realizations you are likely to get from a broad exposure to the intellectual life of other cultures is that, though there may be atheists and agnostics everywhere (I *have* met them in foxholes and in jungle huts), there is no such thing as a nonreligious culture. Certainly there have, in the twentieth century, been societies that defiantly announced their godlessness; some even outlawed religion while treating their sitting rulers as incarnations of the divine. Such variants on the ancient god-king idea demand their own subcategory: "secular religion." But their existence underscores the real problem, which is: if every society practices supernaturalism in one form or another, what then is it that it *does* for a society?

For a group to have any cohesion at all, its members must share belief in something basic. Ethnic identity often centers on shared religious belief. For a multiethnic nation like the United States, that necessary shared belief cannot be religion—no matter how much the members of various faiths decry this fact and how correct they may be in believing that *if* Americans all had the same religion, life would be easier in some ways. There will never be agreement on which religion should be the Official State Church. But no problem. There is sufficient secular ideology to allow people with diverse religious views to agree on how to be Americans, even if they haven't yet.

Which brings up another question: would it be possible to create a society out of people from different ethnic backgrounds who did *not* share any significant secular ideology? Ethnicity always separates you from the rest of the world in an Us/Them dichotomy. Small-scale societies, especially tribes, are typically ethnic in that sense.

The answer is yes, but it is neither easy nor common.

"Stone Soup" Religion

A hobo tells his hungry buddies that he has a magic stone that makes soup out of water. He will share this soup with anyone who contributes to the pot. Soon each one throws in what edibles he has hoarded—a crust of bread, a dessicated piece of chicken, some dry rice, a potato, an onion—

and indeed, by sharing the stone soup they all eat better than they would have if each had stuck with his saved "emergency ration."

The ancestors of Suriname's Maroons had mostly been born in different African societies. When they escaped from slavery, they necessarily did so in the company of some men who had been their enemies in Africa. (The Dutch never hunted slaves themselves; they bought them from the many African nations that did. Recall that the Dutch would not let slaves who spoke the same language serve on the same plantation.) It is difficult to build a society out of men who are enemies. The fact that the runaways did not speak the same language except for their slave pidgin didn't help either. Moreover, they carried a huge variety of different belief systems with them into the South American jungle. They did, however, have a compelling motive to spur them into cooperation: the military expeditions that the planters sent to catch them.

So how did they get from there to today's six healthy, growing tribes?

The military patrols were generally failures: the tropics each time defeated the Dutch and their mercenary troops with hunger and disease, and runaways soon no longer needed to fear them. But the Maroons had their own hungers and hardships, and once the outside threat was gone, there must have been innumerable temptations to sort themselves into tribe-specific smaller groups. There is, however, no evidence that this ever happened. Perhaps the colonists had been so successful in keeping every plantation staffed with slaves from different tribal backgrounds that there were never enough people from any one African background—Ashanti, Ibo, Fulani, whatever—to unite into a social unit large enough to be viable.

Another major problem was the scarcity of women. Unlike the Americans, the Dutch never encouraged slaves to marry and beget more slaves; it was cheaper to buy workingmen fresh from Africa than to raise them locally. There were therefore never enough black women to go around, and the few imported as personal servants often lived comparatively better lives than the men and were not eager to try to survive the jungle without even the scant comforts of plantation existence. For decades, Maroons raided the outlying districts for women and such necessities as they could not procure otherwise.

The runaways appear to have solved their problem by creating what is perhaps the most syncretic religion in the preliterate—if not the entire—world. Whether consciously or as a by-product of intermarriage, they sifted together their polycultural heritage of general and specific beliefs into an intellectual patrimony for each tribe—and even each clan. Over the generations, this wealth of supernatural alternatives has made the members of these societies experts at using religion for virtually every purpose for which Americans turn to law and politics. Although each tribe has a distinct character in the way it "does" religion, all practice ancestor worship, divination and possession; all believe in witches and other supernatural evil-doers; and all believe in whole lists of divine pantheons under the ultimate control of a typically West African creator god. Most of these pantheons have unmistakably African origins, but some are clearly derived from Christianity, and there are even gods and other supernaturals that embody the might of the West India Company, which once owned Suriname and the plantations from which the ancestors fled. What makes it all so typically Afro-*American* is that the whole and its details were constructed and integrated in the South American rain forest.

In colonial days these syncretic belief systems were strong enough to deflect the incursions from missionaries, even when the latter were school-teachers operating as agents for the government. Although the smaller Maroon tribes are nominally Christian in that most of their members have been baptized Catholic or Protestant—and many in both churches; a Maroon can never have too many religious alternatives—they all still fear witches and practice magic and adhere to the prevailing ancestor worship. The two largest tribes deny being Christian, although some of their members are baptized.

In other words, using accidental collections of people from different ethnic backgrounds who did not share any significant secular ideology, Suriname's Maroon cultures managed to create viable, cohesive societies by assembling original, sacred ideologies out of these people's varied belief systems. ✎

Societal Functions

The two primary societal functions of religion are legitimation and integration.

Legitimation. This is the justification of society's nonreligious institutions, agencies and roles. Design problems exist in every society and will destroy it unless they are adequately explained to those affected. Probably the most important of these is inequality. Although in food-collecting societies this generally remained limited to the different treatment and aspirations of the sexes, boys and girls nevertheless had to be given a reason for it that they could not challenge. As cultures evolved into the modern world, inequalities have exploded in type and severity with hierarchies and offices, feudal estates, classes and castes, haves and have-nots. It became a major function of religions everywhere to oil the areas of friction in organized inequality. In the decades before the Civil War, Americans quoted the Bible to defend slavery in innumerable articles and arguments; in South Africa it took until the year 1986 for the Dutch Reformed Church to declare apartheid un-Christian. Every double standard is ultimately justified by supernatural edicts, and so are all hereditary inequalities, be they of power or property, prestige or pleasure.

"But," you may ask, "why not just replace these organizational dinosaurs when the people recognize them for what they are?" The answer is: because functional alternatives haven't yet been thought of, or thought through, or made acceptable. Hereditary inequalities are the basis for the structure of society, and though their victims despise them, those who benefit from them will defend them until something better can do their job, which is to make certain that everything that *needs* to get done for societal life *does* get done. And self-serving though any elite's justification must be, it has a valid core: simply burning down what you don't like does not guarantee that something better will take its place. On the contrary, each time you do, you waste irreplaceable resources. Recognize that most revolutions only supplant one dictator with another, at great cost in blood and property. So far, successful attempts to overthrow a *form* of government have been very rare indeed.

Integration. This term refers to the ongoing process compelling the aspects and agencies of a culture to work toward a common goal instead of the private benefit of their staffs. The integration of society was probably never a problem before people settled down to raise plants and animals. Until then, the family raised children and was the only agency through which culture and humanity survived. It fulfilled every economic, organizational, pedagogic, political, and religious function. But as culture evolved, all except the child-rearing functions were removed from the family and allowed to develop independently. That created opportunities for personal agendas and ambitions to splinter society: for example, those exercising the war-making function could easily overpower those in the political or economic sphere. Religion (and later, secular ideology) imposed the values and goals that still keep the distinct functions of culture integrated. This need, incidentally, is a major reason that religious specialization mushrooms as soon as a society becomes sedentary.

Psychological Functions

The benefits that *you* derive from religion are much more obvious. Fear of meaninglessness goads some individuals into striving mightily to prove that their existence *does* make a difference—and makes others withdraw into asylums, booze and drugs. For the rest of us, every culture explains why, even though death is inescapable, you should bother to live *its* way instead of some other. Religion compels you to believe that existence is better—or at least more meaningful—when you follow the rules and accept what authorities claim to be life's justification. There are indeed good and sufficient reasons (or so culture assures you) that you should spend your time on Earth being cooperative, instead of becoming dependent or predatory on those who are.

If your culture fails to convince you to believe and act on all those things, you'll become a problem to your society and probably to yourself. When any culture fails with enough individuals, then not enough of the things that *need* to be done *will* be done, and its society disintegrates. Without collective agreement there can be no purpose, no organization, no technology, no culture—no anything-you-take-for-granted. No Us.

It is thus no wonder that every society spends so much effort on getting its children to embrace *its* reality and that in spite of its obvious differences from neighboring cultures, yours is utterly sincere in claiming that your belief in its socioeconomic system and the supernatural assumptions that defend it is an absolute necessity.

Faith. When belief is unquestioning and systematized, we speak of faith. Psychologically, faith epitomizes the dependency on culture, while technology and organization must ultimately deal with concrete concerns, faith is a purely mental phenomenon: there is nothing in nature or genetics to base it on; its only foundation is belief. Yet faith is universal. We may not all believe in God, but we do all believe in some things for which we have no tangible evidence: the superiority of our own culture or people or political system, for example. Or progress, science, the perfectibility of humankind, democracy, and any number of other ideas. "Faith," someone once explained to me, "is truly believing in something you know is not true." You could define Faith as unquestioning confidence in an idea or phenomenon whose veridicality cannot be tested.

Faith gives you a reason to stop fearing death; faith gives you a reason to live nevertheless. It helps you deal with your own and others' mortality by assuring you that, for example, there is an existence after this one or that the dead are reborn into infants. It lends meaning to the life you lead here. It gives you reasons for your suffering: you are being tested; endure, and your steadfastness will be rewarded in ways that here, now, trapped in your fleshy envelope, you cannot begin to imagine. *Because* there is a point to life, hope can reasonably spring eternal.

Faith lets you live with inescapable insecurity. If you are a successful person, only you can know just how much luck was involved in your achievement of wealth and power. Why should you have been so fortunate when others, as good or better than you, are still dragging the cart? Culture offers explanations and justifications; believe them and you can live with success. If instead you are a failure (in your own eyes or those you gaze into), faith explains that and legitimizes you also: there is still time to improve, and it may be that the very fact of your lowly status here is evidence of the glory that awaits you after death.

Faith, in short, makes it possible for people to live with the stresses of interaction, interdependence, and inequality that accompany all societal life. It makes possible the whole range of human behavior from superhuman effort to perpetual drudgery, by convincing you to keep pulling the cart.

But mortality is not the only reason that you believe.

There is the insecurity involved in any decision you make.

Choice and alternatives. You cannot make decisions simply on the basis of facts. In the first place, if you have all the facts you need, then no decision is necessary; you simply do what you know is best. In the second, facts by themselves are meaningless. Facts are like bricks: you can build an outhouse with them or a Taj Mahal, but the structure is in the design, not in the material. Meaning is a structuring of facts in that sense, and your decisions require facts that have meaning.

Functionally, you face four categories of alternatives:

1. those you know;
2. those your culture knows but that you don't;
3. those your culture is not aware of; and
4. things that look like alternatives but aren't.

You have often been told that your decision can be no better than your information about your alternatives. But what determines the quality of your information?

Foremost, no doubt, your societal culture. It conditions your alternatives in two ways: by telling you what they are and by loading them with values. Had you been raised in a different culture, you would have had other alternatives, and those would have been differently valued.

Therefore next, equally certainly, is your personal culture.

As you learn more, you become aware of more choices. Still, there is no way for you ever to see all your alternatives, not even if you earned a Ph.D. in every discipline, because tomorrow each field will have unearthed new facts with new implications. You cannot possibly keep up; *there are always more veridical alternatives than perceived ones.*

Consequently no culture imaginable can prepare a Standard Operating Procedures manual to cover *every* situation you will encounter during your life. You'll find this increasingly obvious as the rate of culture change accelerates. It means that you *will* encounter the bandersnatch sooner or later, that you *will* be forced to make decisions for which nothing has prepared you, and that you will *not* have all the data necessary for making an *informed* choice. That must have been understood since before Oma and Opa Backpacker trudged out of Africa, for every culture gives you values, to guide you in situations its manual doesn't cover.

IDEOLOGY AS AGENT OF CHANGE

Secular ideology exists to adapt and redefine the status quo; sacred ideology traditionally stands in defense of it. In the decades between Word War II and the democratization of the 1980s, photographs of South American juntas always showed uniformed generals with grotesquely peaked caps standing on a balcony alongside some bemitered bishop—there to lend sacred legitimacy to the generals' regime.

During the early civil rights marches on the U.S. southern states in the 1960s, almost all the religious dignitaries in the protest movement were Negroes. But once the Supreme Court decided on a new interpretation of the law for the land, one which meant that black citizens had the same rights as white ones, that established a new status quo, and suddenly there were white faces in the front ranks of protest marches: rabbis, priests, ministers, pastors. (One thing that did not change when civil rights supposedly became universal was the second-class status of the female sex. When asked to define the position of women in his movement, a Black Panther spokesman in the 1960s answered succinctly: "Horizontal.")

Missions and Ethnocide

During the twentieth century, every known society was contacted by Western culture. Though a few blossomed from the experience, most were overwhelmed. Missionaries for God and for Profit denigrated local beliefs and customs. Guns and cars and television, tobacco, fast food and alcohol and, most of all, the world market for raw resources have stripped away the old cultures along with the ecologies they were part of. Change assaulted everything of value until belief itself became the last line of defense. Where the old gods died for want of worship, they lie entombed in vanished cultures.

Governments have often used missionaries (with or without their understanding) as agents of induced change. The recent Blackwater case in Canada is an example.

In 1998, the Canadian government officially apologized to the native peoples of Canada for the horrors they had been forced to endure at government-sponsored, church-run residential schools. Tens of thousands of native children had been sent there over the years, for the avowed purpose of assimilating the First Canadians by destroying their aboriginal cultures. Many children were sexually abused, most were physically mistreated, all were punished for speaking their mother tongues. The trial that caused the government to apologize exposed brutal beatings and the rape of children of both sexes by religious officials. In some "schools," the death rate exceeded 20 percent.

For nearly a century, similar outrages affected the Native Americans of the United States. Tribal children were forced into boarding schools, run by one religious group or another, where they were forbidden to speak their native languages or worship in their traditional fashions and were trained to become second-class citizens. Many blame that policy for the hopelessness and alcoholism that typify much of reservation life.

There is certainly nothing original in this use of religion.

In the colonial period, Europeans sent missionaries all over the world to spread the Gospel, that is, to take Christian precepts out of their cultural context and insert them into alien environments not designed to accommodate them. By no means were all these individuals fanatic destroyers of culture; much of what we know today about societies at the time of First Contact we owe to the careful observations and writings of missionaries. Nevertheless, the same Spaniards who described Aztec Mexico for future generations destroyed its temples and burned native believers at the stake. The people who brought us the Inquisition, still caring more about saving souls than lives, leaned over bridges to baptize boatloads of captured Africans being transported down the Congo River on their way to slavery in the Americas. Even in the twentieth century, colonial administrators still used evangelicals as their shock troops in converting native cultures into something more easily "governed" and taxed.

And they found plenty of volunteers. Although the major denominations' missions expected a lot more of their emissaries than burning faith and a willingness to suffer discomfort in the name of God, there were *(and still are)* sects that sent out individuals who conspicuously lack any understanding or appreciation of the culture in which they are to operate. These ethnocentrics have wreaked havoc on native populations, forbidding necessary rituals, damning men and women for adultery because they were married polygynously, destroying the ritual paraphernalia of the local belief system and thereby the social solidarity it served, and hurrying the disintegration of good-enough cultures. The best that an objective observer can say for aggressively proselytizing religions, whatever their dogma, is that they are not as destructive to industrialized, anomie-riddled societies and their marginal individuals as they are to preindustrialized lifeways and people.

Let me hurriedly dispel any implication that religious manipulation of native destinies is an exclusively Christian trait. There may be as many sects within Islam as in Christianity, and some of them are as fanatically devoted to converting the rest of the world as any Mormons or Southern Baptists. In Sudan, Arab followers of Muhammad believe themselves divinely justified to enslave the tribal black Christians and animists in the southern half of that nation, to capture young women and sell them into prostitution, to kill and to pillage, spreading the Word with fire and sword. And then there is Al Qaeda. . . . Gentler sects of Islam proselytize throughout Africa, with greater effect than Christianity does. Elsewhere Hindus drive out Muslims and convert tribal peoples in much the same way as Europeans have. It is characteristic of believers that their faith is strengthened when it is shared—as indeed is true for all of us on every topic based on assumptions.

To an anthropologist (and no doubt to a great many believers of every stripe), the most dangerous thing about the conservatism of faith is that it encourages aggression against those whose worldviews are based on different premises. Most of the 37 nations presently (2002) undergoing wars are fighting over religion. In Indonesia the fighting is between Muslims and Christians. Islamic Pakistanis and Hindu Indians are once more murdering each other and threatening war. The boil of the Middle East, where three of the four surviving monotheisms coexist badly, is again so inflamed that it threatens, at this writing, to be the most likely place for World War III to erupt.

These examples are not meant to imply that wars only grow out of the—apparently insoluble—divisions among fundamentally differentiated major belief systems like Christianity, Islam, Buddhism and Hinduism. Only a few years ago, Yugoslavia's Roman Catholics, Orthodox Catholics and Islamics—people of the same ethnicity and speaking the same language—killed each other as a matter of mutual pest control. Variations in interpretation of dogma within the major belief systems have always led to vicious wars: vide those of the Christian Reformation, and those between Shiite and Sunni Muslims. Meanwhile it appears that Ireland's Catholics and Protestants are doomed to hate each other forever.

Ideological Evolution

Of course change is a two-way street, and ideologies, both sacred and secular, themselves undergo change—some to mature and others to wither. When belief systems come into contact, they come into conflict, and today, with modern media and travel, contact is unavoidable. Consequently belief everywhere is now undergoing rapid change.

What is not changing is people's *need* to believe: we *must* have explanations; we must have our stories.

The crucial fact about belief is that it often works as well—and is as committing—when its content is totally arbitrary as when it is based on incontrovertible evidence. Consequently there are a lot of belief systems that, though they have no more validity than the Tooth Fairy or the Ever-Expanding Economy, are defended to the death by people whose personalities and worldviews depend on them.

But all ideologies, like any other aspect of culture, must eventually adapt their assumptions to the veridical universe. All belief systems change over time.

Two centuries ago, the Constitution of the United States was written by and for property-holding white men; it now applies to both sexes and all ethnicities, supposedly regardless of income. I was still a young man when Roman Catholics were told that eating meat on Friday, something always forbidden them as a venial sin, was suddenly okay and would no longer prolong their posthumous stay in purgatory. I was entering middle age when Mormons suddenly learned that black males could now achieve priesthood in the Church of Jesus Christ of Latter-Day Saints, something until then forbidden only to women and to men with African ancestry. Both Catholicism and Mormonism have handily survived their theological redirections, but now both have their hands full trying to keep women out of their priesthoods.

Which only proves, as women have always known, that the division between male and female goes far deeper than the chasm between black and white.

Thinking It Through

1. Most of the 50+ wars and civil wars presently going on involve the unquestionable assumptions of competing religions. Now consider the idea of "religion as an agent of culture change."

2. In religions that do not promise an afterlife, what compels people to behave like social beings, that is, to forego murder, rape, theft, etc.? Is that also why it is possible for someone without religion to lead a decent life, that is, one not based on exploiting or mistreating others?

3. Why are societies so rabidly defensive in areas of ideation? Do you see any problem in your own society that is illuminated by that realization?

4. Of all modern societies, that of the United States has (by far) the highest percentage of people who go to church or temple regularly. In most European nations (especially in those with a high standard of living) that percentage has been shrinking ever

since the end of the Second World War. Why hasn't this happened in the United States?

5. When belief systems come into contact, they come into conflict; yet a belief system can work as well when its content lacks data as when it is based on evidence that's incontrovertible even in outsiders' eyes. So why is there conflict then? Can you give some examples?

Futures and Alternatives
Cultural Trends

"What could societies achieve if they did things somewhat differently? How much do we still need to find
out in order to comment sensibly on alternatives?
What are the logical traps in setting them out?"

—Cyril S. Belshaw (1921–)

"We're entering into a new way of life, and we're just
as ignorant of this new environment as the Paleolithic
warrior was in his environment. I think we have to
accept risk in our lives. You cannot eliminate all risk
without being dead."

—Alvin Toffler (1928–)

*Your culture is metamorphosing:
once humanity's enabler, it is becoming
your keeper. Expect a more densely
packed world than you and your culture
were designed for, one in which there is
less of everything desirable to go around.
Already the smart money is taking steps to
ensure its own continued comforts:
inequality keeps increasing as wealth and
power—and control over information
about both—are concentrating into ever
fewer hands. You, meanwhile, get more
shows with laugh tracks.*

*Y*ou now live in a global economy, and you can travel the globe and never leave its nice new global culture. Everybody speaks English, and Big Mac is understood in places you've never even heard of. What can go wrong with your brave new world?

Only three interrelated things: the population bomb and its fallout—environmental collapse and terminal inequality. Like the Medusa in Greek mythology they are so scary that no one wants to look at them but, unlike the Medusa, they exist, so we must.

THE POPULATION BOMB

According to official U.N. estimates, one-half of all human beings, thus three billion people, are forced to survive on incomes of less than two dollars a day. Optimists point out that when populations become urbanized and achieve economic security, their fertility rates drop. And indeed, in many areas of the globe the fertility rate is starting to level off. But in most cases that is not because the locals have achieved middle-class nirvana, but because they have already run out of options in terms of space and resources. As the slums that make up much of the world's largest cities attest so graphically, urbanization does not guarantee economic security. What's worse, a decline in the rate of population increase does not mean a decrease: even if the entire world suddenly limited reproduction to replacement (one child per person), the human population would continue to double and redouble—albeit more slowly.

The tide of children welling up behind you is the single most important pressure for change in your physical environment. With ecological disasters of unimaginable proportions stalking its life raft, humanity now adds another 100 million more passengers every year. There are already three billion more people than the Earth can support; except for China (which enforces its one-child-per-couple policy with serious sanctions), no society has shown itself willing to come between people and their desire for babies.

But why do people *want* babies?

Some major reasons that people get married include sex, politics, love, economics, kinship obligation, security and personal competitiveness. No doubt there are dozens of others. Throughout history and across cultures, marriage has been a must if you wanted children without being ostracized for dooming your offspring to half the life chances a child with two families has.

Sure, a female can conceive and deliver without being married, but *all it takes to stay poor and dependent and exploited down the generations is for a woman to have one more child than she can raise alone.* Even women who are married when they have children may find themselves involuntarily ensuring the permanence of our underclass because one of every two American marriages ends in divorce.

That underclass is the indispensable basis for hierarchic, hereditary inequality. Without it, without people living on the streets or forced by their sense of parental responsibility to take the jobs no one wants, ruling elites would have had to give you better reasons than "You want to live like *them?*" for why you should pull the cart while the driver, who has never taken his turn, sits easy and whips you onward with threats of unemployment and homelessness.

From that perspective, producing children you cannot afford is not just irresponsible, it is a truly antisocial act, because it perpetuates and intensifies inequality. But no prevailing culture has ever allowed that perspective to gain popular recognition in any stratified society. In yours, you cannot safely even mention it. You'd risk being called a Commie or worse.

You can see why.

But *why* do people want babies?

The question is not as fatuous as it may appear. For many (most?) individuals and couples, especially in competitive economies, accepting the responsibility for a child means trimming your dreams and accepting a lower quality of life, working for the money in a job that wouldn't otherwise be tolerated, having less and expecting less of almost everything, including fun. In the 1960s, technology came up with the perfect answer, one humanity has been looking for since forever: a safe and effective way to separate sex (the dominant cross-cultural reason why men want women) from reproduction (the dominant cross-cultural reason why women want men). Nevertheless, half a century and a few billion births later, birth control is still anathema to many people. But the idea that children are an unavoidable by-product of the sex drive is simply no longer true. You are able to separate sex from reproduction. So again, why do people *want* babies?

Determinists remind us of the powerful biological urge driving women to reproduce. But women and men have lots of drives that they do control, including sex: most men are not rapists; most women don't fling themselves at any sailor. Besides, a drive is not an instinct. Some women abort; others kill their infants and children; still others give them up for adoption. If motherhood were instinctive, none of this would be possible. So if there *is* a compelling urge to have babies, it is either not species-wide or not equally coercive for all individuals. More likely, then, the urge has been culturally induced: women in most societies are taught that they are "not complete" unless they fulfill their reproductive potential— even if that costs them every other potential they have. In the late 1990s, the U.S. Census Bureau reported a great increase in the number of post-35-year-old women who got pregnant out of wedlock. These, presumably, were mostly women who had "made it" in the rat race, heard their biological clocks ticking, and decided to have a baby without becoming dependent on a man.

The urge for fatherhood is even less universal than that for motherhood; there are in every urban society many men who never want children. Those who do, generally want a son, perhaps for the chance to make him what they wanted to become themselves—an investment as guaranteed to succeed as a lottery ticket in a hundred million dollar jackpot.

In many cultures it is the first-born son who inherits, or who is responsible for taking care of elderly parents. Consequently most societies tend to value the birth of sons more than that of daughters. This holds especially true for China and India, each of which has over a billion people and cannot afford them all. In India, moreover, the kinship system ensures that any female child is culturally defined as an economic drain on her father, because her eventual marriage will require a dowry to be paid to her future husband's family. Modern China, of course, broke with its ancient traditions of sexual inequality when it limited each family to a single child. But, just as predicted, that one child is far more often a male than would be the case in any natural birth-sex ratio. This explains why young Chinese men now have the unusual problem of trying to find marriageable women—a development that will eventually change Chinese society far more than is now being anticipated.

Elsewhere, the preference for male babies leads women to continue risking pregnancy and tolerating abject dependency until they have produced a son, and ideally at least one spare. Not only does this foster sexual inequalities of the most brutally exploitive sorts, but it inevitably leads to more people than there is room and opportunity for—that is, to explosive overpopulation and a general lowering of living standards.

But you are not living in India or China, so let's bring the question home without getting personal. If you ask your unmarried friends if and why they want children someday, you'll discover their answers group into a limited number of categories. Some people want a baby because of what you could call the Dynastic Urge ("I want to make sure there will always be somebody with my name/values/roles"). Others subscribe to the Teddy Bear Ethic ("I want a talking doll that wets and cries and loves me unquestioningly"), or to the Small Pet Owner's Compulsion ("I want something little and defenseless that will always need me"). Devout believers bow to the Moral Imperative ("I'm a sexual being and marriage is the only context in which my God wants me to express that fact," or, "Having children is my duty").

There are, of course, many other reasons for wanting children, and some may even be defensible. But if you do ask people their main reason for wanting a baby, you will notice that remarkably few of them ever say anything like "The future looks so good that I want to share it with some lucky kid."

It could be argued that any answer short of that one deserves an "F."

Unless major readjustments are made, not only in people's reproductive attitudes but in the way food is produced, and where, the world will face shortages of grains and other staples. That will force nations (including yours) into wars with weapons of mass destruction—either to acquire what they need, to defend what they have, or to reduce the human population to numbers the planet *can* feed and house and occupy usefully.

I live in California, a place so mythologized through the movies that surely, if they could, most people on Earth would settle here. Apparently they're trying to: I've seen our population grow from 20 million to 35 million. As more people crowd in, they drive up the price of real estate, make solitude and quiet more difficult to find, increase crime and insecurity, overwhelm tax-supported services, corrupt government and business, destroy much of the state's natural beauty and wildlife, and press for a continuous lowering of educational standards. There is absolutely no doubt that our population will reach 40 million in the next few years, become 48 million by 2020 and then 60 million and then 100 million and on until all of California will look and feel like Los Angeles—except for the weather.

Will we be better off when California's population doubles? And then doubles again in still less time? That would make this state as densely inhabited as Japan, but without Japanese culture's homogeneity, manners and lack of firearms. Think that'll work here? *There is not a single way in which our increasing population density has improved the quality of life for most of the people already here.* But immigration of both the legal and illegal varieties continues because it benefits "developers" whose campaign contributions corrupt city councils into overriding the advice of honest planning commissions.

From crime to war to inequality, from unemployment to terrorism to starvation, from constricting breathing space to the destruction of the very ecologies that make your oxygen; *every problem humanity faces is made worse by adding more people.*

ENVIRONMENTAL COLLAPSE

Through culture, you affect your environment far more than other creatures. But modern cultures are much more destructive of the environment—and of your children's life chances—than the technologically simpler ones they replaced. As societies industrialize, or more precisely, as their cultures industrialize, their production of all sorts of waste overwhelms nature's capacity to recycle. Already, the Greenhouse Effect is no longer merely a theoretical possibility, but an ongoing event with horrendous effects on the climate and weather, and frightening economic and political implications.

In spite of that, the wasting of Earth's resources grows more rapidly than their actual use. In the late 1990s, something long thought to be physically impossible was brought about through human perversity: tropical rain forests burned out of control in the Americas and in Asia. While these irreplaceable repositories of genetic diversity are hurriedly being destroyed to make temporary hardscrabble farms that soon turn into deserts, the acreage used for growing food is shrinking worldwide—because more (*and more productive*) land is (even more rapidly) being engulfed by urbanization. Many countries already can no longer feed themselves and must depend on imports.

Driven by advertising and rising expectations, people are no longer satisfied with rice and beans. Pork, beef and chicken are raised largely on grains, and there seems to be an insatiable demand for all three. But already, inevitably, rising prices are beginning to cut the per capita consumption of these "luxury" proteins in the newer markets of Asia and Africa. The world's most populous nation, China, has recently converted from being a grain exporter to the world's largest grain importer—at a time when the vagaries of weather have reduced the world's grain surpluses to their lowest levels in half a century. Poorer nations find it therefore much more difficult to buy grain. In 1998, Indonesia tried (and failed) to buy half of the world's rice crop. Soon food riots occurred in its major cities.

Imagine what will happen when well-armed China, even though it has practiced reproductive responsibility, discovers (as it eventually must) that there is not enough surplus grain for sale in the whole world to feed *all* of its 1.3 billion mouths. Think of the business opportunities for the U.S. defense industries! (And think of who all those profitable guns and planes and smart bombs and lethal microbes and poisonous gasses will eventually, inevitably, be aimed at.)

Meanwhile, all other recognized resources are being overexploited right along with farmland. Humanity now uses half of all accessible freshwater supplies on the planet—twice as much as in 1960—and is depleting freshwater ecosystems at a rate of 6 percent per year. (What will you be drinking in 15 years?) As wetlands habitats dry up, their species go extinct and their function in human ecology—the purification of water—has to be performed by less effective but more expensive civil engineering.

Even the oceans are proving not to be inexhaustible after all: in spite and because of the doubling in size of the world's fishing fleets, and the use of electronic technology that won't let a single cod escape to breed, harvests of the most important food fish—herring, cod, pilchard, haddock, hake—have all declined between 65 percent and 95 percent from their peaks around 1988. Next year there'll be still fewer. There is little hope that these and hundreds of other species will ever recover while the pressure on them keeps increasing.

The fact is, the era of absolute limits that economists and ecologists have warned us about is now here. This is true particularly for most of the societies that couple high birth rates with low resource potentials.

Natural systems are responding to the ecological disturbance unleashed by human activity: the three hottest years since the 1400s occurred in the 1990s. World temperature averages for 2000 and 2001 were higher still. (Do you see a trend here?) Weather extremes are increasingly common: "once-in-a-thousand-years" floods now occur with some regularity; the smoke from out-of-control forest fires in Indonesia irritates lungs and throats thousands of miles away; causing a huge brown cloud to hang above the Indian subcontinent to damage crops there; killer tornadoes devastate North America's heartland; there are floods in perennially dry regions and droughts across Amazonia and the American South and Southwest. As resources run out, you can expect competition to increase to the point where it usurps your present life chances— unless you come up with a way for your culture to trade competition for personal responsibility and cooperation.

Inequality in the Third Millennium

So far no one has been able to imagine a way in which most of the world's people can live as well as the average American. Already there is not enough clean water, fresh air, tillable land and cheap energy to go around.

In 1997, with the human race at 5.8 billion members, the total economic wealth in the world was estimated to be 23,000 billion U.S. dollars, that is, at $23 trillion. Seventy-eight percent of that, or $18 trillion, belonged to the so-called developed countries, which collectively had 20 percent (1.16 billion) of the world's people (I'm rounding down here), whose average per capita wealth was thus $15,517. That average included homeless people and Bill Gates.

The remaining 22 percent of the total, $5 trillion worth, was the wealth of all the developing countries combined. They contained 80 percent of the entire world population, 4.65 billion people whose average per capita wealth was therefore $1,075. *Nowhere* was the money spread around equitably; there were some unimaginably rich people in even the poorest of nations—in fact, it was usually their wealthy rulers that kept these nations poor.

There were 358 billionaires in 1998; their combined wealth reportedly exceeded the combined incomes of the 2.3 billion people who were lowest on the economic totem pole, wherever they lived. So on average, if you use finance as your yardstick, *each unelected billionaire had more economic and therefore political clout than 6,400,000 human beings.* And that's only an average again; some had a lot more. Do you realize what that meant in terms of "one man, one vote?" But things have gotten a lot worse in the years since then. Nearly half a billion mouths have been added, and every environmental marker has declined.

Feel-good bumper sticker slogans notwithstanding, human beings are less equal than ever. Maybe, conceivably, someday they could be made equal for certain limited purposes in certain nations, but so far that process has been completed nowhere, and there exist no plausible plans or even theories for realizing any such ideal. Especially not here in North America, where distribution of the Four Ps is the most unequal in the Western world, and inequality is far more extreme than is either functional or sustainable.

It is in that unsustainability that danger lurks for you.

FUTURES WE HAVE MANAGED TO AVOID

Which brings us to planning and visions of the future.

The 1800s ended with a great interest in stories and predictions about the world of the twentieth century. Especially in America, the mood was hopeful: the new marvels of machinery and electricity encouraged people to dream of ever more cunning devices for easing labor and producing necessities. The nineteenth century had been an age of social thought and experimentation; New Harmony, Indiana, and a spate of other utopian communities had been attempted; social philosophers from Edward Bellamy to Karl Marx taught that human nature was perfectible if its condition was humane. Jules Verne and H. G. Wells flooded the Western world with stories of a future that would have flying machines, trips to the moon, submarine ships, and time machines.

Then came the cold reality of the twentieth century with its hijacking of these wonderful futures by demagogues and bureaucrats, its ethnic and ideological wars and its bestial genocides. Demagoguery and ethnic wars were not new to the twentieth century, but they had never been so efficient. After World War II proved that people and society are infinitely corruptible, the dreams of tomorrow turned ugly and bleak. The best-known novels of that age's angst are Aldous Huxley's *Brave New World* and George Orwell's *1984,* both definitively antiutopian or dystopian portents of what could go wrong with the world. Meanwhile other writers fed an insatiable demand for futuristic what-if stories and wrote a few serious extrapolations of existing trends.

One thing almost totally absent in all this literature is the recognition that *any* deviation from Life As We Know It is, at some level, dystopian. Do you believe that the Founding Fathers would be pleased with how their vision of America turned out? Do you think they would be proud of a nation in which 50 percent of all babies are born out of wedlock, in which 12-year-olds become mothers without their inseminators even being prosecuted for statutory rape, in which children carry guns and commit multiple murders? Do you believe that the signers of the Constitution had in mind the insatiable venality and corruption of today's political institutions? That they risked their fortunes and their sacred honor for a society in which only millionaires or those obligated to millionaires can run for public office, in which the worst fate that can befall an honest person is to fall into the hands of lawyers, and society is prevented by legal stratagems from removing sociopathic predators from its streets and boardrooms? And yet *you're* comfortable in what they would have considered hell, are you not?

Another characteristic of both fictional and nonfictional futurists is their failure to comprehend that though culture change may begin in technology, it must ultimately be expressed in values, thought and behavior. The unwarranted assumption that human nature is a constant, and somehow separate from culture, is still accepted almost universally and is still nonsense. If you had been raised in Nazi Germany as a member of the Hitler Youth, or on an Amish farm with no more than the permitted 8th-grade education, you would be very different from the person that is now you. Human nature is malleable. It expresses the way in which a specific culture has sculpted an individual; it is not some steel girder on which a culture can be painted.

But back to the future. One reason people today avoid seriously thinking about it may be that most futures you see on TV and in the movies were imagined by pessimists with tunnel vision. Most are labeled "post-Holocaust," which tells you something right off. If these dystopias are the only futures held up for you, they may turn out to be self-fulfilling prophecies because you won't be able to visualize and work toward an alternative.

A dose of culture history may help. The predictions made 50 years ago about the age you live in now were hilariously off base. Not just because they assumed that technology would fix all problems and that more technology would fix the problems technology caused. Not just because they seldom even anticipated that technological fixes could have unanticipated results or that they didn't foresee the transistor and the microchip. More especially because their characters and social situations did not evolve, but were frozen to norms more than half a century old. Feminism, Japanese cars, the black middle class, lobbyists, Southeast Asian street gangs, drug addiction, the World-Wide Web, unwed teenage mothers, the home office, illegal immigration, gay rights, E-mail, HMOs, state lotteries, Indian casinos, growing illiteracy, shopping malls and other facts of social life were never anticipated. Given the history of prediction, can you really believe that today's projections are any more accurate and complete?

There is a warning in this, and I will heed it: I won't try to tell you what your life and your world will be like. You were born surfing a wave that is still rising, one that's already higher than any swell of change ever recorded. I was lifted on that breaker when its crest was lower than it is now, but already higher than it was for my parents. So is this the Final Tsunami? Is change now coming so fast that virtually no one will have time to adapt? Nobody can answer that. On the one hand, so far human beings have proven themselves more flexible than they expected. On the other, homelessness and drug addiction indicate that more and more people have found themselves simply unable to deal with their evolving culture.

Look. That alleged Chinese curse that everyone, including myself, quotes so freely, "May you live in interesting times," has been applicable to every time and place. Opa Backpacker was terrified of cave bears; your grandfather was terrified of the Bomb. But Grandpa had a lot more options in life than Opa had, and you've got more than he. There are now more ways to live a human life than ever before, and in many ways life has never held more promise. Ancient scourges like cancer and heart disease are being understood and can often be defeated if not avoided. Western European nations haven't warred amongst themselves in half a century, and you can cross borders there without any hassle.

True, there are also greater risks. Wars have become unimaginably deadly, crime is ubiquitous, a thousand things your ancestors never imagined can kill you now, and every day more of your privacy is invaded by individuals and institutions that do not have your interest at heart. Control over information—the heart blood of independent thought, the power base for every tyrant—is being centralized, lost to the tycoons and corporations who buy up the world's publishing houses, newspapers, television and entertainment empires. The balance between private right and social power is once again shifting as governments and corporations become ever more effective at getting you to do what they want.

9/11 didn't help.

We've managed to avoid many of the apocalyptic futures that have been predicted. But does that mean the seers saw imperfectly? Or that by making their predictions public, they woke the rest of us up in time to wrench the cart away from the edge of the precipice? Whatever the case, it appears that any respites we've enjoyed were temporary. Business efficiently invades your privacy with hi-tech devices and techniques, in order to streamline the process by which it transfers your life chances to its bottom line and the wildly excessive "compensation" of its managing class. Business does so legally (and essentially without restrictions) because laws to control its outrages have not been passed and will not be passed as long as business determines who gets to make the laws. Nor does the assault come only from multinationals; your government is catching on, and up, rapidly.

Today, Big Brother is watching you even more closely than Orwell imagined in *1984*, because the War on Terror "justifies" draconian laws that minimize your ability to protest in word or deed your government's actions and attitudes, and because new secrecy laws, centralization of control over the news media, and the ever-increasing percentage of irrelevant information limit your access to relevant data.

So where does this leave you? If you are not satisfied with being manipulated efficiently and usually almost painlessly, what alternative do you have? To hide in the woods and live off nuts and berries until the freeway comes through? Good luck.

Here's a better question: What alternative do you *want*?

Odds are you haven't thought enough about that, because it is difficult to know what you want when you have never seen anything better than what you've got. Yes, that is why people prize inventors and why we read those originators of ideas, the science fiction writers. But even they have found that it really *is* difficult to imagine workable alternatives. But not impossible.

You do need to figure out which world you are facing and what would make it livable. More than anything, you need realistic cultural scenarios so that you can map out a good way to use your time and resources and make your Plan B.

But first you have to excavate one more layer of your existence to understand how you relate to the culture that fashioned and sustains you and from which you must get a life.

THE ETERNAL DICHOTOMY

You, like every other human being, are a battlefield for an ancient contest between your culture's and your own needs. In religions this conflict is described as the eternal confrontation between good and evil, creation and destruction, yin and yang. The prize has variously been described as your soul, your loyalty, your honor, your faith, your sanity. I want you to consider a cultural interpretation.

You were evolved (or designed by your creator; the ideas are not mutually exclusive) to be the supreme decision maker in the animal kingdom. Your organic equipment lets you recognize alternatives, extrapolate their short- and long-range implications, and compare their costs and benefits. You have a physical need to exercise that equipment, for if you don't, if you let it atrophy from disuse like the muscles of some chained prisoner, your health will suffer. It is the essence of freedom to be able to choose, and although you may not be able to define freedom, and even though you may recognize that it is always conditional even where it is not an illusion, you still need at least that illusion to lead a tolerable life.

But you are also a member of a societal species. You cannot survive without other people because you are dependent on culture through them. Moreover, you live in the most complex society in human history, one in which the division of roles is so complicated that much of your potential behavior has to be circumscribed by rules to keep you from accidentally screwing up the social machinery.

There is an ancient irony here: you are better equipped for making decisions than any other type of creature, but you can't be allowed to exercise that capacity freely. That was already the case in simple societies, because even there cooperation demanded some fitting of the individual to necessary roles and because any deviation from what worked created at least a supernatural risk. Oma Backpacker no doubt already had her hands full getting her unwilling brood to suppress their natural urges in favor of social convention. But the limitation on individual freedom can seldom have chafed as much as it does today, because under technologically primitive conditions you're expected to make meaningful decisions if you and your people are to survive.

We—all of us, but especially anthropologists—who have personally experienced life among preindustrial people often came away with the impression that they seemed on average to be smarter and more adaptable than the folks back home. Part of that respect is no doubt due to the very human tendency to admire those who befriend you in bewildering and dangerous situations, as fieldwork almost always is—or at first appears. But it is also true that in societies lacking police, child labor laws, welfare, orphanages, emergency rooms and other social safety nets, the incompetent are forced to depend on their limited wits and the conditional kindness of relatives, and are therefore less likely to survive to be noticed by ethnographers.

Here, however, we can and do keep the physically and figuratively brain-dead alive. For decades sometimes, without their assistance, just because we can afford to. For now. Your culture does far more for you than Opa Backpacker's did for him, but where preliterate societies can be as complicated as a Swiss watch, modern industrial nations are as complex as a nuclear submarine. Therefore your culture is vulnerable in vastly more and different ways than his—and demands your cooperation accordingly. Consequently, though it's impossible to measure such things, there is probably far more pressure on you to conform than there was in Opa's days.

It suits neither the community nor the individual if you wind up feeling that you are being denied the free exercise of your will, your choice, your independence. Especially because by the very purposes of inequality it would be strange indeed if *some*body didn't profit personally from your submission. As cultures (and elites) evolved, they therefore came up with some highly imaginative ways to deny that there even *is* a conflict. Few have done as well in this endeavor as the mass societies of the twentieth century.

Consider Freedom

Freedom is the area of choice between Must and May Not. The form freedom takes is always relative to local culture.

In the United States, for example, you are free to do anything that's not specifically forbidden. That makes freedom part of the commons, a privately exploitable communal good. But those who manage societies see freedom, like any other unfenced territory, as at least potentially dangerous. That perspective is undeniably rational, because criminals in the United States can safely commit novel crimes—like creating designer drugs that cannot be defined as illegal until chemically identified and are therefore legal by default for the duration. Unsurprisingly, American freedom is under continuous assault by legislators who praise it mightily while busily trying to restrain it with laws.

In China, on the other hand, you are free to do anything that is specifically allowed. If it isn't, don't. So from the point of view of most Americans, there is no freedom in China. And from the Chinese point of view, Americans chop away at their freedoms much like Brazilians cutting down their rain forest. In both societies freedom is necessarily restricted, but Chinese know it and Americans deny it.

You do understand *why* society *must* minimize your decision making? True freedom of choice would render you unpredictable, and then society—with its trade and traffic, its maintenance and marriage, its work and war and all those other important cooperative enterprises—would become impossible. If you were the only deviant around, and society could afford you, you might be tolerated as a mere eccentric, until and unless you did something dangerous. But what if "everybody" (meaning one too many people) ignored the rules? The reason every society has those rules is survival—not just yours, but its own. *So life comes down to a paradox: you were built for choosing, but you cannot usually be allowed to do so.*

Nevertheless you have that very real need to exercise choice, and when conditions change, it becomes occasionally necessary for you to do so. Whenever that happens you are supposed to remember your values. Just as in earlier and simpler times.

Still, in a complex society such as yours, such occasions are far too few and far between for keeping your decision-making equipment properly tuned. Illusory or veridical, freedom of choice is a necessity not only for you but also for society at large. Therefore, as culture grew increasingly complex, it developed "pacifier" choices for you to practice your decision making on. These safe options don't make a bit of difference in the actual running of society or your own survival, but they do afford you the comforting illusion of being in control of your life without letting you get in the way and endangering others.

Spurious Alternatives

The current technique for keeping you from making significant decisions became perfected with the advent of mass production and is now a major aspect of your culture. Like Imperial Rome's "Bread and Circuses," it is a conscious attempt to prevent your involvement in meaningful alternatives by keeping you busy with spurious (phony, inconsequential) ones. A relentless trivialization now blankets every aspect of your life, from irrelevancies such as

Fashion—Can you wear black socks with brown shoes?

and

Sports—Does it make any difference in the Grand Scheme which bunch of millionaires scores most often in a ball game?

to vital arenas such as

Politics—Should you vote for the crook or the idiot after each has proven that the other is venal and incompetent?

and

Education—Should you get college credit for remedial courses?

And what have you received in return for surrendering your capacity to choose in areas that directly affect you?

Entertainment—Five hundred channels and nothing to watch!

For many people, the cultural fluff of spurious alternatives is all there is to life. These are the spear carriers in the pageant: the dedicated consumers (normally a transient maturational stage in most of us, but a permanent condition for many victims of culture). Dedicated consumers function as the garbage disposals of industrial society: they convert irrelevant products into waste without ever becoming satiated. They are the preferred customers of the corporations that actually run your society and that will spare no effort in triggering and inflating your desire for things you don't need.

Note that spurious culture is not limited to phony alternatives; it permeates value systems. The same sort of people who tell you straight-faced that you have the best system of justice in the world, and that yours is the best-educated generation that ever lived, also tell you that you can be anything you want, as long as you exercise your free will.

What free will? Can there even *be* such as a thing as "free" will unless and until you have genuine alternatives to choose among, and know enough to recognize them and understand their implications? The ignorant cannot have free will: for them the term is a meaningless slogan—good enough to die for, not good enough to live with.

On Consumerism

So there are two trends influencing your freedom to choose: first, the attempt to keep you from participating in the running of your society; second, the effort to convert you from an enlightened citizen into a mere consumer. These come together wonderfully in the phenomenon of advertising, which has become the dominant reason for programming and content in the print and broadcast industries.

Modern media seem intent on drowning you in irrelevancies so that you cannot ask important but potentially dangerous questions. Commercials never tell you how the car fared in government-conducted safety tests or what *Consumer Reports* shows its repair record to be. Instead, beautiful half-naked women drape themselves on and around it, implying promises that if verbalized would amount to solicitation but that, for some reason, almost no one in your culture equates with prostitution. (In other societies, including yours not so long ago, they did or still do: Jewish, Islamic, and Christian fundamentalists denounce this linking of sex and mercantilism as a form of whoring, or worse.)

And then there is news, one of the triumphs of the art of the spurious. Up to half of it is sports scores, which make no earthly difference to your existence. For the rest, if it bleeds it leads, as long as it is something you can do nothing about. News stories give no explanation of the resolutions Congress is debating, only of congressional scandals presented in repetitive sound bites designed to give you a profitably exploitable view of yourself as a victim. International news is essentially nonexistent: there is no profit in telling you about the rest of the world—it would only give you ideas.

Advertising, the unindicted insatiable corruptor of your culture, is feasible only because all sorts of people of both sexes, from children to the aged, have been taught to cheerfully lie for pay about the qualities of goods and services they are not qualified to judge. Odds are *you* would jump at the chance to make money that way too; yet you probably resent having your character questioned. You've come a long way, baby, but do you know where you're going?

Relevant Alternatives

The crucial fact about spurious alternatives is that they are *not universally* blinding. There *are* people in your society who *do* constantly make important decisions, ones that affect you directly but from whose deliberations you are excluded. Think here of policies and politics, of who decides how to get your money and what should be done with it—and even with your life if you are drafted into some war, or whenever considerations of public safety meet the trump card of private profit.

People you have never heard of and who did not consult you have gradually converted the collective resources of your society into private property—theirs. See, for example, the role of the U.S.

Forest Service in the destruction of America's forests; consider the mass extinctions in every part of the natural world; the blatant rape of every resource in humanity's commons. Think of the public airwaves being given to corporations for private profit making; reflect on how television, the most nearly perfect medium for education, has been debased into a purveyor of violence and irresponsibility, the ultimate depressor of public intelligence and morality.

Remember the savings-and-loan bailout? Remember the lies that got America into Vietnam? Remember the World Trade Organization nixing America's decision to limit imports from nations that enslave human beings or destroy the environment? Remember that corporate welfare—the tax monies spent to aid corporations in such worthy endeavors as advertising American cigarettes in the Third World and maintaining price supports to grow sugarcane in the Everglades and rice in the Californian desert—runs five times as high as all the money spent on all the programs designed to help poor people? Remember Enron and the other energy wholesalers turning California's 12 billion dollar surplus into a 12 billion dollar deficit—all so some of that money could go to a few breathtakingly antisocial superpredators? Remember Arthur Anderson, the accounting firm charged with protecting the public from such crimes, hurriedly destroying tons of records in an effort to make prosecution of the criminals legally impossible?

Oh yes indeed, highly relevant alternatives do exist, and decisions about them are being made every day.

But without you.

THE SLIPPERY SLOPE

You were no doubt taught in high school that "an informed electorate is a necessary prerequisite to a democratic society." That's still an inspiring shibboleth, but let's face it, it's probably neither an accident nor an *unanticipated* by-product of change that every generation since World War II is less literate than its predecessor and makes lower scores on all standardized proficiency tests after more years of education. The average number of words in the written vocabularies of 14-year-old Americans in 1945 was 25,000, in 1990: 10,000—about average for preindustrial tribesmen. Now it's probably less.

This rise of spurious alternatives, cloaked by relevant ones, was no accident. Predatory elites today are the most efficient in the history of inequality. It is they who pay for the shows you watch on television rather than reading about what goes on in the world; it is they who underwrite the insanely expensive elections of their representatives in both parties so that the wholly-owned incumbent usually wins; it is they who ensure that election reform and accountable government remain pipe dreams; it is they who whip up your righteous indignation at anything that could stand in the way of unfettered exploitation of the human masses, such as a responsible population policy; and it is they who have therefore continuously dumbed down education.

In any foodchain-economy like capitalism, when you're not the diner, you're the dinner. From one perspective, your culture is constructed as an artificial reprise of the natural ecosystem, benefiting the meat eaters at the top at the cost of the plant eaters at the bottom. In this view, America is not a feudal kennel but a giant ranch. Ignorant consumers graze fondly on ever-novel, never-perfected products, are kept fenced by law and order, milked for profit and services, and periodically led to slaughter. The cattle are allowed to elect their own herd bulls because that cuts down on stampedes and the need to hire cowboys. Never having seen the absentee owners of the ranch, they cannot even imagine their existence.

Analogies can be instructive, but this one, too, has its limits. People are a lot more unpredictable than cattle, and although the interaction between predator and prey cannot be denied in your culture, various checks on the rapacity of elites have evolved. Unfortunately these can only be applied post-facto, and therefore wind up with the taxpayers being presented the bills for cleanup and correction, instead of those who profited: management and investors. Early in 2002, the president announced that the grand effort to clean up superpolluted industrial sites all over the nation would no longer be paid for by the corporations that poisoned the land and the water for profit, but by you.

Unaccountable elites persist, everywhere. But no longer in castles on the hill where the revolted peasants can locate them and burn them out, as they did in the old Dracula and Frankenstein movies. (I think European vampire legends are allegories about the scourge of feudal aristocracy.)

In any ecology—and a complex modern society is functionally just that—predators evolve as prey gets smarter. The marvelous adaptation of today's predatory elites is that none of them can ever be held accountable because they are invisible entities: like the vampires of legend, they are not mortal. Corporations, timeless associations of individually unanswerable persons, pursue the bottom line: their profit at your expense.

Must things stay this way? Not necessarily; the pendulum swings, and we are once again witnessing how the collective can suppress a truly great evil.

In the 1990s, the tobacco cartels (who have hastened the deaths of more people during the twentieth century than all its wars combined) felt the lash of belated public disapproval. Yesterday it fell on slave traders, the intellectual ancestors of tobacco executives; today it is being considered for the thieving corporate executives who in 2002 had collapsed the stock market and cost the citizenry and its retirement funds 7.7 trillion(!) dollars; perhaps tomorrow it will castigate some other institutionalized parasites.

Yet slavery continues here and there: in its familiar form in places like Sudan (whose dominant Muslims still capture black people to sell them) and in its older sexual guise almost everywhere. Children and young women bought in Third World countries and the old Eastern Bloc nations are being sold to brothels all over the world, usually with at least tacit government approval at both ends of the supply line.

Nicotine addiction is another form of slavery. It, too, is far too profitable to be allowed merely to vanish. Some of today's popular actors and actresses get paid to make smoking look sexy in the movies and on television shows. It's called "product placement," and proves that in your society, at least, money trumps morality. Too many young women, willing victims of a dysfunctional aspect of culture, smoke to stay thin. Too many young men become addicted to nicotine, the most difficult of all readily available drug habits to overcome, in order to look tough and to celebrate the sense of immortality that the young of all species seem to be cursed with. Too many advertising agencies look upon youth's innate vulnerabilities in the same way as animal predators picking out their next meal.

Money is its own legitimation.

But also note that the relentless effort of a few respectably deviant *individuals* finally brought the depravity of both slave traders and tobacco executives to public awareness. *Respectably* deviant individuals also forced an end to the marketing of infant formula to women in the Third World, where an irresponsible campaign against breast-feeding caused the deaths of tens of thousands of babies because their mothers lacked access to the sterile water needed for diluting the formula. Respectably *deviant* individuals have forced most of the other improvements in public policy and private accountability.

And that should make it clear that the question "Should I ever make decisions at all?" has to be answered affirmatively. True, there are whole arenas in which you should not: public safety demands that you cannot be allowed to choose to drive on the wrong side of the street, for example, or perform major surgery without medical training. But if you want to be a cultured person rather than a mere creature of culture, there are important areas in which individual choice is not just relevant, it is critical. The trick is to know enough so that you can make an informed decision instead of mindlessly rooting for what you fondly hope is "your" team. The danger is that your knowledge will be outdated by the time you want to use it as the basis for your judgment. You cannot possibly ever know enough to make informed decisions in all the areas that will face you, but you can learn where to find out what you need.

You live in a culture that knows more about the universe than all the others that went before it combined; yet you possess a smaller percentage of that knowledge than any previous generation did—an unavoidable side-effect of technological complexity and role specialization. After all, the whole point of the division of labor is that individuals won't *need* to know their whole culture. You trust and believe that there are people who do know things and that you can hire one if you ever need to. So the main thing you believe in—odds are, you've never considered any other because you haven't known how to judge it—is your own culture.

If you are thinking of America, then I do, too. Not least because here I can say my piece without being put up against the wall for it. I've experienced that alternative; I understand and appreciate the difference, that's why I'm a *volunteer* citizen. Despite its dark history (black slavery, Indian genocide, laissez-faire capitalism, Vietnam, a hundred wars in South America), the United States has held a torch for others to see by; it saved the world time and again, and it gave me a life worth living. I still believe that America is humanity's last best hope.

But I can also see that America is in decline on almost every measure except military might. I understand that "decline" has always described any status quo when a new culture is aborning. Still, I would not be a responsible American if I blindly accepted the steady diet of spurious crap that we are being fed by those who direct the evolution of this culture without our input.

Is a new and better model of America now gestating? I can't see it yet; I can no longer even believe that the nation-state is a perfectible means of organization for a world with six billion people. But that does not mean that I despair. Only the very rich can afford to be pessimists, because they know that whatever happens, *they*'ll be taken care of. I, like everybody else, need optimism to help keep me going until *you* develop a viable alternative to the downward spiral of exploding populations, wars and crime, resource waste and environmental collapse.

KILLER CULTURE

Culture, you now know, is humanity's primary means of survival; it's what makes the way you live possible, and what places you midway between ape and angel. What's not usually acknowledged is that culture is also the primary cause of human suffering and death, and of extinction for other species—often at the cost of people's quality of life.

When the typical age at death was still 45, people died of all sorts of things their cultures did not have the means or the will to counteract. Your life expectancy is far better now, but soldiers are still killed in meaningless battles, and civilians still die from accidents, diseases of opulence, and disorders of inequality. And *you* still risk perishing through and for technology, ideology, and organization.

Two generations ago (1963), Jules Henry examined this idea in his book *Culture Against Man*, but he was certainly not the first person to realize that we die because our culture fails to keep us alive. His bald proofs that culture is not an unalloyed blessing created a brief flurry of interest. But soon anthropologists, historians and philosophers returned to their fascination with how cultures produce their cornucopia of ways to be human and of things to do, to feel, to know and to believe. After all, there was not much anyone could do with the knowledge that your culture will likely cause your death. But that doesn't mean the insight is not important.

Though every culture may occasionally kill some of its bearers, it's usually not by design but as a by-product of that culture's imperfections: misunderstanding and misapprehension lead to mistakes. But once ideologies have turned into dogmas and institutions have lost their adaptive flexibility, any culture may become a lethal risk to the people it exists to serve.

The primary reason every culture sooner or later fails its bearers and winds up killing them was introduced in chapters 9 and 10: each culture necessarily defines its own nonveridical reality, and sooner or later but inevitably, each culture's specific way of deviating from veridicality has led—or will lead—it to a test it must fail. Typically, that moment comes in culture contact between societies with wildly different institutionalized assumptions.

It is easy to see that happening when the First World meets indigenous, preindustrial, small-scale societies, and eliminates or absorbs them. Such differences as modern weapons technology, mass communication and bureaucracy are all that's needed to explain what happened there. It is less obvious why complex civilizations—the Chinese, Egyptian, Roman, Incan and Aztecan empires, Napoleonic France, Hitler's Thousand Year Reich, the Soviet Union—are no longer with us. For these, it was not so much technological inadequacies as their ideas and assumptions that ultimately caused their fall.

Consider, for example, the Aztecs. When they met the Spanish Conquistadors four centuries ago, the Aztecs constituted the flowering phase of a sequence of cultures in the Valley of Mexico and were a nation-state already older than Spain. Aztec society was as accustomed to warfare as Spain's, it outnumbered its invaders astronomically, and it was fighting on its home terrain. It is true the Spaniards had horses and guns, but surely these should not have canceled out their extreme numerical disadvantage.

Of course the invaders did (unknowingly?) carry a secret weapon: smallpox. Once Aztec warriors captured an infected Spaniard, the deadly plague spread through the native population faster than the Conquistadors could advance, decimating Indian resistance in their path. Even so, the Spaniards were still outnumbered by thousands to one. The idea that a handful of foreigners who understood neither the local culture nor even its language should vanquish an empire was absurd, and not anticipated by the Spaniards themselves.

The explanation for the fall of the Aztecs lies not in what they did, but in what they believed. Aztec theology included powerful myths about a bearded and light-skinned avatar of one of their culture's most important deities, and Hernando Cortés, the leader of the invading murderers and robbers, fitted that image. Moreover, the Aztecs engaged in warfare largely to capture living bodies for their institutionalized human sacrifices, the terrible offerings which were absolutely necessary, they believed, to ensure their harvests and to keep the gods on their side in battle. Even though their wars were as political as any you're used to, the Aztecs battled to gain captives. The Spaniards fought to kill. As Cortés and his disciplined psychopaths moved west across what is now Mexico, the Aztecs in their capital city of Tenochtitlán sacrificed ever more human beings to propitiate their heedless gods. Finally (the record shows), on the day before the Spaniards rode into the city, its heroic but critically overworked priests cut and ripped the hearts out of some 20,000 living men, women and children in a last, great, glorious but doomed effort to appease the White Avatar of Quetzalcoatl. At that point it must have been clear to the people in the streets of Tenochtitlán that their culture was killing them.

Afterwards, the Spaniards' lust for gold made them do things to the locals that were every bit as vicious and venal as what the Indians had done to each other to appease their gods. The Aztec empire became a Spanish colony, Catholic churches were built over the bloodstained ruins of native temples, autos-da-fé brightened the darkness of heathen superstition, and the gold of Mesoamerica filled Spain's coffers for its wars against fellow Christians in Europe.

What killed off Aztec culture—and the cultures of the rest of that part of the world—was not the military might of a country unimaginably far away with only the most tenuous of supply lines, but a set of perspectives on the social, natural and supernatural worlds that failed to produce the anticipated results in men armed with totally alien cultural premises.

Spain, ruled by pious people who well understood that only God's grace could explain their nation's inordinate good fortune in the New World, felt duty-bound to enforce, throughout all the territories under its control, its harsh views on how life should be lived. Spain instituted the Inquisition, and exported it to the Low Countries to abort the birth of Protestantism there. The Dutch, unable to stop the Spanish legions on land, fought back by hijacking the gold and silver fleets sailing from America to Spain, always reinvesting the gains into more ships with more cannon and more men. After eighty years of war, Spain's economy was in ruins, its non-American territorial possessions (and those of Portugal, which had joined Spain in the war against the Low Countries) now belonged to the Netherlands and England, and Iberia's leading role on the world stage ended with its peace treaty with the Dutch in 1648.

What destroyed the Iberians was not superior military might (Holland was a tiny country), but their inability to "think outside of the box" in terms of religious tolerance and military tactics. God, rich Spain knew, was on the side of the biggest fleets and armies. Victory, the impoverished Dutch proved, came with hit-and-run tactics, with starving the Spanish armies and armadas of supplies and gold.

The Netherlands, ruled by pious people who well understood that only God's grace could explain their incredible victory over the most powerful nation in the known world, now faced the homecoming of generations of their own men—who had few skills but sailing and killing. The Dutch turned disadvantage into advantage by ordering their fleets outward to look for profit where no Europeans had gone before. That turned Holland almost overnight into the world's leading colonial power. Capitalism, which under different names had been the ideological component behind Holland's success in defeating a far more powerful foe, was converted from a military tactic into an economic philosophy, with all that the term still denotes about exploitation for private profit at public expense. England, which had allied itself with the Dutch once it was clear who was winning, immediately adopted the

Dutch corporate model of global business and colonization, and soon war between these two powers became inevitable. Great Britain won its third and most important war with the Netherlands, neutralized their further territorial ambitions, traded Holland Suriname for New York, and set about creating an empire "on which the sun never sets."

What eventually destroyed the Dutch hegemony was not British militarism, but Holland's inability to see colonies as anything but money-making resource bases for a ruling elite. By the time the Dutch realized that there was more to colonies than short-term profit and taxing the natives, the Second World War arrived. Soon thereafter all the European colonial powers were shorn of their captured overseas territories: India, Indonesia, and most of Africa and the Caribbean all became independent.

Note that each culture's success was also the source of its undoing: we stick with things that apparently worked for us, even when our cause-and-effect reasoning is faulty, even when new circumstances demand new approaches.

Unfortunately but predictably, almost all of the newly independent countries now have their own insoluble problems. Some of those—overpopulation, resource waste, unemployment, and environmental collapse—they share with their old colonial masters. Others—ignorant exploitive elites, ineffectual civil services, anti-democratic governments—they suffer precisely because they were ruled by outsiders for so long, and because powerful countries depending on them for raw resources (oil, copper, uranium, cobalt, coffee, cocoa, lumber, etc.) have found it "productive" to acquire these goods through local regimes that understand business and profits and know enough to *stay* bought. Most ex-colonial governments are based on a European model whose prerequisite is a locally nonexistent educated electorate, a model that simply does not fit the assumptions underlying local cultures. The future of Africa may closely mirror the past of South America—except that Africa's crises are deeper and its resources already inadequate. India, since its birth in 1948, has been threatened by its own minority religion, which now menaces it from Pakistan, and by conflicting demands from its religious and its secular institutions. Indonesia (whose founder, Sukarno, referred to Western New Guinea as "Our colony West Irian" when the Netherlands, under U.S. pressure, eventually surrendered it to him) is a critically unstable collection of cultures in permanent crisis from population pressures, and with a simmering uprising in West Irian.

So when you look at the nightly news and see people starving, governments and economies collapsing, and poverty-stricken nations wasting their resources on warfare against each other and their own peoples, you should recognize that each of these events indicts a locally dominant culture which, inadequate to its tasks, has turned killer.

The reason is almost always the same: the culture's ideology, its system of definitions (remember the trouble with definitions?) about the world, society and the individual have grown so divergent from veridicality that only extreme measures can force the culture bearers to remain integrated into the society and its institutions. None of these empires fell because they were too weak to resist change; they are no longer with us because, in spite of heroic but doomed efforts to cram square pegs into round intellectual holes, they were each weakened by the loss of internal ideational congruity, and therefore fell to more determined and self-assured foes.

So what about the U.S.A.?

It is the last and greatest superpower because it bankrupted the Soviet Union before it could bankrupt America, but its problems have grown overwhelming. It would take another book to identify all the design flaws that became visible during the twentieth century under the stresses of adapting to explosive change. Here is an example from the ideational aspect of culture.

How Much Justice Can You Afford?

In a world that has almost 200 nations—each with its own laws and constitutions, traffic and trade, victims and criminals, contracts and courts, prisons and attorneys—*the American "justice system" employs one of every three lawyers on Earth*. Does that make you feel safer? It shouldn't: most of America's problems today are made worse by that fact.

By converting Law into a for-profit enterprise, the Judicial Branch has become the dominant power in government—the exact opposite of what the Founding Fathers wanted. For-profit law and privatized government are responsible for such vicious misdirections as "Capitalism = Democracy," for the sale of Congress to corporations, for our continual-crisis economy, and for the hardening of inequality.

This self-proclaimed "fairest legal system in the world" depends for its functioning on uncompensated amateur juries, drafted from people who are unable to avoid involuntary servitude but who are able to convince prosecution and defense that they know nothing relevant about the issue at hand. They are selected by specialists looking for those who can be manipulated into seeing things as the lawyers want them to. The "adversary system" for deriving at Truth and Justice, so fanatically touted by those who grow rich from it, means only that whoever can afford the best lawyer wins, regardless of justice, fairness, or the well-being of society at large. Killers go free, innocents are executed, those caught swindling and pauperizing thousands may be sent briefly to country-club prisons, while those who commit victimless crimes such as smoking pot may face decades of incarceration, rape and degradation in hell-holes that put teenage car thieves, child molesters, mass murderers and drug offenders in the same prison population. Lawyers get paid either way. And then there is the insanity of the Drug War, which flatly denies that there were any lessons to be learned in the failure of Prohibition. ◅

Were dead cultures pushed, or did they jump?

No other nation can hope to defeat the United States on the battlefield, but that does not mean that the world's sole surviving superpower is safe from annihilation. Historically, the most common cause of death for dominant cultures has been through suicide.

Cultural suicide occurs when a society is driven by some irrational self-indulgence to waste resources faster than they can be replenished. When that occurs on an island, it becomes a laboratory example. Easter Island in the South Pacific was covered with tropical forest when Polynesians discovered it. A population explosion followed. The evolving culture coupled endless internal warfare to the continual creation of massive, economically dysfunctional statues. The natives cut down the forest until there were no more trees left to make the canoes needed to escape from their doomed, literally denuded island. After the now unavoidable massive die-off, the culture was essentially lost to its pitifully few survivors.

Islands only show more dramatically what is happening all over the world. Does anyone learn from them?

Around the time you read this, the last tree in Haiti should be turning into charcoal, right on schedule. The Haitians are clear-cutting their country because people there need fuel for cooking food to put into all the hungry young mouths that will soon be having babies of their own—for whom there will be no jobs and no opportunities except illegal emigration to the United States. Long after Haiti has become a desert, Haitian women will be bearing children to become economically dependent on handouts from other countries.

But it is not fair to single out Haiti as a problem, because there are dozens of other countries, in Latin America, Africa, Asia, and Eastern Europe, where populations have outgrown their resource base but keep on having children for whom there is no room, no water, no food, no school, no work, no medicine, and no hope other than emigration.

And still the United States refuses to defend itself and its people, whose life ways can only be negatively impacted by this perpetual "Invasion of the Surplus Breeders." Why doesn't it? Because some people here, the important ones, profit from it. America's is a subtler, less noticeable manner of suicide, as pills are subtler than guns or gas.

Theoretically, American culture could be adjusted to cope with the 12–20 million illegals who are already here, if the influx were stopped effectively NOW. And certainly we have the armed might to do so. But even though our medical, educational and judicial institutions have been stressed beyond their capacity by immigrants and are failing us all, there is no hint that the people who run the United States (for profit) are even willing to *consider* any alternatives to the status quo.

A culture's past success is often the source of its future undoing, and surely the most visible success of American culture is the cornucopia of "consumer goods" (do think that phrase through) that industry produces whether anyone needs them or not. But that very abundance has its costs in irreversible environmental degradation and a constant shrinking of the life space for other creatures, and therefore of alternatives for our own descendants. In other words, the technological sector of American culture has evolved at the cost of its organizational and ideational sectors.

Prognosis? See the Aztecs and the Easter Islanders, add automatic weapons and a sea of blood. Without a major readjustment of America's nonveridical assumptions in law, governance, business, inequality and education, you must expect to experience the implosion of this nation, and its tsunami effect on the rest of the world. The events of 9/11 may prove to be a sufficient impetus for a reassessment of American culture, but there is no guarantee that those who run the nation (and benefit so disproportionally from its culture of inequality) will not steer you into fascism instead of correcting the flaws in your culture's assumptions.

Reassessing Your Culture

Like many people, you may have ideas about what is wrong with your culture, what should be changed and what should be preserved about it. When not kept pruned, the tree of culture throws up so many suckers that its fruit-bearing branches starve and break while its life chances are wasted on pointless, unproductive growth. Unfortunately, pruning is not a popular idea just now. President Dwight D. Eisenhower said it this way:

> Every gun that is made, every warship launched, every rocket
> fired, signifies in a final sense a theft from those who hunger
> and are not fed, those who are cold and not clothed. This world
> in arms is not spending money alone, it is spending the sweat
> of its laborers, the genius of its scientists, the hopes of its chil-

dren. This is not a way of life at all in any true sense. Under
the cloud of war, it is humanity hanging on a cross of iron.

These words, first spoken half a century ago (by the very general who directed the Western victory over Nazi Germany, a man who understood better than most the benefits and costs of weaponry) are as appropriate now as when they were uttered. With clouds of war and terrorism thick and perilous, the threat of terminal disaster looms from more directions than in any previous era. The waste of human and environmental potentials for private profit has never before benefited so few at the cost of so many. There are many Killer Cultures now, and they are on the march as the world's indisputably best-equipped, best-trained and mightiest military power is playing Whack-A-Mole with people who are in most ways very much like yourself, except that they are ready to kill themselves for a chance to kill you.

And you ask, in straight-faced innocence: "Why do they hate us so?"

No matter how satisfying your answer to that question may be, it might lead you to ask its corollary: "Even if they are crazy or evil, could we, could our culture, be less than perfect?"

But once you ask *that*, a flood of other questions follows. Like:

- If this is indeed the Land of the Free, why do we, of all the nations on Earth, warehouse the highest percentage of our citizens in prisons?
- Why are they disproportionally black and poor?
- If we have the most equitable legal system in the world, why is justice too expensive for all but the very rich?
- If we have the best medicine, why do tens of thousands of people here have to choose between food and medical care, when no one needs to do so in the 16–20 other countries whose citizens outlive ours?
- If ours is the best educational system, why have literacy—and most people's understanding of the world and our culture—declined in every generation since World War II?
- If ours is the best political system, why can no one win public office without becoming wholly indebted to those who do not have the common welfare at heart?
- If America is so fair, why do its CEOs who, a generation or two ago, made 10–20 times as much money as their average worker, now make 500 times as much by robbing employees' pension plans and legally (!) pauperizing people who have worked hard all their lives?
- If the corporations, whose profits all come from your wallet, don't pay taxes, why do you have to make up the shortfall?

- If other countries cannot or will not limit their birth rates to the carrying capacity of their lands, but send their population surpluses to you without your permission, why should you be forced to feed and clothe and educate and medicate and far too often incarcerate their citizens at the cost of your own life chances?

Reaction to Action

Theoretically, the saving grace in culture, even Killer Culture, is that once you understand that some underlying premise is non-veridical, you can change it. But, like breaking a lifelong habit, that is never easy: even though cultures change randomly all the time, the prerequisites for any serious attempt to influence the direction of cultural evolution include exceptional understanding and uncommon courage.

It's never enough to shout, "Burn it down so something better can grow!" because any seeds for improvement may not survive the fires. Vandalism is never a functional form of protest. Instead, ask yourself: Is this the American culture I want? If it isn't, what would you have different? How and why would that make it better? What are the underlying motives and values connecting the phenomena you object to? Can those values be changed? Into what? What would it cost you? Us? The rest of the world?

Be forewarned: questioning your own culture's unspoken assumptions is very dangerous. Culture patterns follow the same survival laws as organisms do. Realities try to survive; they will defend themselves. Challenging your society's "Self-Evident Truths" means unleashing the tigers of doubt—and finding that everything, *Everything!* has suddenly become unstable. If you, alone, doubt and reassess, you will be judged a mental case, but as long as you do not act upon your quaint deviance you'll probably only be sidelined and ignored. (The odds are just as good in democracies as in totalitarian regimes.) But if enough people dare challenge the Givens, *no matter on what basis*, that will interfere with the smooth workings of culture-as-you-know-it, a true revolution could be unleashed, and those in power could lose it.

Therefore, such questioning is everywhere made dangerous to the questioner. When fundamental social change is advocated in any culture, those who benefit from the status quo will defend it to your death, if necessary. Anything that interferes with the traditional transfer of life chances from the producing population to the decision makers and resource owners will be met with the awful power of the State—which in every stratified society exists, after all, as *their* agent. That aggression was amply exercised on the first Abolitionists, the first Labor Unionists, the first Suffragettes, the first Integrationists, the first Freedom Riders, and the first Anti-War Demonstrators—none of whom even considered questioning the most fundamental assumptions that still underlie inequality in North America and the rest of the world.

If you did succeed in organizing such a challenge, then, history teaches, its violent persecution will be officially rationalized with the (quite cogent) observation that, if left unchecked, efforts to change the nature of your society's division of labor and its rewards must lead to deprivations, dislocations and suffering. Representatives of the ruling class will dismiss, as insulting and inflammatory, any suggestion that their objections are self-serving, and will make that very proposition punishable "for the good of the country." They will be ready (to quote a celebrated slogan from America's longest war) "to destroy the village in order to save it." In the name of Freedom, not just yours but all our rights will be curtailed; in the name of Security, not only you but all of us will be made less safe in our homes and our persons. This eventuality is as predictable in class systems as in feudalism or caste systems; just read your newspaper for proof. Or board an airplane.

Most of us will therefore be your enemies, especially if you decide to *forcibly* convert us to your way of thinking. But even if your organization does nothing nasty, even if you merely advocate viable alternatives but do so convincingly, you will be seen as a threat to the status quo, and therefore most men's hands will be raised against your organization. Since the dawn of social stratification, every attempt to fundamentally restructure an existing hierarchy and its ideational scaffolding has met such responses. Most people understand this at some almost subliminal level: ours is a nation of immigrants after all, and it was always so in the stratified societies we or our ancestors left. That's one reason why most people cannot even imagine questioning their culture's assumptions.

Yet *somebody* must, because as change accumulates, every existing culture's every assumption will sooner or later prove itself deficient in veridicality. The archaeological record is largely composed of societies that disappeared because they failed to change adaptively in time, of cultures that responded to challenge by defending too long their treasured assumptions and traditions. *Two basic lessons of evolution, whether in biology or culture, are "Adapt Or Die Out," and "There Are No Permanent Adaptations."*

But if reassessing cultural assumptions about injustice and human exploitation is always so risky, why should you do it? And when?

Any culture's self-defenses include arguments against directed culture change. The commonest is the advice to "Postpone it as long as possible, patch things up, make do with what you've got; it was good enough for your forefathers in the Golden Age, let's bring that back!" (But the conditions under which that Golden Age flourished are gone and can never return.) In societies undergoing rapid change, as yours is, you also hear that "If it works, it's obsolete; we can do better!" (And so Unachievable Perfection becomes the enemy of the Achievable Good Enough.) Between those extremes lie all those perspectives that ask, "Is this the right time to risk the devil we know for the devil we don't?"

That question is unanswerable except through hindsight—which you'll acquire only if you survive what's coming. You cannot know what to do, what road to take, what alternatives to pursue, unless you have some idea of where you want to be. So perhaps a more salient query would be: *"If you still have time to design an alternative to the culture you have, what is it you want it to do and to be?"*

Thinking It Through

1. As a modern urbanite, you do not grow, collect or kill your own food; you do not manufacture your own shelter, clothing, or even entertainment; you are untrained in survival skills beyond those required for city life; so in fact you are not responsible for your own existence, but dependent on the operation of individuals and institutions over which you have absolutely no control. Would I be wrong to label you as an evolving hive creature that (necessarily?) insists on wrongly calling itself merely a social or solitary being?

2. Do you believe that the mass extinctions now taking place are what the Creator had in mind for his Creation? Do you expect your god(s) to forgive mankind for eliminating, forever, every potential use in every species we extinguish without even bothering to analyze it and evaluate it for its possible contribution to us or our descendants?

3. There is no way imaginable for the whole world to live an American lifestyle, in part because there simply isn't enough of the Good Stuff to go around, but in the main because we use up far more than our fair share of the Earth's resources. Those facts determine our foreign policy, and are the primary reason why some of "them" hate "us". Can you defend your right to live well at the cost of "their" poverty and despair? If you cannot, can you suggest a viable alternative?

4. For immigrants, the idea of America is often far more attractive than the reality of the United States. How would you draw the distinction? Can the United States be made more like the Amer-

ica foreigners dream of? Should it be? Are we moving toward or away from America? What is steering us?

5. Any culture's self-defenses include arguments against directed culture change, yet undirected culture change is becoming more and more dangerous. How do you react to the idea of a Cultural Editor, an official agency staffed by cultural and technological experts trained to determine and evaluate the probable effects of every new invention, (re)organization, entertainment, weapon, marketing ploy, proselytizing religion, educational fad, etc., and empowered (like, say, the Environmental Protection Agency) to regulate or prohibit the introduction of new traits into your culture?

Prepping for the Third Millennium

Improving Your Odds

"Only the man who finds everything wrong and expects it to get worse is thought to have a clear brain."

—John Kenneth Galbraith (1908–)

"Never doubt that a small group of thoughtful, committed citizens can change the world. Indeed, it is the only thing that ever has."

—Margaret Mead (1901–1978)

❧

In an old story, a captive gladiator is given a chance at freedom. Alone in the arena he faces two unmarked doors. Behind one waits a young lady the emperor has selected for him to marry; behind the other, a maddened tiger. He doesn't know which door hides which fate, but he knows that his paramour, a fiercely proud and famously jealous aristocratic woman, does. If he opens the right door he will be free, but lost to his jealous lover. If he opens the wrong one he will die, but she will not have lost him to another woman. Leaning over the wall of the pit she points to one of the doors. What will he find behind it, the lady or the tiger?

There will be a lot more doors in your own life's arena, and behind most of them will wait tigers. Is your information better than his?

❧

So now you know that culture is the major factor in how you got here and turned into the person you've become. You understand that culture is first of all language and then everything that language makes possible: the ways people organize, the things they make and use to change their environments, how they figure the universe works and the reasons they think up to justify their behavior.

All that's left for you to worry about is the rest of your life: is it just going to happen to you as an aging creature of culture, or will you have some say in how it plays out? Let's restate the question. Are you able to make decisions when:

- so much of what and who you are has been decided for you;
- your alternatives are defined by your environment; and
- both you and it are changing all the time?

Bringing It Home

You are not the person you were ten years ago—or yesterday; and tomorrow you will be more different yet. Over time, your physical capacities wax and wane; you cannot yet do at fifteen what you easily manage at twenty-five, but at sixty you can no longer do what you took for granted at thirty. Intellectually you know that to be inevitable—we all do, but emotionally most of us are afraid to consider it. You should, though. So you can plan ahead.

Whether your mental capacities decline in that same period is more debatable: barring a serious genetic handicap or massive trauma, if you keep using your brain and don't pickle it, it'll probably outlast the rest of you.

What *will* change, however—and this is the most difficult to accept—is your values. I would never have believed it, as my age-mates didn't and you probably don't, but it is a fact: many people and ideas you would have died for at twenty or thirty will seem almost irrelevant when you're fifty or sixty. There are things I now prize inordinately—like comfortable routines and time to think in solitude—that I used to disparage. Judging from the literature on maturational stages, that sort of change is pretty standard.

And it is also where hope lies, not just for your culture but also for you.

As you age, you grow more and more in charge of the specific contents of your personal culture—and, in the process, more alone. This fact coordinates with another: gerontologists have observed that as people grow older, they increasingly differentiate themselves in appearance, attitudes and behavior. By the time you die in ripe old age, you should be—and look—almost totally unique. To a peer-pressured teenager that may sound like a curse, but there is much to be said for living long enough that you can finally be you in your own way: this "social organism" stuff goes only so far. *The trick lies in not just succumbing to the process of individuation but in directing it.*

Attitudinal change creeps up on you; you usually don't even know that you've reoriented your compass until somebody else points it out, and then you wonder why you ever thought the way you did. That's normal also, and healthy enough—even if it does sound like hypocrisy or sour grapes from youth's perspective.

Obsolescence

What's harder to live with, and brand new in human history, is that you will, almost inevitably, become culturally obsolete. Most of that is due to technology and the ways of working with it. The stuff you grew up with remains obvious and comfortable no matter how it evolves, because you can keep up. But you never become as cozy with gadgetry that enters the culture when you're fifty or older, unless you just happen to be that one in a thousand who's bent that way.

Even then, everywhere else in culture the cards are still stacked against you. Each generation has its own music, its own dance, slang, attitudes and beliefs. You invest yourself in your age, you learn the things your age cohort identifies with, you keep up with its evolutionary trends. But to do so, you have to ignore what comes with the next cohort. They tumble into existence ever closer on each others' heels—Depression Babies, Boomers, Gen X'ers, Echo Boomers, Millennials—all with their own cultures. Their technologies overlap but aren't identical; their organizations are consciously separatist to emphasize their (largely spurious but identifying) differences; their value assumptions become ever more wildly variant.

The term "generation gap" was invented in the 1960s to describe the cultural chasm between parents and offspring that showed up during the Vietnam War. "They" remain your parents, but already you may no longer have much in common with them. The lifestyles of your own children will sometimes seem frighteningly weird—at least until you let yourself discover what the kids are concerned about. As culture changes ever more rapidly, generation gaps widen; the lifestyles of parents and children grow apart even faster than those of age cohorts.

And you, the individual, remain unavoidably alien to most of them—and therefore, you gently obsolesce.

That isn't *necessarily* such a bad deal *if* you have collected, from the cultural bazaar spread out around you, the stuff it'll take to keep you comfortable and interested in life. As Ashley Montagu, a wise old anthropologist, put it: "The idea is to die young as late as possible."

Options

So, given these circumstances, what are your options? Sorry to say, you've only got a few, and most of them look pretty bleak.

1. *Play the game.* Try to be the best profiteer you know how to be; live off others without adding to the social kitty. Statistics suggest that to get filthy rich, you should try banking, insurance, or real estate. Join the rat race: get your MBA, pass the Bar, but do so in the full realization that when everybody does, not everyone can become a mover and shaker. Your entire existence will have to revolve around work and consumption, and work will be a sort of combat without any armistice—until you become a casualty or are put out to pasture.

2. *Go into crime.* Choose hi-tech; being a physical predator is for losers. With a larcenous soul and any brains and charm at all you can expand into politics and business to become a shaker and mover in the old feudal mold. Odds are you will spend more of your life in prison or looking over your shoulder than in enjoying your booty, but that's just paying dues. For a smart, ruthless individual, crime pays very handsomely indeed—not least because most of your associates will be ignorant and incompetent. Live hard, die young, have a beautiful corpse.

3. *Stay drunk, stay stoned, get cable.* Dropping out is the easiest response to an unattractive present and a threatening future, but also the least rewarding and most degrading. Addiction is only a weasel-word for being enslaved; expect to face hard and chilling times between highs. Better to overdose now: die while you still have options about when and where and how to cash it in.

4. *Make it work your way.* Learn what the traps are and how to recognize them, and walk your own path. This is the most demanding alternative, for to bring it off, you need to understand how the system works and how to get by—short of dropping out—with the least interference. You will need to learn how to defend yourself against predators, how to make alliances, and how to make do with Good Enough instead of The Best. You will need to learn a lot of things. But you would have to anyway, even without hope.

But hope does exist. If you manage to remain culturally flexible and creative about your options, you *can* live well and prosper.

SURVIVING WELL IN INTERESTING TIMES

Apparently you have decided that being responsible for your own life (that *is* what making meaningful decisions comes down to) is an acceptable way to get through it; otherwise you wouldn't still be reading this. Since life is habit forming in every sense of that term, you probably also intend to emulate Ashley Montagu and stay young forever or die trying.

The advantage of a long life is that you get to satisfy a lot of curiosity and to experience a lot of different ways of being you, not all of them unpleasant. Eventually you may grow so tired of it all that you won't even have to be dragged into your final good night. But don't count on that: if you work things right, you may never grow bored enough.

The downside is that you'll have to make do without people of your own age, the ones who intuitively understood you because they shared your cohort's cultural perspectives. If you live long enough, you will almost inevitably become culturally obsolete and personally isolated. In the final analysis, in spite of carefully nurtured marriages and friendships, the elderly generally die alone.

But then, who doesn't?

Their simpler cultures once bound your ancestors to other generations in a seamless continuity of life. But in today's consumer society, once you're old enough to have become satiated with stuff, you are at best useless to the economy and at worst a dangerous example of how one can live well by accepting the idea of "enough." The same culture that once tried to overwhelm you with its glut of alternatives will now try to separate you from the rest of society, probably so you won't infect it with your unprofitable attitudes.

But you need not *accept* this isolation. There are more of the competent elderly around every year, and with the Internet, distance is no barrier to networking. One welcome attribute of the ever more complex society you live in is its apparently endless subdivision into interest groups. Another is that the hi-tech anonymity of modern life makes it easier than ever to create a *personal* culture. When you combine those two ideas, you can belong to a variety of groups that are as age-tolerant as your ancestral Backpacker societies and that can separately or collectively provide you with every psychological satisfaction that you require as a member of a social species—with the added new benefit that you can turn it off whenever you need privacy.

Best of all: You don't have to wait until you're old. Your personal culture is typified by your interests, attitudes, possessions and behavior. It is your personal selection of items from the cultural bazaar. Though you share its traits with others, your profile of them is yours alone. Indeed, *you* are all that holds your personal culture together, for it's strictly up to you to decide how many different clubs or interest groups you join, and whether you join physically or electronically, and to what degree of commitment and participation.

Building Your Personal Culture

Your greatest problem at present is that you are always being forced to make choices before you have a chance to figure out where the alternate forks in the road might take you. No matter how many of those situations you have acted on already, there will always be a hundred more for which you are not prepared. The only thing you can be sure of is that your answers will affect how you live and die, and with whom.

- Drop out of high school or endure it to graduation?
- Take a dead-end job or go to college and risk flunking out because you don't really *want* to go yet?
- As you now understand yourself, what sort of work would make the best career for you?
- Is it likely to support you and bring you social recognition?
- What kind of person should you marry? *Should* you marry?
- Should you *plan* children or let them come "naturally," however that may impact you—or them?
- When you move away, which church will you join—if any?
- Do you really understand what the political parties stand for, if anything?
- What's worth working for? Dying for? Living with?
- What do you really need to know, and why bother?

When the alternatives are spread out before you in college, you can have a shot at almost anything. The possibilities are so dazzling that some people sometimes (and a few all the time) see the very need for choosing, not as a set of magic doors, but as a burden. In response, they reject possibilities—sometimes all of them, and drop out too early. That's not advisable. As with unwed motherhood, the decision is usually irreversible, and denying yourself a good look at your alternatives simply freezes your life chances and lifestyle to those you have when you drop out of the game.

The world is full of people who will be delighted to do your selecting for you—for a fee, which is usually money but may cost you your soul. All you have to do is follow their instructions. Investment brokers will happily churn your account, making all your financial decisions. Politicians will promise literally *anything* for the opportunity to make rules for you to live by and them to live off. Television evangelists offer to open a direct channel between you and God, and all you have to do in return is forego independent thought, eat your vegetables, pray a lot, give up sex and, to activate The Promise, send them your money. Then you will surely go to heaven, where you will never have to decide anything again. Guaranteed!

Sarcasm aside, it is obviously true that choosing has never been more difficult. You have more alternatives, and more of them contain nasty surprises. When you are forced to choose among unfamiliar alternatives, increasing the number of options only increases your level of stress. And with options increasing almost as rapidly as populations, you are encouraged to gamble blindly rather than to choose intelligently.

Technology remains the impetus for increasing the complexity of culture and its options. The evolution of the other major aspects of culture (organization and values) lags so far behind technology that instability is now the norm, long-range planning is no longer considered realistic, and ever-increasing segments and percentages of the population are unable to adapt to the pace of change—and are therefore at risk for everything from drug addiction to unemployment to mental illness.

Culture lag refers to the different rates at which the aspects of culture evolve: technology is fastest; ideation is most resistant to change. Culture lag is the major factor stressing the social fabric today, because technology presents you with opportunities and alternatives for which your culture hasn't prepared you, and yet you need to consider them in your decisions and plans.

The computer is now the dominant element in reorganizing society. It has eliminated jobs for middle managers and workers and closed a gate between those able to use the technology and those who cannot. At the present rate of change, many individuals cannot keep up. Those who cannot are pushed out or drop out. Then they become everybody's problem: you already know that most of society's "safety nets" fail.

So dropping out is out for you.

Or is it? There are few absolutes in culture; most measures are relative to some continuum. You want to live; yet you can imagine circumstances under which it would be better to be dead—like learning that you are entering the last, drawn-out stage of an incurable disease that reduces its victims to mindless agony or, with medication, to vegetable obliviousness. That might lead even the most devout of believers to violate a taboo on suicide or euthanasia. So could the specter of being publicly responsible for a horrendous calamity. You know other examples.

Similarly, many people accept *lifeways—asylums—in which some responsibility for decisions and their results is surrendered to Authority.* Asylums vary in the degree and duration of commitment they require: Enlisting in the armed forces obligates you to years of automatic obedience to orders, dictates your meals, dress, location and occupation and revokes some of your civil rights. Taking final vows in a cloistered religious order not only extends that commitment for the rest of your life, but also adds sexual abstinence and other demands. Academia and government service are at least partial asylums, and prisons and mental hospitals are largely involuntary ones.

After treading water in your culture's sea of relevant and spurious choices without ever getting clued in on which are what, you may well learn to find voluntary asylums attractive. They offer a structured life that focuses your concentration. Some encourage hard work and reward dedication, others tolerate sloth and incompetence, but they all reduce your spurious alternatives and minimize the shock of the new and the need to make decisions—and thereby your risk of failure.

Furthermore, many people benefit from a couple of years of enforced discipline: in higher education, ex-GIs typically outperform civilian students. Others, like tenured teachers, appreciate the security of lifelong employment, even in situations where they have virtually no input into the conditions of their work. For the security is real: governmental asylums from the municipal to the national level all guarantee health insurance and retirement benefits, necessities that often remain only unsecured promises in the private sector. But there are never enough asylums to go around.

In any case, the determining factor in your suitability for such a lifestyle is not physical or mental capacity so much as attitude. And that is also the key to your personal culture.

Your Tool Kit

The key to surviving well in interesting times is to remain flexible and creative about your ever-changing options. That means understanding what they are and how they function, and that, in turn, means education. To evaluate your interaction with formal instruction, you need to know what education is actually *for*.

The irreducible purpose of schooling (no matter how often that may be forgotten by school boards) is to standardize the knowledge and behavior of a society's young so that they can become adequate replacements for those who now do what needs doing but who will inevitably die off. That means that children need to be taught certain essentials, especially reading, reasoning and the basic communication and cooperation skills that determine their fitness for further instruction. There is a lot more to life today than the three Rs, but when schooling fails at that basic level, a child's life chances are severely reduced, and it is essentially wasted to the community.

The ability to communicate and cooperate adequately now involves some minimal knowledge about a lot of things that were of no interest to your ancestors: knowledge about the origin and evolution of the common culture, including its geography, history and ideas, the ability to operate its universal technology, and so on. So although high schools offer a far wider range of subjects than grade schools, their reason for being remains the same: to turn out people who can be trusted to behave predictably and at least minimally competently as co-citizens, employees and parents.

Higher education was traditionally restricted to a few members of the upper classes—usually younger sons who would not inherit titles or lands. In the Middle Ages, the earliest colleges and universities offered only two degrees: in sacred law (and theology) and in secular law—the very devices through which elites still rule and stay in power.

Today's right to go to college even if you are not well born was earned for you by the generation that won World War II. Beginning in 1941, civilian men in the United States were drafted to serve "for the duration"—often five years or more—in the largest war in history. For this extraordinary service, veterans were rewarded with the opportunity to get up to four years of college paid for by the taxpayers. The resulting democratization of higher education resulted in a tremendous explosion of new ideas and behavior and made it impossible to return to the old class exclusiveness of college life. Only the fraternity system survives from the old ideology. The GI Bill for the Korean War was even better, but then the social upheaval caused by all these newly educated low-borns began to threaten the Establishment, and slowly but surely the benefits were reduced. Today's military service personnel are all volunteers and guaranteed only a governmental copayment for higher education.

Where the purpose of schools is enculturation, the instilling of the shared culture beyond what the parents have been able to impart, the purpose of college is more complex. Higher education exists to serve three social functions.

1. *To create an educated electorate.* This is, of course, its most dangerous function from the perspective of any ruling elite. Note that government support for higher education in general (rather than for specific fields of study) increases during wartime (because no one knows which idea in what field may turn out to give our side an advantage) and decreases in peacetime (because it raises wage demands and reduces profits). Although it remains true that democracy would require an educated electorate, democracy has been avoided in all but name since the Founding Fathers stipulated their preference for a republic with themselves in charge, and it is not likely to be realized without a profound rethinking of national priorities and a true revolution. Nevertheless, this function is the excuse for funding state institutions of higher learning.

2. *To produce the specialists society needs.* That's pretty self-evident, until you remember how much of your culture is spurious. Indeed, the reason why the college degree is now the functional and status equivalent of your great-grandfather's high school diploma is that so much of higher learning has been watered down and diffused with spurious subjects that contribute little to your comprehension of the universe around you.

3. *To produce cultural "mutants."* This is the least-understood and least-appreciated role of higher learning. Physical evolution requires and produces some individuals whose genetic variation from the norm usually handicaps them—but from among whom, occasionally, some particular oddity proves advantageous in the battle for survival. In that same sense, your society needs enough *competent* oddball intellects that it will have an adequate supply of brand-new alternatives to fall back on in those novel situations that interaction with other evolving societies inevitably produces. (Note the emphasis on competence: only in fantasy can an ignorant, unprepared hero contribute anything worthwhile.) In biology, the role of mutants is to field-test functional physiological alternatives. In culture, the role of the offbeat intellectual is to spontaneously generate original alternatives.

As with biological mutations, the production of useful cultural mutants is cruelly inefficient; it wastes the lives of innumerable also-rans and "wannabes." Whether in biology or its cultural analog, most mutations are lethal, meaning they won't spread into the gene pool or the trait list—they make no difference. But species and complex societies cannot survive without them, and higher education is the most effective way to produce them culturally, even if the process may churn out a hundred semiliterate, self-styled poets and half-baked philosophers for every genuine original thinker it produces.

But what do *you* get out of investing five, ten or more years in higher education? Well, it offers very attractive *individual* rewards.

1. *A good living as a specialist.* This is probably why most people go to college. Higher education opens up a whole library of alternatives that Opa and Oma Backpacker never dreamed about, including a lot more ways of being human and contributing to society than they could have imagined. On the minus side, unfortunately, the college degree has been devalued to where it is now the minimum prerequisite for any but technicians' jobs, which means it now takes at least four more years than it took your grandfather to get to the beginning of your career path, and 16 more than Opa had to endure before he could be a man and do a man's work. (Has it ever struck you that today's longer life spans just barely compensate you for the ever-lengthening list of demands you must satisfy before "they" let you loose at life?)

2. *Increased adaptive potential.* The anticipated result of a successful education is that you get to partake of the Four Ps at a more advantageous level than you can without it, because you know things and can do things that society needs—or that make you less dependent on society. But you also know that job security is a thing of the past, that the only answer that counts when heads are being lopped is the one that satisfies the question, "What have you done for me lately?" and that the computer can reduce all but the most esoteric specializations to at best temporary survival strategies. Nobody's Statement of Purpose for the Admissions Office ever began with "I want to attend Frisbee State to improve my adaptive potential." Yet in times of great change—that is, for the rest of your life—knowing about alternatives gives you a leg up, helps you adjust your cultural fit. Which brings us to the nitty-gritty.

A Functional Education

Given that things *will* change, your best investment strategy for higher education must recognize that you have short-term and long-range costs and benefits. Often an immediate advantage, like early specialization and the part-time job that comes with it, turns into a long-range cost, like vulnerably narrow specialization and an inability to deal with related disciplines and materials. When culture change was glacially slow, early specialization gave you an advantage. Under rapid change, your best strategy is to remain flexible and adaptive, which means you should *avoid specialization as long as you can.*

The *best* strategy in becoming educated for long-term flexibility is to take the introductory course for every discipline on campus. That will expose you to the maximum number of different perspectives and insights. Of course that's impossible: you have economic limitations. You have to graduate sometime before your money runs out, and you ought to finish a double major along the way. And not in sister disciplines—pick them so each can be a source of employment when the bottom falls out of the other. I know that everybody resents having to take general education courses, but they offer the most direct way to broaden your perspective and your adaptive potential.

"Oh, but I can't do such and such subjects," you protest.

Nonsense. If you've been able to read this far, there isn't an introductory course on any campus that you should be afraid to tackle. Remember: *profs want to be understood as much as you want to understand.* Of course there are lemons in the professoriate as there are in any other enterprise, which is why you should do your homework on any class you consider taking. The world-famous expert is not necessarily the best lecturer, nor are his courses necessarily well organized—or even taught by him; you may sign up for Einstein's section of 101 and get lectured by a first-year grad student learning the trade. So find out who is actually going to be teaching you and talk with ex-customers. "She's hard!" should not be a turn-off; "He's boring!" or "He's pedestrian!" ought to be.

The best thing college can teach you is how to learn, because you will be learning as long as you live, and you might as well be efficient at it so that you'll have time for other things. You should come away from your official education with a long and complex perspective, the ability to see alternatives, and an active and functional imagination. Oh yes, and a way to make a living, come hell or high water. To achieve all that, you'll need a better plan than hoping to hit a lucky major in the career sweepstakes.

So what *can* you do to maximize your potential?

First, find out what that potential is. It probably won't pay you to try to become a professional athlete: most of them barely make a living as javelin catchers for the exceedingly talented. What else are you good at? Find out! There are testing facilities that can measure your potential in a variety of areas. Then find out what you could *become* good at that you could like, and get the education and training that it requires. Here again, your best exposure to the choices is through general education.

Second, figure out what you need, now and forever (which means: the rest of your life). The key here is to realize that "need" doesn't mean "want." Admit to yourself that it may mean changing your culture, and *that* can be a lifetime job.

Third, recognize that "there ain't no freebies," that anything beyond "enough" will somehow cost you more than it returns and will draw the unwanted attention of those who never *can* have enough: criminals and the pathologically competitive.

Fourth, prepare yourself to be culturally flexible: learn enough about the basics of everything that you will not be clueless whatever happens; become good enough at a couple of things that you can make a decent living at them.

Five, go for it.

And Now a Word from Our Sponsor

But first you have one major decision left to face.

The idea of "Culture as Choice" is not limited to your selecting items from the cultural bazaar to maximize your life chances and customize your lifestyle. It also implies that you have an opportunity to contribute consciously to the construction of a culture worth living in and, if need be, dying for.

So the question is: are you to be a reactive creature cannily surviving your culture, or a creative one trying to make something better out of it than what it now is? This is the updated version of the choice between affecting the future through your genes or through your behavior. No doubt personality and talent will play some part in how this choice strikes you, and it is obvious which is the default position.

In any case, you know that your culture is in trouble and needs adjusting.

Its most obvious impacts on your personal universe are its implementations of two basic but debatable value assumptions: that it behooves every fish in the aquarium that is your class system to gobble up as much of the resources of nature and society as possible, and that the personal worth of a fish is measured by how far up the food chain it swims. Television, radio and the print media repeat these messages ceaselessly through that catechism for consumerism you call Advertising. As corporations compete for your money (and they truly don't care if that's disposable income or your irreducible subsistence), everyone involved, even you, understands that each new marketing campaign necessarily must be more expensive and persuasive and invasive than the last. Because once you have spent your wad and gone into hock, the next candidate for separating you from the earnings that represent your life chances will have to bombard you even harder and longer if it is going to be noticed at all.

Think about that for a minute. The world has already become plastered with advertising. Cityscapes—the places where you *live*, after all—are flickering with neon and noise-polluted with jingles and Muzak designed to "choreograph your shopping experience." Highway scenery is hidden behind billboards. Almost everything you read and hear and see is interrupted by advertisements. Primeval forests are felled just to be turned into junk mail for you to throw away unopened. Hysterical hucksters shout at you from your car radio; and the technical perfection of TV ads is far subtler than any show grudgingly tossed you as chum so that you will bite on the commercials.

You've got one nasty, ugly, exploitive culture there.

As the world runs out of space, resources and alternatives, Those Who Own The Ranch are hurrying the process of transferring wealth—which in your society translates into life chances—from the cattle to themselves. Their brilliantly promoted ideology has already turned citizens into "consumers"—a demeaning term signifying that your main value to society lies in your capacity for converting their surpluses into their profits. On top of all the ear and eye irritants *already* unleashed on a helpless public, their highly paid specialists labor ceaselessly to perfect new methods to get your money. You have been under continuous assault, all your life, and there is not a damn thing your culture, as it is now organized, can or will do about it. It's legal! That's all that counts!

Is this really why U.S. children repeat the Pledge of Allegiance? Does the inscription "In God We Trust" prove only that Money Is God, and we should worship Profit no matter what its pursuit does to the quality of life for *most* of us? Is it true that Capitalism Equals Democracy? That to be rich, at *any* cost to others, is the goal of life?

Hey, it's not part of my job description to tell you what the meaning of your life is—or should be. Only you can decide that. But let me say it again: your decision can be no better than your alternatives, and *those* are being siphoned from you for the good of the few and replaced with phoney ones that don't work.

Your culture, especially your societal culture, has been allowed (or encouraged, it depends on your tolerance for conspiracy theories) to evolve willy-nilly. There is in the modern world no institutionalized editor or watchdog—as there sometimes was in simpler societies—to control the probable impact of new traits posed to enter the common realm. Consequently the evolution of twentieth-century cultures has been mostly reactive: when new traits—advertising on television, illegal immigration to provide necessary labor, assault weapons for children—enter, society *responds*. Usually ineffectually, because it has been overwhelmed with the range and number of such "innovations."

As things now stand, there is no realistic chance of founding such an editing institution, and if there were, then no chance of giving it any power to arrest threatening new traits.

And as things now stand, your future is projected dead-ahead as one bleak and scary place in which children commit mass murder; in which the big print giveth and the fine print taketh away; in which government of the rich, by the rich and for the rich is wholly owned by corporations and utterly unaccountable to you; in which your every defense is checkmated by lawyers; and in which the only excuse for your existence lies in your willingness to serve some neofeudal bandit who has been lucky and ruthless enough to gain control over something you or those you love need for survival.

You know that certain devoutly-to-be-avoided changes are already occurring in everything that is important to human welfare. You know that avoiding the wreck awaiting you at the end of history's downward spiral will require vastly more drastic alterations in the fabric of culture than any ever imagined before. You *know* that, because it has already been *proven*: no measure attempted so far has redirected the evolution of culture enough to change the odds in humanity's favor.

Nevertheless this fashionable scenario, realistic though it may be, is not the only *possible* alternative and therefore not inevitable. The grim and bloody future of your fears need not be a self-fulfilling prophecy. For one thing, your societal culture is not as efficient at determining the way you look at the world as your ancestors' cultures were; your societal culture is choking on self-doubt and alien inputs and mutating at a fantastic rate. When a societal culture *is* effective at channeling your perceptions, it seems natural and is unquestionable—which means that you literally cannot even imagine an alternative to the way you see and think and evaluate and classify your experiences. But yours hasn't been that efficient for generations. Be grateful for that!

Any lasting problem a society hasn't solved by now—war, inequality, population pressure—will remain unsolvable until and unless its people learn to look at it from a perspective in which it *has* been or *can* be solved. And such perspectives are available; both ethnography and science fiction detail exotic ways of looking at familiar problems. Of course not every change in perspective will bring an answer you need; the trick is to gauge which ones hold promise.

SCENARIOS

I like the dreams of the future better than the history of the past.

—Thomas Jefferson

What the world—and you—now needs more desperately than anything else are scenarios for alternative futures: logical, plausible models that can be evaluated rationally and adjusted and improved. Obviously you cannot inflict experimental societies on living people—that sort of evidence takes more time to gather than you have left, and who would be the guinea pigs? But nothing prevents "thought experiments." *One logical role for cultural anthropology is the conscious design and simulation of cultures for mass societies.*

Science fiction has failed you there: it has brought you culturally impossible futures in which only technology changes, and dystopias that, like Medusa, turn your mind or heart to stone.

If humanity is to be responsible for its own evolution (as the Fall from Grace perhaps implied), then we humans need to discuss what we want to become. What do you want to go into your culture? What should be thrown out? Consider, for example, some changes I consider necessities if the world is to survive to see 2100:

- *Involuntary population control*—a universal Responsible Birthing Act if you will;
- *A reduction in human inequality* to the minimum necessary for each society to produce the specialists it needs;
- *Undeniable accountability* for every official and representative in government and business;
- The establishment and arming of *an international authority capable of defending the interests of the species* against any hostile national, corporate or private interest; and
- A new form of government employing the opportunities implicit in modern communications technology to produce genuine *participatory democracy*.

No doubt you can think of others; no doubt also you can see the oxen being gored by my proposal—and judge whether their welfare outweighs your own. If you can imagine more adaptive goals, then do! Add and subtract whatever you like; the issue is not whether anyone's list of specific adjustments to the culture is ideologically correct or organizationally palatable, but whether it would lead to a better future for your children than the poisoned environment and the ferocious competition for table scraps they'll face if nothing—or only something ineffectual—is done.

One clue: whether you focus on the societal or the individual level, work backwards. Describe what you want your life to be (after analyzing why); figure out how that would work if everybody had your rights, obligations and properties; and then figure out the cultural steps necessary to get (us) there.

"But this is ideology," I hear you object, "not science!"

True. Ideology is not dead; nor should you try to kill it. It is a necessary part of culture at every level from species to individual. The trick is to make it work for humanity instead of having humanity work for it.

A plethora of assumptions—sacred and secular ideologies into which you've had no input—have forced you to this precipice with billions crowding you. Your future is a step into the void. To avoid annihilation, you need to design an ideology of your own to bridge that void. Now that you grasp what ideology is, you must help shape one for a world you would *like* living in—and the odds are that if you do, your value system wouldn't be that unattractive to others. Share your scenario, your vision, for only a new vision—a new ideology—can save you and those who press behind you. Goals need to be established; alternatives need to be imagined; priorities need to be ordered; means need to be agreed upon. If you accept responsibility for your own alternatives, you're going to be busy.

Culturally, you are a victim of the past; try not to be a tyrant to the future.

You can do better than was done for you.

Thinking It Through

1. Consider your ability to make decisions when so much of what and who you are has been decided for you; when you only get to choose between Column A and Column B in politics, classes and careers; when your alternatives are defined by your environment; and when both you and it are changing all the time. That vaunted Freedom you may be willing to die for, is it veridical?

2. One thing new under the sun is that elder generations no longer automatically adapt to the technological cultures that younger

ones grow up in. Does that mean there is a limit to how much change anyone can take in a life time, and that if you live long enough, you'll reach it? What does this do to the idea that culture is handed down from one generation to the next? How will an ever-faster pace of change kill modern culture?

3. U.S. population policies prohibit the UN from spreading information about birth control to Third World countries that are running out of every resource except weapons. Is this a good idea?

4. "Why can't we all just get along?" Is our prized multiculturalism at least in part responsible?

5. Most people don't have a clue about how cultures work, how theirs is organized, by whom, for what reason, or who pays. They don't know that (or how) their buttons are being pressed. They cannot change things except to make them worse. You, however, have now been introduced to Culture. Does that change anything for you?

❧ Index ❧